# THE COMPLETE
# EQUINE
# TRAINING MANUAL

A comprehensive guide to schooling,
for horses of all ages and abilities

David and Charles

A DAVID & CHARLES BOOK

First published in the UK in 2007

Layout and design © David & Charles
Source material courtesy of *Your Horse* magazine © Emap Active

The publishers would like to thank Nicola Dela-Croix editor
of *Your Horse* magazine, and Susan Voss, and her team at Emap Licensing.

David & Charles is an F+W Publications Inc. company
4700 East Galbraith Road
Cincinnati, OH 45236

A catalogue record for this book is available from
the British Library.

ISBN-13: 978-0-7153-2642-8 hardback
ISBN-10: 0-7153-2642-2 hardback

Printed in China by Shenzhen Donnelley Printing Co., Ltd
for David & Charles
Brunel House    Newton Abbot    Devon

**Commissioning Editor**  Jane Trollope
**Assistant Editor**  Emily Rae
**Project Editor**  Jo Weeks
**Designer**  Jodie Lystor
**Production Controller**  Beverley Richardson

Visit our website at **www.davidandcharles.co.uk**

David & Charles books are available from all good
bookshops; alternatively you can contact our Orderline
on 0870 9908222 or write to us at FREEPOST EX2 110,
D&C Direct, Newton Abbot, TQ12 4ZZ (no stamp
required UK only); US customers call 800-289-0963
and Canadian customers call 800-840-5220.

# CONTENTS

# BEST TRAINING PRACTICE

Good basic training is vital, whatever you intend to do with your horse – jumping, dressage or simply hacking. A horse may be born bursting with natural talent, paces to die for and the ability to jump over the moon, but on its own that isn't enough. As soon as a rider sits on his back, he is put off balance and he has to learn how to move well all over again. In training a ridden horse we're showing him the best way to re-balance and carry himself and his rider. We're teaching him how to perform to the best of his ability, moving with lightness and ease, without restriction or tension.

Before – and then continuing alongside – ridden work, a horse must learn what is expected of him in the yard and stable, how to lead, how to accept the farrier and how to load into a trailer or horse box. All these are skills that horses do not automatically have and it is our duty to ensure they are taught carefully and clearly so we end up with a horse that is happy to do anything that is asked of him.

# EFFECTIVE SCHOOLING

**The key to success in any schooling session is to ensure that you and your horse are capable of achieving what you set out to do. Many problems a rider faces are caused by one of the basics being out of place. For example, if your horse won't do flying changes, it may be that he is unbalanced in the canter and is not able to collect very easily. In these circumstances, it is no wonder he is unable to change legs.**

## CHECK YOUR ABILITIES

Can you clearly communicate what you want from the horse? Often a horse does not respond satisfactorily because the rider is either giving him confusing aids or is blocking him in some way. For instance, imagine asking your horse to strike off into right canter, and as you do so leaning forward and looking down. The added weight over the horse's shoulder will unbalance him, and he may strike off on the wrong lead or rush away in a fast trot. The horse is not being awkward; it is the rider who has caused the problem.

## ASSESS YOUR HORSE

• Does he go forward willingly?
• Does he respond to the aids?
• Is he balanced over his four feet and keeping an even rhythm?
• Does he bend and turn softly in both directions?
• Does he move in a straight line?
For him to be able to learn more advanced movements, the answer to all these questions needs to be yes. If any are no, then you need to work on that skill before moving on.

## DOES HE GO FORWARD WILLINGLY?

The most fundamental requirement of a horse is that he goes forward genuinely and willingly. If asked, many riders would say their horse does respond in this way, but often they are mistaken. Perhaps the horse goes forward, but in a grudging manner. The legs may be moving, but the horse is mentally switched off. This is a key point to note, as if the horse is not responding genuinely to your forward and controlling aids, all other schooling is of little value.

*Your horse should go forward softly and respond willingly to your aids*

## TESTING THE FORWARD AIDS

Try this exercise, which is best done on a loose rein so there can be no confusion from the rider's hands. Walk the horse around the school on a loose rein, and then at A, B, C and E ask him to lengthen his stride in the walk for four or five steps. Note the quality of the reaction. Did he immediately lengthen his stride with increased activity, perhaps stretching his head and neck a little further? If he did, slow down the walk and give him a pat. Your horse is responding genuinely to the leg. If, on the other hand, he tightened against your leg, made a sluggish effort or brought his head and neck back towards you, he is not responding genuinely.

*Ask your horse to lengthen in walk for four or five steps*

## GETTING IT RIGHT

• *Focus on learning one thing at a time, in simple stages.*

• *Keep it simple. If you are unable to do something in trot, try it in walk; if you can't do it in walk, do it in halt.*

• *Listen and watch other riders. Make sure you watch good riders. Don't fill your mind with pictures of bad riding.*

• *Have fun! A playful, exploring attitude can take you a lot further than a rigid, serious one.*

• *Be grateful for your mistakes. They let you know what you need to do differently next time.*

• *Stay focused when you are riding. Horses know when your mind is wandering.*

• *If the session is not going well, give your horse a long rein and have a rethink during a relaxed walk. Try to come up with a different approach that your horse might understand more easily.*

## PROBLEM SOLVER

**Q** I have recently bought an ex-riding school cob. He is lacking in energy and enthusiasm and generally ignores my leg aids. How can I encourage him to be more responsive?

**A** Riding school horses often switch off mentally to cope with being ridden by many people of varying ability. Given time to get used to being owned and ridden by one person, your horse will soon relish his new life.

Take time to make friends with him. Don't go for a ride every time you see him, but spend time grooming him and generally making him feel special.

When you ride, make sure that you sit correctly in the saddle, in an upright position, and that your aids are correct. Try not to clench your seat muscles in an effort to get him to go forward. Pushing him along with your backside will discourage him from using his back muscles and he'll be reluctant to move. Quick nudges with your calves, pressing rather that kicking, will work best.

It may help to give a short, sharp tap with a schooling whip just behind your leg if he doesn't respond straight away. If he's slow to react, halt, and ask him to walk on, repeating the same aid with your legs and using your voice. Maintain a firm but friendly attitude.

He must just notice your leg aids and nothing else. Once he's responding to them, you can start thinking about your rein and weight aids. You can do this exercise while hacking. Your horse has probably spent a lot of time in an arena, so he'll benefit from a change of scene.

*Most horses enjoy a break from arena work*

# THE PARTNERSHIP

Everyone wants to create that all-important bond with their horse, a sense of mutual trust and partnership that gives both horse and rider confidence in each other. This takes hard work, common sense and, most importantly, an ability to understand what makes your horse tick. The good news is that everyone is capable of improving their relationship with their horse.

## ACCEPT THE DIFFERENCE

Remember that horses see life very differently to us. They are experts at living in orderly, co-operative herds and appreciate that group living is vital for survival. They have evolved to run away from problems, while humans have evolved to work problems out. They understand complex body language that we are often blind to, and they are simplistic in the way they deal with field squabbles, while human relationships are more complicated. The next time your horse 'misbehaves' ask yourself why he's acting that way: spooky behaviour is the horse reverting to his flight instincts and it's perfectly normal for a horse to feel stressed if he is left alone in the field as, in the wild, being left alone would mean danger. The more you can learn about equine behaviour, the easier it will be for you to understand your horse's actions and develop a more sympathetic, effective approach to riding and handling him.

## KNOW YOUR HORSE

An excellent way to improve your understanding of your horse is to really get to know him. Sounds obvious, but you can learn a lot by studying every aspect of his existence. How does he fit in with herd life? Does he tend to get bullied or is he always in the thick of the action? Is he protective of his own space in the stable? Is he ticklish when you groom him? Just like us, every horse is an individual with his own personality. Knowing what your horse likes and dislikes, spotting when he's genuinely frightened and when he's just playing around, and recognizing his needs and moods are essential to the bonding process. For example, if you know your horse is ticklish under his belly, groom him only with a soft brush or cloth in that area. If he doesn't like to be handled while he's eating, leave him alone. You wouldn't set out to deliberately annoy your friends, so apply the same logic to your horse.

*You will know when you have a good relationship with your horse*

*The secret of a good partnership is to understand and accept each other and to learn how to work together*

Getting to know your horse's individual foibles is also a good idea from a safety point of view. When hacking, for example, some horses like to look at strange objects, make up their own mind that they are safe, and carry on. Other horses constantly look for something to be frightened of and are better if you take no notice of what they've seen and carry on as though there is nothing to be afraid of. Being aware of your horse's preferences means that your rides will be much more enjoyable.

## YOUR SIDE OF THE BARGAIN

• Choose the horse you ride with care. It is all very well taking on a 'problem' horse but make sure you are capable of dealing with him. It is far better to buy a horse you can cope with and like.
• When training your horse, make sure he understands what you are asking. Once you start an exercise, follow it through, repeating it three or four times. If he's struggling, think of another way to explain what you want.
• If you have had a bad day, don't take it out on your horse. Just groom if you are too stressed to ride well.
• If things go wrong with your training consider having lessons. A good instructor will help you to work out the cause.

## SUCCESS STORY

• Cassie is an 11-year-old Thoroughbred mare. She was bought as a first horse for a novice rider, but proved too lively and, after a spate of rearing, was put up for sale. When Lisa went to try her she hadn't been ridden for months but, despite her history, Lisa could see that she had a lovely nature and decided to take her on.
• Once home, Cassie's behavioural problems began to emerge. She was extremely anxious if separated from her field mates, even trying to break out over her stable door. She ran sideways and reared every time Lisa tried to get on, jogged out on hacks and wouldn't let the farrier anywhere near her back feet.
• Undeterred, Lisa set about retraining Cassie, adopting a patient, methodical approach to each problem. To conquer the separation anxiety, Lisa brought Cassie in with another horse every day, groomed her, fed her, then turned her out again. Then she gradually progressed to bringing her in on her own for short periods. Slowly, Cassie began to settle in the yard on her own.
• Lisa then began lungeing and long lining to build Cassie's trust in her. She also led her out in-hand and practised walking over scary obstacles in the school. With time, Cassie's confidence in Lisa began to grow and, in turn, her anxiousness became less of an issue.
• 'Cassie still won't stand completely still when I get on, but she's miles better," says Lisa. "Basically, I just used repetition to help solve this problem. I'd put one foot in the stirrup, she'd walk away, so I'd go with her and try again. I just kept on and on until she let me get on without a fuss. It would have been easy to shout and kick and get angry with her, but I knew I had to be patient.'
• 'It took two or three months until I started to see a change in Cassie, but now she is much more relaxed. She is an affectionate horse and she loves people, so I'm glad she's had the chance to relax and improve. I think building a relationship with a horse is as much about us getting to know them as them us. I know what winds Cassie up, so I make sure I avoid those situations.'

*Slow, patient and repetitive work is the best way to achieve lasting results*

# THE WHOLE HORSE

No matter what your riding ambitions are, when you are training your horse it is well worth considering varying his work as it will not only make him a better all-round performer, it could boost his motivation and protect him from injury. Known as cross-training, this type of approach has its roots in human athletics and has steadily increased in popularity. Many athletes now train in two or three activities to develop all-round body fitness, improve strength and keep their motivation and interest in their particular specialization. Cross-training pays off in other ways: for example, runners who substitute part of their running exercise with other activities, such as cycling, weight-training or swimming, suffer far fewer injuries – and their running performances improve.

## PRODUCING THE ALL-ROUND ATHLETE

Specializing in a single riding activity is likely to maximize only one or two aspects of your horse's ability. For example, working over poles and jumping grids will improve his suppleness and technique over a fence, and control and balance between fences. However, if all you do is jump or do flatwork for jumping, he will only develop certain muscles and will never achieve all-round fitness. Ultimately, his body may not be able to cope with the repetitive stresses involved in jumping, and he could incur injuries that result in time off work.

You can introduce cross-training at almost any time. However, if you compete it is best to begin well before the season starts (at least a month in advance), so your horse is a strong and capable athlete by the time the competitions get under way. Introducing cross-training does not mean you have to increase the amount of time you ride. Simply spend some of the time you put aside for training in your particular area on cross-training instead.

There are three areas to consider when producing an all-round athlete: working the muscles, heart and lungs, building up bone and tendon strength, educating your horse and improving his flexibility.

### MUSCLES, HEART AND LUNGS

The muscles and heart adapt fairly quickly and retain their fitness for up to two weeks without training. The lungs also adapt quickly to training, but revert if work is not maintained. In fact, within two weeks of stopping work, the efficiency of the lungs will decrease to pre-training levels. This is an important consideration if you are planning to compete at speed, for example in hunter trials. Muscle strength and heart and lung fitness will

### All-round fitness

Train your horse using a variety of activities, such as
• Lungeing or long lining
• Flatwork
• Jumping
• Road work
• Riding on bridleways and tracks
• Hill work
• Fast work

*Hill work is probably the best way to increase your horse's fitness*

increase with regular hill work or short periods of fast work. Working your horse hard over a long period of time will tire him unnecessarily and increase his chances of injury. Instead, use short periods of uphill or fast work, interspersed with short walks to allow him time to recover.

## BONE AND TENDON STRENGTH

The bones and tendons take two years of consistent and progressive training to reach optimal strength. Studies have shown that the temperature inside the tendons reaches over 44°C (111°F) during exercise, and that ridden horses experience some cellular changes to central fibres in the tendons, which can damage the tendons if they have not been strengthened through suitable fittening work.

Hacking on roads and bridleways gives you the ideal opportunity to develop bone strength. Long periods trotting on roads or hard ground will result in concussion to your horse's limbs, so use predominantly walking exercise to stimulate the bones to harden. Working over a variety of surfaces (from roads or stony tracks to rough or soft, muddy going) is good for developing overall tendon strength and elasticity. Road work produces stiffer, stronger tendons. Rough, uneven ground causes slight twisting of the limbs, which stimulates the tendons to adapt to different strains. The effort of pulling the limbs out of soft going encourages elasticity and overall fitness in the tendons.

However, too much road work will result in your horse's tendons not being flexible enough to cope with soft going. Similarly, working on soft going every day will not develop your horse's bone and tendon strength on harder ground, and may result in tendon strain. It follows that work on a combination of surfaces will produce the best bone and tendon strength.

## EDUCATION AND FLEXIBILITY

Schooling your horse in an arena develops flexibility and suppleness, and educates him to your aids. You can teach him to move correctly and develop lateral work or jumping. Vary your schooling programme including polework, lateral exercises and lungeing or long lining each week.

Focus on doing several different activities each week. Decide when you will be training for bone and tendon strength, when you want to concentrate on flexibility, suppleness and educating your horse, and when you will be doing fitness work for the muscles, heart and lungs. Build up the time you spend on each of these activities so your horse has a chance to adapt. Keep a record of what you do and set some objectives so that you can track your progress. See pp.214–218 for more information on fittening a horse.

*Lungeing is a good way to exercise your horse and test his responses*

---

### Sample weekly schedule

**Day 1** Ridden schooling, including lateral work (flexibility and education) – 30 minutes

**Day 2** Hacking including two bursts of hill work (heart, lungs and muscles) – 45 minutes

**Day 3** Long lining or lungeing (flexibility and education) – 30 minutes

**Day 4** Rest day

**Day 5** Ridden schooling, pole work or jumping (flexibility and education) – 30 minutes

**Day 6** Hacking with road work at walk only and other surfaces at walk and trot (bones and tendons) – 45 minutes

**Day 7** Rest day

*Strengthen your horse's tendons with gentle road work*

# HOW FIT IS YOUR HORSE?

**A fit horse is capable of carrying out the demands placed upon him. This is true whether you show jump, do dressage, event or compete in any other discipline. If you can monitor how fit your horse is throughout the year, you can tailor your training programme to suit you both and it will enable you to get the most out of the partnership. Monitoring the fitness and general health of your horse will also mean you can spot signs of illness or injury earlier and deal with them before problems worsen.**

## THE PULSE

Taking the pulse (number of heartbeats over one minute) is the best way to monitor your horse's immediate response to his exercise programme. Using either a stethoscope or heart monitor on the left side of his chest, just behind the elbow, take his pulse at rest before exercise in a quiet environment. Alternatively, take his pulse by gently resting two fingers on one of the pulse points, such as the top of the lower jaw or the inside of the knee joint, counting for 10 seconds then multiplying by 6. A normal resting pulse rate is 36–42bpm (beats per minute), although some horses have resting pulses as low as 25bpm. Get to know your horse's normal resting rate.

*Pulse rate and recovery time are excellent indicators of horse fitness*

To test whether your horse is fit enough for the work you are doing, exercise him as normal, and take his pulse when you return to the yard. It should not be over 64bpm as this indicates fatigue and a lack of fitness, and it should return to around his resting rate within 20 minutes. A pulse rate in the high 50s is an indication that your horse has worked hard. The only exception to this would be on very hot, humid days when it will be higher if he is still hot after exercise. You can lower the pulse more quickly in these conditions by washing down with cold water over his neck, saddle area and between the hind legs.

If you are in the process of getting your horse fitter and want to measure his progress while out riding, use a heart rate monitor. During fast canter or gallop work, his pulse may reach 160–180bpm but it should drop to below 120bpm within a few minutes of returning to slower work. Do not repeat the fast work until his pulse has dropped to 120bpm.

## STANDARDIZED EXERCISE TEST (SET)

Another way to monitor your horse's fitness on a regular basis is to do a standardized exercise test. Plan a specific route that involves a hill or some fast work, or use one of your schooling sessions (just be sure to carry out the same periods of walk, trot and canter in the same order each time you do the SET).

Take your horse's resting pulse before you exercise, and then take the pulse again immediately after you have finished exercising. Continue taking your horse's pulse every 10 minutes until 30 minutes after finishing exercise. This will give you a set of readings for the fitness of your horse. Do the same SET on a regular weekly or fortnightly basis.

Your horse's fitness is improving if the pulse rate taken when you first return to the stable is lower and/or the recovery time (the time it takes the pulse to drop to the resting rate) is shorter than previous SET readings. Higher pulse rates and a longer recovery time indicate that your horse is losing fitness or overtraining (see box, right).

## RESPIRATION

Respiratory rates (the number of breaths taken over one minute) are slightly easier to measure than pulse rates, but they are a less reliable indicator of fitness. To take the respiratory rate, either hold a wet hand by your horse's nose and feel the air as he breathes out, or watch his flanks moving and count each movement in and out as one breath. Your horse's resting respiratory rate should be 8–12brpm (breaths per minute).

Measure his respiratory rate after strenuous work, such as cantering or uphill exercise, to monitor his fitness. Many horses will take a high number of heavy breaths immediately after hard exercise, followed by lighter breaths, gradually dropping to the resting rate. Fitter horses will take lighter breaths and their respiratory rate will fall more quickly and return to normal sooner after exercise.

## BUILDING UP BODY TONE

We can all see the basic difference between a fat, unfit horse and a sleek, fit one. However, there are many levels of fitness in between these two examples. By looking at body condition and taking measurements of your horse's weight, it is possible to assess subtle changes that occur. A horse that is fit to compete in most disciplines will have:
• A level back
• Ribs that can be felt easily (although not necessarily seen)
• Rounded withers
• Sufficient coverage of the neck and shoulders
• Well-covered hindquarters with the hips still able to be felt easily
There are always conformational differences between horses, so get to know your horse as an individual and monitor his condition on a regular basis. Measuring your horse's exact weight requires special equipment, but changes in weight can be monitored with reasonable accuracy using a weightape. Drop the weightape over the lowest part of the wither, then pass it underneath the belly, making sure it sits as close to the front legs as possible (just behind the elbows). Measure your horse's weight like this on a regular basis so you are immediately aware of any changes. It is particularly useful if you have recently changed your exercise programme or the discipline you are training for, especially when coupled with the recordings of pulse rates, respiratory rates and general body condition.

### AVOID OVERTRAINING

*If your horse's pulse is suddenly much higher (double the normal reading) during or after work, without an increase in speed or duration of exercise, he may have been overtrained. Overtraining occurs when the exercise programme is too strenuous and his body cannot cope. Overtrained horses are less likely to show a lack of performance in short, fast work, but may lack stamina. If you suspect overtraining call your vet for advice.*

*Ensuring your horse is fit enough to do the work you are asking of him means he is less likely to suffer injury or stress*

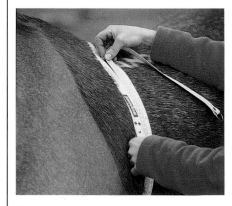

*Each time you use a weightape ensure it is in the same place as before as it is easy to get inconsistent readings*

# THE SOUND HORSE

A horse that works correctly is not just a pretty sight, but is physically more comfortable, economical and healthy than one that does not. The good news is that anyone can learn to ride in a way that will keep their horse athletically competent, sound, happy, long-lived and free-moving. Every rider owes it to their horse to school according to good, solid form and function, not fashion or performance goal. Your aim is to avoid injuries and discomfort in the horse caused by unequal stresses on his locomotor structures. On a daily basis, the horse should gain the confidence, strength and co-ordination to carry himself in a balanced and efficient manner and avoid many of the wear-and-tear stresses that may eventually disable him.

*Correct movement can be achieved with correct schooling*

## MENTAL HEALTH

To be physically sound, a horse must be mentally sound. To school in a truly effective way, you must remember that your relationship with your horse is at the heart of the process, with competition performance at the periphery. Developing the horse's confidence is as important as developing his physical prowess, because only when he is calm and focused on you can he pay attention and learn. Emotions are strongly related to physiology. What we want to recreate when we ride is the lift, posture, energy and balance you see in a horse that is mentally stimulated – think of a horse at play or one suddenly focused on an outside distraction.

## IMPROVE HIS POSTURE

Lameness is defined as asymmetrical motion. This uneven way of moving may be caused by a physical injury, which can be located and treated, or it may be caused by poor posture, for which there may be no visible injury (although the strain of moving unevenly over a period of time may well create a physical injury or ailment). Teaching a horse to carry himself straight is not about getting good marks for your centre line entry in a dressage test. It's about keeping his motion as symmetrical as possible so he moves evenly, with each limb taking its fair share of weight.

Most horses have a preference for loading their weight on one side or the other. When you stand straight in front of a horse, it's usually quite clear which shoulder is taking more weight: the head swings the opposite way to the direction in which he is leaning (just as your head might if you were carrying a heavier shopping bag in one hand than the other). Pulling the head 'straight' will not correct the uneven stance elsewhere in the body, which is what is causing the problem. A horse will express this preference in other more subtle ways, too, such as always looking at you with the same eye first as you walk towards him.

*The inside hind leg should land directly under the horse's navel*

The structure and conformation of the horse is hardly ever the problem when it comes to obtaining straightness – it's posture. A horse is straight when his sternum is centered between his elbows. His lower limbs or feet may not be straight, but structural problems higher up, through the shoulders, chest and elbow, are very rare.

## THE 'UNDERLINE'

Any reference to developing topline and a correct outline is misleading. In order to round up, you need to stimulate the 'underline' of the horse – the belly, lower neck and pelvic area. By doing this, you will be engaging the 'postural ring', a set of consecutive muscles that run from the poll, down the neck, over the back, round the haunches and under the stomach, then up through the front legs to the throat. These interact with each other and stimulate correct posture. When the horse's abdominal muscles contract and lift the back, the haunches will naturally lower and the head and neck fall into place (see diagrams below). Without the release that comes from lifting the lumbar vertebrae and engaging the postural ring in this way, the horse will have restricted use of his hindquarters and will not be able to work as freely and comfortably.

Strengthening the horse's underline simply involves stimulating the musculo-skeletal system in as varied a way as possible, using as many transitions, changes of pace, stride length or direction as you can, and using of ground poles to increase balance, co-ordination and muscle fitness. This is why circles are an essential part of schooling, because they encourage equal use of the inside hind leg, which should always swing so that it lands directly under the horse's navel. Every transition is a complete gymnastic exercise in itself. The horse needs to gather himself for a moment, or half-halt, so that the limbs can change the direction, speed or length of their swing. Every half-halt requires a small lifting of the loins which, in turn, increases the degree of roundness and collection. Transitions train the horse to flex his joints and maintain some flexion in reserve, so that he can carry you and himself with less risk of injury and with more energy.

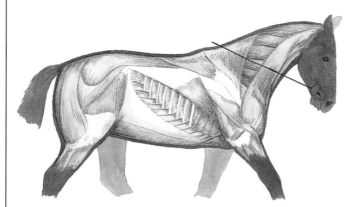

*When the horse's abdominal muscles contract to lift the back, the haunches naturally lower*

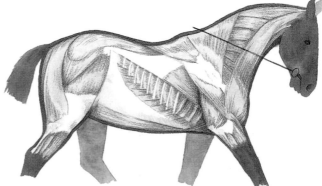

*If the lumbar vertebrae do not lift, the horse has restricted use of his hindquarters*

## FIVE BASIC GOALS

1 *Before asking anything of your horse, help him to be calm. This means that he is comfortable and confident with you, his equipment and his working environment. Any tension or activation of the horse's flight responses are contradictory to the result you want, both physically and mentally.*

2 *Ride by feel, not form or position. Horses care less than you might think about where your hands and feet are. Riding from a mental, rather than a physical, perspective will open you up to better feel, so ride with interest and keep the horse interested by offering support and direction.*

3 *Time your aids perfectly. Make any suggestions to your horse while he is still OK, rather than waiting until he is wrong and correction becomes necessary.*

4 *Ride in balance so you interfere as little as possible with your horse's efforts.*

5 *At every moment help your horse to carry himself straight.*

## FOCUS ON THE LITTLE THINGS

Goals can make riders blind to key aspects of their horse's behaviour. Imagine that it doesn't matter if you never saddle your horse and ride. Keep your training objectives at the back of your mind; abandon all ambition and schedule. As you carry out your schooling session, be sensitive to the horse's mental and physical state, and adapt to his response – don't expect him to adapt to yours! Many riders believe that trying something different will confuse their horse, but it could explain things better to him. If what you're doing isn't having the desired effect, change it – repetition without result isn't good training, it's a sign the horse isn't getting the information he needs.

*A horse that moves well demonstrates lift, posture, energy and balance*

In the moment, forget going anywhere and focus on each single step instead. In an ordinary halt, for example, the overall goal is to induce the horse to stop. But a horse can only stop one foot at a time, and with a soft feel through the muscles of his neck. Therefore, to get a change you don't actually have to stop; you can half-halt, hesitate, or merely begin to change direction, all of which require the horse to yield in the neck and feet. This means you are inducing the horse to change the overall shape and movement of his body, which has all kinds of side-effects, including redistributing his weight.

*When you ask for halt remember that a horse has four separate feet to bring to a stop – concentrate on each one*

### RIDING YOUR HORSE SOUND

**1** *Remember it is riders that are ambitious, not horses. Your bravery and confidence don't help him; what he needs is help finding courage within himself.*

**2** *Never ride without a thorough warm-up, and don't do too much work at any one time. Remember that your horse learns upon release and reflection.*

**3** *Hardness of muscle deprives your horse's joints of a range of motion, and the vast majority of leisure horses don't need to be 'hard' fit.*

**4** *Never pull your horse's head and neck away from the direction of his attention. His feet should be pointing where his eyeballs point.*

**5** *When you want to halt, think of stopping the feet and not the face! This is the route to collection – not holding onto his mouth, bending his neck, pushing him forward from the seat and leg into a fixed hand. A horse is on the bit when every change in the rein creates a change in the hindquarters.*

## PROBLEM SOLVER

**Q** I rescued a horse that was painfully thin and in bad shape. Two months on he has gained weight and condition and I have started trying to ride him. When I tack him up he resists the bit and refuses to leave the yard for a ride. I have tried riding out with other horses and he still panics. He has tried to rear, he pulls his head down, bucks and spins round. He bares his teeth and shakes his head as if the snaffle is hurting him. I ride him in a flash noseband and a running martingale. Is there any other tack that could help me with his problems?

**A** There could be several factors influencing your horse. Firstly you have improved his general condition and health. A newfound feeling of wellbeing often results in the problems you have described. You know little of your horse's past – it could be that your horse's behaviour originates from fear and it may be long standing. Horses have a good memory and you will need patience to solve these issues.

The first thing to do is review his health. Pay particular attention to his mouth and back to make sure he is comfortable. Check all his tack fits well and try to use the simplest equipment possible. Avoid gadgets, they may achieve a quick result, but it doesn't tend to last.

The next step is to start a re-schooling programme that will encourage your horse to work in the correct way and allow him to gain confidence in his rider. You may need to start at the beginning. Lunge him without any tack and establish forward movement with a relaxed attitude. Gradually introduce the tack and work with it until your horse has the same relaxed attitude. Then is the time to re-introduce the rider.

When he accepts the rider, the correct response to the aids can be established. When you are confident that your horse is obedient, introduce the situations that he finds more difficult to cope with, such as hacking out, preferably in the company of another horse, at least at first.

*Sometimes the only way to help a horse through his troubles is to restart his training from the very beginning*

# RESPONSE AND REWARD

In your training it is vital to keep your horse motivated, and the best way to do this is to reward him when he does the right thing. The most important aspect of reward is that it is appropriate and instantaneous. For example, if the horse moves off your leg satisfactorily, you should relax it straightaway. If the horse gives in the mouth, soften your hand instantly. Consistent responses and rewards like this are beneficial to both the horse and the rider. The horse gains confidence because he is given clear messages. Also, like people, horses tend to move towards pleasurable experiences, so if he gets a pleasant result – a softer hand, for instance – the horse is more liable to repeat an action.

## RECOGNIZING RESPONSE

When you are consciously looking to reward your horse, you will become much more aware of what's happening between you. This leads to you being more tuned into him, and making better choices about what to do next. It is so sad to see a horse give in the mouth, and the rider's hands still jiggling about, oblivious to the fact the horse has responded. To the horse, this means he has not found the required response, and so he will try something else, dropping behind to avoid the hand, for instance. If, instead, the 'give' is rewarded instantly, he will know that this is what is wanted and is much more likely to remain soft in the mouth.

When you are teaching your horse something new, or he responds particularly well, you may want to give him a bigger reward, such as a friendly pat. In all your training, work on really noticing your horse's reactions. Reward every good response you get with a pat. Focus on softening every time he gives, and relaxing your leg when he goes forward. These responses will soon become automatic, and riding will become more like a conversation and less like an argument. If the horse puts in extra effort, reward him with walking on a long rein and a pat. Most horses respond to such treatment by going with a renewed willingness and a more positive swing to their step.

*One of the earliest and most important things to teach a youngster is that whenever he does what you ask he will be rewarded*

*If you work on achieving a good relationship with your horse – including balancing training time with fun rides out – he will want to please you*

## TAKING UP A CONTACT

Try this exercise when teaching a horse to soften to the bit – it perfectly illustrates the effectiveness of instant reward.

Walk the horse on a long rein. After a few moments, pick up the reins and, with sympathetic hands, use gentle contact to soften him. The moment he softens genuinely, give him a long rein again and a pat. After 15 metres (50ft) or so, pick up the reins and repeat the exercise. After five or six repeats, most horses are quite happy to go straight on the bit the moment they feel the reins being picked up. On the sixth time keep the contact and ask the horse something new – to go into trot, or to make a circle. Although it will need repeating at a later date, the initial lesson has been learnt, and it is time to move on.

*Horses really enjoy a gentle appreciative pat and it tells them that they are doing the right thing, which gives them confidence*

## THE GOLDEN RULES OF TRAINING HORSES

*Trainer Michael Peace has these golden rules that he applies to his own work.*

• *In an ideal world, it would be great to operate a reward-only approach to training, but in real life this does not work. There needs to be a balance between positive, reward-based training (giving the horse a stroke to say thank you) and negative-association training (pushing a horse back out of your space when he pushes into yours, for example). As long as you never bully and always strive for a 50/50 balance in your relationship, correcting a horse is perfectly natural to him and mirrors the behaviour he expects from other horses in a herd.*

• *Horses are masters at reading body language. They are experts at living in groups and can read the tiniest of signals. If you are positive in your actions and make it clear exactly what you want your horse to do, this will help to cement your relationship and build respect.*

• *Always motivate your horse to work well. This does not mean walking round with a pocket full of treats – instead, let him know when he has done well with a gentle pat and let that be his reward. Horses are social animals, so a genuine rub on the head is as effective a reward as a mint.*

• *Be a good manager and always remember to think carefully about your own behaviour before you try to manage your horse's.*

• *It is a fact of life that horses prefer the company of other horses to that of people. Where possible work your horse in an environment away from his friends, so there is a better chance of gaining, and then keeping, his attention.*

• *Horses are logical creatures, so apply logic to your training methods and use your common sense at all times.*

• *Make every training session interesting and upbeat for the horse and keep the pace of the lesson moving forwards all the time.*

• *Try to finish every training session on a high note and make each goal easily attainable. Lots of tiny, minor achievements are far more productive than one damaging failure.*

• *Horses appreciate quiet, consistent handling. If you are relaxed one day and sharp the next your horse will lose his trust.*

• *Don't allow the relationship with your horse to become muddied by emotions. If you are leading your horse and he pulls away, for instance, don't take it personally. Instead, work through the problem and take time to understand why he is behaving like this.*

• *Gain as much knowledge as you can about the way a horse thinks and behaves so you understand his actions.*

• *My training philosophy is all about achieving and maintaining a 50/50 balance – something that calls for constant, minute adjustments to the relationship. This means your horse has to work just as hard as you, whether you are handling him on the ground or riding.*

# TRAINING A YOUNGSTER

Taking on a youngster is not an easy option; training young horses requires a lot of time and patience. However, the wonderful thing about working with a young horse is that you have the opportunity to ensure he learns what you want him to learn and in the way that you want him to learn it, and when he is ready to be ridden you have the deep satisfaction of knowing that you have achieved something very special. This section outlines the most important things your youngster needs to know and how you can go about teaching them. If you lack experience in this area, and even if you have worked with youngsters before, it is worth considering getting in a professional to help you teach some of these skills.

# FIRST STEPS

Young horses need thorough training, from learning to stand still when tied up, to being groomed, shod and having their feet picked out. Begin with general handling around the yard. Take your time, make friends with your horse and don't rush. Groom him and lead him in-hand around the school, perhaps also training him to go in and out of a lorry or trailer. When he is ready to be backed, his lessons can include in-hand work and eventually lungeing, schooling and safe short hacks. Tackle schooling exercises logically. If your horse doesn't understand what you've asked, return to a simpler exercise you know he can do well to build his confidence. In early schooling sessions make sure you keep turns and circles large, avoiding sharp turns, which can cause a young horse to lose balance.

*One of the key stages in a youngster's training is ensuring that he is happy to be with you*

## MAKING THE RIGHT CHOICE

Before committing to a youngster it is well worth asking yourself some searching questions to ensure you are doing the right thing:

*1 Am I going to be able to commit enough time to him?*

*2 Is he going to meet my needs? It is important that your youngster will mature to a horse that is a suitable match in terms of size, temperament and ability.*

*3 Have I got access to the right facilities? Whether you keep your horse at home or at livery, it's important that the fencing is safe, there's company (preferably plenty and of mixed ages) and plenty of turnout. A yard with a manège and access to quiet country roads and tracks is preferable (a quiet, safe area in which to train your youngster is essential).*

*4 Who else will be handling him? Continuity is important when it comes to handling young horses, so if you are going to have to rely on other people to handle your*

*youngster, make sure you can trust them to follow your instructions.*

*5 Have I got the necessary experience, knowledge and common sense to bring on a young horse successfully?*

*6 Do I have a network of knowledgeable friends who can support me? Help must always be on hand when you are training and especially backing a young horse. Youngsters are unpredictable. You must take steps to ensure you are as safe as possible when you begin the backing process.*

*7 Have I got enough money to pay for his keep? A youngster may appear to be the cheaper option, but if you send him away to be started, you must have the cash to pay for the best possible training for him. It can be very expensive to have a horse professionally backed.*

*8 Does he have any health problems? As with any horse, it is important to get a youngster vetted before you buy.*

*9 Have I given serious thought to the fact that I may not be able to ride for some time? Most horses are backed at the age of three or four, which means at least two years without riding if you buy a yearling.*

*10 Am I confident enough to handle a young horse?*

*Youngsters need the company of other horses of a variety of ages so that they learn to socialize*

# CASE STUDY: **FIRST TIME LUCKY**

Sheryle Elson bought 15.2hh TBx Maddy as an unbroken four-year-old.

'My first horse was a sensible, middle-aged Fjord, so I went from one extreme to another when I bought Maddy,' explains Sheryle. 'But it had always been a dream of mine to buy a young Thoroughbred and bring her on myself.'

'I bought Maddy from a local dealer. I chose her largely because she had such a loving temperament. Even though she hadn't been handled much, she was gentle and easy to do – although it was nerve-wracking for the first few weeks. I'd never handled a youngster before and kept worrying that I'd do the wrong thing.'

'I spent the first couple of months taking Maddy for walks around the village in-hand so we could get to know one another. I had a bit of trouble leading her at first because she insisted on walking right behind me, but luckily the owner of the livery yard where she was stabled was experienced with youngsters and gave me lots of advice.'

Working with a youngster can be time-consuming and challenging, but it can also be immensely rewarding

'Maddy is quite laid back for a Thoroughbred – most of the time – and this has been my saving grace. She was pretty calm as a youngster and wasn't bothered about any of the usual "scary" things like traffic. I started to back Maddy a couple of months after I bought her, with help from the livery yard owner again who long lined her for me.'

'To get Maddy used to wearing tack I started to lead her, in-hand, in a bridle, and then I led her round the village in a saddle too. I was the first one to sit on her in the school and everything went smoothly. There was no bucking or wild behaviour – although she's made up for that since! I did a bit of work with her in the school, introducing her to the basic aids, and started to hack out on quiet roads and tracks, with an older horse for company, more or less straightaway.'

'I love Maddy and I've never regretted buying her. She can be lively out on hacks, and if she's in season she can be naughtier now than she was when she was a youngster, but she's mine. I gave her a good start in life and I'm very proud of her. My only ambition now is to win a rosette in a showing class. If that happens I'll be made up.'

# A REAL BABY

Anyone who has ever taken on the responsibility of a foal will be aware of the multitude of theories relating to how best to handle a newborn. Some experts believe you should leave your mare and foal alone to bond in the first few hours and days, intervening only to carry out the essential health checks and make sure they are happy. Others consider it a good idea to handle young foals all over to get them used to being touched and to desensitize them to human contact. Every owner's goal is to produce a healthy, friendly, well-balanced youngster and so, whatever approach you adopt, common sense and sound horsemanship must be applied.

## NEWBORN

Trainer Michael Peace believes that in the first few days after birth, mare and foal should be left alone in the foaling box to bond, with as little human intervention as possible. Obviously your vet will need to perform the necessary physical checks immediately after the birth, but otherwise there should be little interference from you – no matter how cute and cuddly your new arrival looks.

Stick to basic, essential, routine handling for the first five days, giving your mare and foal a helping hand only when necessary. For example, you may need to get hands-on to help the foal suckle. If the mare is used to you she won't mind you being around and, provided you are sensible, aggression is rare. Make a fuss of the mare first before you approach her foal. Maiden (first-time) mares can be overly protective of their foals. If this is the case, ask an experienced friend to help and hold your mare with a headcollar and rope while you check the foal, making sure she can see him at all times.

There is no point trying to do any educational handling with a very young foal. However, it is well worth quietly observing your mare with her offspring to ensure things are developing normally. If you are inexperienced you can learn a lot from a good book on stud work, which will explain what is normal, healthy behaviour. For example, a foal should attempt to stand within a few minutes of being born and be on his feet and suckling within an hour. Having an understanding of these basic 'landmarks' will help you spot quickly if something is wrong.

## EARLY HANDLING

Initially your aim should be to reach the stage where the foal is happy to be stroked all over by you – mirroring the touch of his mum. Once you've gained his trust you can start to manipulate his movements.

If you're dealing with a timid foal who runs behind his mum whenever you enter the foal box – and this is common – back up the mare

## Test your know-how

**What is imprinting?**
Imprinting is a process where the foal is handled all over in the first five days of life to desensitize him to stimuli. This is thought to prepare him for potentially disturbing encounters with people, such as shoeing, bitting and clipping. Done correctly, it can be beneficial. However, it can easily go wrong and, if overdone, will remove the flight instinct we rely on when training horses in later life.

## FITTING A FOAL SLIP

Stand to the side of the foal, loop the slip under his neck and hold the loop in front of his nose. The foal may reach down to look for it and you can then slide the foal slip on. Alternatively, unbuckle the noseband as many foals will object to having things placed over their nose. Buckle the headpiece around the foal's neck, then gently slide the slip up the neck, and buckle up the noseband once it's in place.

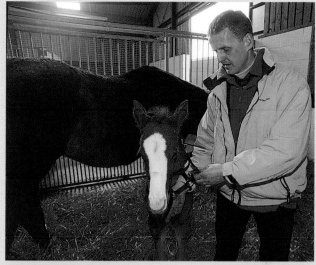

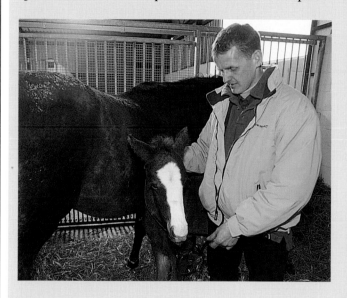

• *Don't worry if you can't do up the foal slip properly at first. You can sort out the keepers and so on later.*

• *Once the foal slip is in place, leave it on for a short time so the foal can get used to the feel of it. You can put it on and take it off at a later stage once the foal is more comfortable with you and it. Never leave a foal slip on for long periods as it may rub.*

• *Don't put any pressure on the foal slip. A foal's head and neck area is very fragile and you could do a lot of damage.*

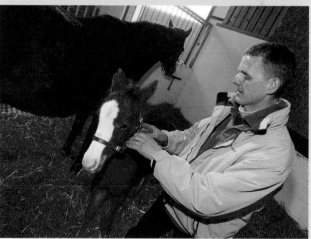

• *Foals have a strong urge to be with their mum, and mares often like to keep their foals in front when they're on the move so they can see them. Bear this in mind when leading your mare and foal.*

to help block his movements. Then gently squeeze him forwards onto your side of the mare so you can introduce yourself. Once the foal is facing you, his natural inquisitiveness will probably work to your advantage, as he's likely to come over to investigate. If you're struggling to encourage the foal out from the opposite side of his mum, try getting a sneaky touch on his neck by fussing the mare and then sliding your hand underneath her chin.

When the foal is five or six days old, weather conditions allowing, you can start to turn both mare and foal out in a safe, well-fenced paddock for a few hours each day. At this stage you can introduce a foal slip (see box above). When he is happy with wearing the slip, start to get him used to being led off it.

Initially it's handy to have someone standing behind the foal, to gently encourage him forwards as it can be dangerous to pull on a slip. Keep a hand on the foal's neck to prevent too much forwards movement while maintaining momentum with an arm around his quarters. Subtly teach your foal to yield to pressure – a touch on the hindquarters means move forwards while a touch on the sides means move sideways and so on. To turn the foal, place one hand lightly on the foal slip and your other arm around his neck and gently guide him round.

## WORK AND PLAY

There's a fine line between giving your foal a positive view of humans and over-handling him. It's important to deal with him in a practical manner and not treat him like a baby, which may cause problems once he grows into a strapping young horse that sees humans as play things. Biting and nudging, for example, may seem funny when done by a foal, but they must be discouraged as they will be unpleasant and annoying once he reaches maturity.

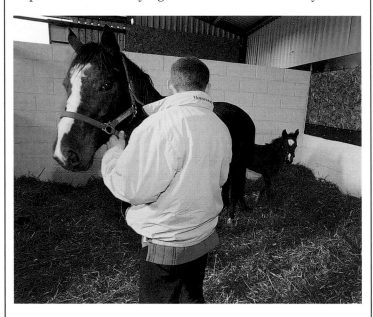

*When a foal is hiding behind his mum you can persuade him to come out by gently backing her up and squeezing him out of his hiding place*

If a foal lives out all the time with the minimum of handling he may become a bit 'wild'. However, Michael Peace says he would much rather deal with a two-year-old horse that hasn't been handled, than a youngster that has been over-handled and spoilt.

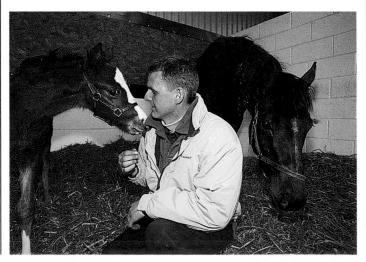

## PROBLEM SOLVER

**Q** My 18-month-old Welsh Cob has started to nip me when I pick out his front feet. He has a lovely temperament so I'm sure he's only playing, but I want to put a stop to this behaviour before it gets out of hand.

**A** Young colts play by nipping each other and will often try to bring each other down by grabbing at a front leg. It's all a big game to them so it is likely that your youngster thinks you are playing when you pick up his front foot. You need to make it clear that you are not playing but, at the same time, don't be too firm with him. It is very important that you do not let your colt's behaviour stop you from picking up his foot. If you drop his foot and turn to remonstrate him, he will soon learn that biting gets results.

There are two stages to curing this problem: first, get your positioning correct. If you stand well out to the side of your colt to pick up his foot, it will make it easier for him to reach round and bite you. Instead, position yourself slightly in front of his shoulder and tuck yourself in as close to him as is safe. This way, he won't be able to reach round so effectively. Second, when picking out your colt's nearside front hoof, hold his foot with your left hand and use your right elbow to bump his nose out of the way if he tries to nip.

*Nipping is all part of a youngster's life but he needs to know that it doesn't include humans*

*Brave foals are easy to deal with as their curiosity often gets the better of them and they come and check you out*

# EARLY EDUCATION

For the first months of his life a foal has a lot of growing and developing to do and, apart from ensuring he is happy to be approached by people and understands the very basics of what is required of him, this is what he should be allowed to do. However, after a couple of years your young horse will have outgrown his 24-hour playtime in the field. Although he is too young to be ridden, there are plenty of exercises you can do with him in-hand. These will help to keep his mind occupied, prepare him for later life and strengthen your relationship.

## LEADING LESSONS

If your horse has been handled correctly from a foal, by the time he is two years old he should be friendly enough to allow the basics of handling. So where should you go from here? The first and most important step is to teach your horse how to lead correctly. This is the foundation for everything you do with him later. If he is leading well he is listening. If he is pulling he's not listening.

Remember, young horses have no idea what they should be doing, so follow these guidelines and give your horse every chance to get things right. (This work assumes your horse is used to wearing a headcollar – if not, you need to work on this first.)
• Find a small, safe area, for example a pen or large, roomy stable, and begin your training using a headcollar and long rope.
• Lead from the near side and stand slightly in front and to the side of the horse, so you act as a visual cue for him to follow. Horses like to follow, so make it easy for your youngster to do just that and don't be too insistent on where he goes. It's all about compromise at this stage. If you need to turn, ease him round – don't pull.
• How you hold the rope is important. Have it loose enough so that the horse doesn't feel as though you are challenging him, but make sure it is short enough to be able to redirect him if needs be.
• Keep each leading session short and praise your horse with a rub on the neck when he follows politely. Always finish on a relaxed, confident note, if you don't, you won't have achieved anything positive.

Young horses are often flighty and excitable, so make lots of circles and changes of direction to focus his attention on you and be gentle, but definite, in your actions. If he tends to be bargy, remember he is young and this is only high jinks, so back him off a little but don't overdo it. When dealing with youngsters, it is important to keep everything low-key. If you get unnecessarily tough on them you'll cause confusion and negativity. Instead, strike a balance between being firm but fair. If you feel intimidated and nervous, ask someone more experienced and knowledgeable to help you with his training.

As soon as your horse has grasped the basics and is following politely in response to a soft feel on the rope, you can move on a stage. Make the pen larger, move out of the stable into a bigger area (the yard for example) and walk further. Eventually, you will be able to lead your horse around the field. (If you are having problems leading any horse, young or old, see pp.30–33 for a leading masterclass.)

*Teach your horse to lead well – it is a key foundation skill*

# NEW EXPERIENCES

Once your youngster is leading well in a larger area and responding to a light feel, you can begin to expose him to new things, which will increase his knowledge of the world and help him to learn to trust you. Choose exercises like 'Stepping over a log', below, that encourage a horse to think forwards and gain confidence in himself – something that will come in handy when you start to ride him and ask him to take the lead. If done correctly, work like this will build and strengthen your relationship; you can't teach a horse anything unless you're working well together. There are no set rules. Vary his routine, use your common sense and find the right balance. If your horse is progressing at the right pace he will look forward to his work and positively enjoy it.

## STEPPING OVER A LOG

This is a simple but effective exercise. Lead your horse up to a low log or other small obstacle and ask him to step over it. At first he is likely to be suspicious, so let out the rope, stand on the other side and let him stop and sniff it. You are not teaching him the art of stepping over a log, you're teaching him to consider this new obstacle and co-operate. If he stares off into the distance or fidgets and gets excited use the rope to gently draw his attention back to the log. When he makes the decision to pop over the log, this is a big step for him. His blood will be up after all that excitement, so walk him back down to the point where you started and work through it all again, calmly and gently. As your horse becomes more comfortable with this exercise his movements will be more relaxed. A horse that storms ahead wild eyed and rushes over the log is not keen, he's worried.

*Allow your horse to look at each new thing he meets and then tell him what you would like him to do. Don't worry if his response is a bit rough to begin with: as you repeat the exercise he will become more confident and so calmer*

## TURNING SKILLS

The next stage in your horse's training is teaching him to turn away from you. Standing on his left side, to ask for a turn to the right:
• Loosen the rope in your right hand so you are slightly in front, but still to the left of the horse. Have the rest of the rope, loosely coiled, in your left hand.
• Briefly and gently, raise your left hand to the side of your horse's face, this will encourage a movement to the right, and at the same time guide gently him round to the right with your right hand.

Initially, you should look for only a couple of steps in the right direction. Build on this until you can take more strides around to the right, and progress to doing serpentines across the field or arena. Gradually use subtler aids. Eventually you will reach the stage where your horse will stay behind you and move away politely when you turn.

*A turn to the left is easier for the horse to understand than a turn to the right as he can merely follow you round*

*Look on leading practice as a way to really get to know your young horse, and have fun doing it*

## STOP

A vitally important part of leading work is to teach your horse to stop when you stop. This is difficult with young horses: they are naturally impatient and expecting them to stand still on command may lead to a battle.

If he doesn't want to stop, walk him around and wait for him to relax – a relaxed horse will drop his head and lick and chew. Then slow your walk, wait for him to stop naturally, stop with him, reward him with a rub on the neck and walk on. Don't expect the halt to last for more than a second – this is something you can build on at a later stage. If you keep everything calm and matter of fact your horse will soon learn that when you stop, he stops. Remember you can't use force to get a horse to stand. (For more advice on halt, see pp.78–83.)

# LEADING MASTERCLASS

Imagine this: you can lead your horse – a young, strapping Warmblood, flighty, reactive Arab, headstrong Cob – anywhere without any worries or problems. There is always a big loop in the leadrope and the horse walks happily alongside you. Both you and your horse are completely relaxed, even when horses in adjoining fields are charging around, or a bird scarer goes off, or a low-flying jet goes noisily by.

Or does this sound more like you? If something distracting happens when you are leading your horse, you have to hang on to him for grim death. In fact, you are always worried when leading your horse – and the horse never looks very relaxed either!

So how do you achieve the first and say goodbye to the second? The answer is simple and something that anyone can follow.

## AN ESSENTIAL SKILL

The truth is that leading well is an essential skill for a horse. If a horse has been taught well he will be a pleasure to own, if not he can be a nightmare. Horses that become excited and dance around will put the handler in danger, and those that pull away and get free put themselves, and potentially other people, in danger. So, if your horse is not exactly an angel to lead, follow this plan to turn him from monster to superstar.

## HELP YOURSELF

• Keeping control of your nerves is vital as your horse will sense any doubt or fear you have. Practise deep breathing and notice how this helps you to become calmer and more focused.
• Work through the leading exercises to build your confidence in your ability to get and keep a horse's attention and respect.
• Start small and build up. Teach yourself to see a setback as a training opportunity rather than a complete disaster.
• Work through any personal fears or worries with the help of an expert, such as a NLP (Neuro Linguistic Programming) practitioner or a sports therapist.
• Use Bach Flower Remedies (mimulus for known fears and larch for lack of self-confidence) to improve your mental state.
• Wear protective clothing. As well as being sensible and safer, this will make you feel more confident.
• If your horse really frightens you, it is better to get suitable help than to try to resolve the leading problem yourself.

**1** *Have slack in the lead rope and position yourself in front but to the side of the horse. It is easier for your horse to see you in this position than if you are back by his shoulder. Take a few steps and see if he follows you. If he does, let him know that's the right thing to do by giving him a rub on the head.*

**2** *If he doesn't follow, take the slack out of the rope and gently draw (not pull) the horse towards you, rewarding him with a rub when he takes a step towards you. Be aware of where you are standing – you do not want to block his movement by standing in his way.*

**3** *Work in this way until you have your horse taking several steps when you ask. Now add in lots of changes of direction so that he has to concentrate on you in order to know what to do next. Remember to keep the rope slack.*

You and your horse need to learn to respect each other's space, and you must be consistent in how you handle your horse and always be quiet and courteous with him. If something does frighten him, you must not panic or pull on him or shout. You must teach yourself to stay calm (see box, left); your horse will immediately sense this and take courage from it, as will other horses you handle. You also need to prepare your horse for situations he may meet which could worry him.

## THE CLASS

The method described below works with all horses from youngsters to older horses, those that are sour and those that are confused. Start your leading lesson in a confined area, such as an arena. Use a normal headcollar and a longer-than-usual rope. Once you are doing well in the arena, try leading your horse in a larger area. For example, lead him around the yard or down to the field, putting in the occasional halt, ensuring that he stops where and when you ask. The important thing to remember is to be consistent with this today, tomorrow and every day from now on. As well as teaching a horse how to pay attention to you and to respect your space, this leading exercise also helps a horse move from a negative mindset (such as the horse who always misbehaves when led) to a more neutral state of mind. From this point you can then show the horse that there is an easier and much more enjoyable way to live – that is, to be led easily rather than dancing around.

**4** *Work on halts, too. Your aim is to have your horse stopping when you do and standing with his head in line with, or just behind, your shoulder. If he stands too close or goes too far in front, just back him up into the correct position and praise him by giving him a rub on the head.*

**5** *By now your horse should be paying attention to you – you will know this as he will be responding to your every move, following you with his head lowered, body relaxed and a soft look in his eye.*

## TROUBLESHOOTING

Horses learn good and bad behaviour equally well. If your horse has learned that pulling away results in freedom, he will employ this tactic whenever he decides that he'd rather be somewhere else. To change this behaviour you have to break the cycle and show him that being with you is better.

• Use a much longer rope than usual so that you can feed it out if necessary rather than have it pulled out of your hands.

• Avoid getting yourself in a position where the horse can pull on straight in front of you (right). Keep to the side so that if he takes off you can step to the side and put yourself at 45 degrees to him (below). You can then use this leverage to get his head round to you, so unbalancing him and giving you the opportunity to bring him round on a circle. Then back him up, position him where you want him and try again.

• Don't shout at him, jerk on the headcollar or jab him in the chest. Just show him he's wrong by putting him where you want him to be.

• At no point in this process should you get into a tug of war or a confrontation with the horse. We all know that horses are much stronger than we are so there is no point trying to beat them.

• If your horse shows frustration it may be that he doesn't understand what you want. Take time to consider the task from his point of view.

• Some people advocate using bridles or stronger halters for horses that pull away. However, a bit or a pressure halter can cause discomfort and you may find that your horse fights you even more. In addition you are not really dealing with the root cause of the problem.

## PROBLEM SOLVER

**Q** My Thoroughbred x cob yearling mare is difficult to lead. She walks to the field in a headcollar, but as soon as I try to lead her across the field she pulls away and runs off. She is the same if I try to lead her in the school. She either squashes me into the fence or spooks and pushes past.

**A** Teaching your horse to lead properly is a vital part of her training, as it will help her to learn manners, co-operation and trust in her handler. Always work her in a headcollar with a long rope, and position yourself out in front and slightly to the side of her. When working with young or problem horses, out in front is the safest place to be should they rear or barge into you. It also gives them an idea of where they should be going next. Before you begin make sure she knows what pressure is and that she should yield to it, as horses will naturally try to resist pressure.

As you lead, make changes of direction and regularly stop and start to keep her attention. Don't pull her around: use a long rope and plenty of turns to teach her to stay with you. If your horse is dragging her heels a little behind you, for example, make a sharp left turn so she's by your shoulder again. If she leaps past you, don't make a fuss, just give her some slack on the rope and step to the left so she can find you again. Constantly use subtle moves like this to reposition her and teach her where she needs to be. By leaving her alone when she's right and correcting her when she's wrong, she will soon learn where she should be going.

Another good exercise is to stop, back her up, give her a rub on the neck to say thank you and then walk on. This will get her thinking about stopping rather than just pushing past you or barging.

All the time you're leading, she should be focusing on you and anticipating your next move. If she isn't concentrating and barges into you, stop and wave the rope at her to back her off. Once she is the correct distance away, give her a rub on the head to say thanks and then carry on. This teaches the horse that it's her responsibility to respect your personal space. Make your intentions clear and be deliberate in your actions, both when you're leading and when you're pushing her out of your space. If a horse barges into another horse in a herd situation he will be pushed back, so you are mirroring horse language.

Young horses often try to rush past you while they are being led if they are worried by something. They haven't yet learned how to rationalize situations, so if something spooks them their instinct is to run away. If this is the case, you need to gain your horse's trust and confidence and teach her to put strange noises and so on into perspective. This takes time and patience. Asking a friend to lead an older, quieter horse alongside yours can help.

*If the horse barges into you, push her back out of your space*

# KEY LIFE SKILLS

Once your youngster has accepted a headcollar and is happy to follow you on a leadrope wherever you go, it is time to introduce a few more challenges. Each one of these will build on this foundation and help him to understand and be content with his working life. Being handled, tied up, accepting the attentions of strangers such as the farrier and vet, and learning to lunge and long line are all part of his new world.

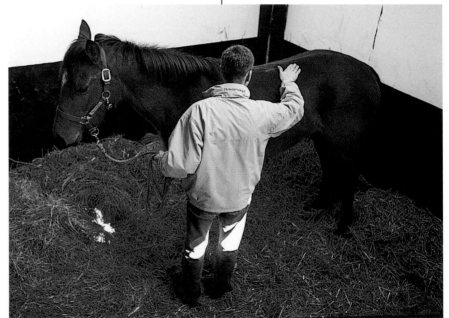

*Teach your horse that being handled can be pleasurable and is perfectly safe*

## BEING HANDLED

It is important for his future wellbeing that your horse will tolerate being groomed and touched all over his body. Careful handling at this stage will prepare him for later work and strengthen his trust in you. The introduction of tack, boots and rugs will come as less of a shock to him if he has been well handled from a young age.

Always remember to touch him equally on both sides and, at this stage, avoid very ticklish areas as you will only annoy or frighten him. If he swishes his tail at you or lifts a leg because you've hit a ticklish spot, don't jump away but back off gently and leave well alone. Never make him feel uncomfortable, or get to the stage where he tells you to back off, but teach him that you are going to touch certain parts of his body – and you are going to do it politely. Running your hand along his wither and back, along the front of his shoulder and from the top of his tail to the back of his hock is as far you need to go at this stage. Touching his legs (apart from the areas you need to handle when you pick out his feet) and any really sensitive areas can come later.

## VETERINARY VISITS

It is a fact of life that your horse will receive veterinary attention at some point in his life, so he needs to learn to tolerate the vet so visits can be as stress-free as possible – for all concerned. It is your job to make sure that your horse is as prepared as he can be for a visit from your vet.

Many youngsters live a sheltered life, rarely seeing anyone other than their owner and a few yard regulars. If your horse is wary of all strangers, invite a few of your friends over so that he can become accustomed to seeing new faces. Set up the situation so that he learns that a visit from a strange person can be pleasurable. If he is in his stable when your friends come over, for example, ask one or two of them to quietly say hello to him over the stable door and give him a gentle stroke on the nose – anything that he will view as a positive experience. Repeat this activity regularly with different people so that he gets used to accepting attention politely and without getting stressed. Leading work will also teach your horse to trust you, which will help when you need to hold him for the vet.

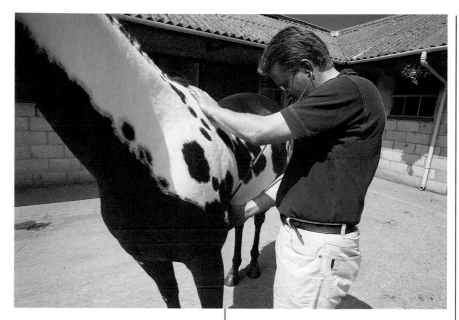

*When your horse is relaxed around strangers and used to being handled, a visit from the vet is far less stressful for both of you*

## FARRIER VISITS

Any work you do preparing your youngster for vet's visits will also help him accept the farrier. However, with the farrier there are the additional skills of learning to pick up his feet and hold them up, and allowing the farrier to rasp them and eventually put on shoes. When he picks up his feet the biggest problem is maintaining balance, so help him by making sure he's standing square before you lift one of his hooves. If your horse picks up his foot then slams it back down, chances are he's unbalanced rather than being deliberately obstructive, so give him time and practise picking up his feet at least twice a day – in the field and in the yard. Ask someone to hold him for you, run your hands down his leg, tug under his heel and say 'pick up' or 'up'. Bring his foot up gently, gradually lifting it higher each time and always go round all four feet (for more on this, see pp.63–65).

There are lots of other things you can do to prepare your horse for the farrier. You can simulate the shoeing process by tapping his foot gently with a hammer and getting an old shoe and holding it against his foot, hitting the metal with a hammer so he gets used to the noise. Throw the shoe aside like a farrier would. Bring him in when another horse is being shod so that he can become used to the sights and sounds of the farrier.

When the time comes for him to be shod, it is most important to choose a sympathetic farrier. Have a chat with him before he comes to shoe your horse and explain that you have a youngster and may need extra time and patience. Always be there when your horse is being shod and have him shod for the first time in two stages – front shoes first, then back shoes a couple of weeks later. Sometimes it is a good idea to have youngsters cold shod for the first couple of times as the smoke and smell of hot shoeing can be off-putting.

*Make sure your farrier is prepared to spend some extra time on your youngster for the first few visits*

35

## TYING UP

Being tied up in the yard is something that all horses have to accept and most are happy to do so, provided their introduction to being tied is done in stages.

At first, slip the lead rope through the tie ring (or preferably a piece of string or bailer twine that is tied to the ring) and hold the loose end. Allow your horse to move and get used to the feeling of being restricted, but slacken the loose end if necessary so that he doesn't start to fight the rope. Leading work will have taught him how to find a release from pressure. If he gets concerned then go back to practising leading to ensure that he really understands what is required. Do this work for a few minutes at a time to begin with and give him a friendly rub on the neck when he stands quietly and correct him when he moves, telling him to stand. Eventually he'll get used to the idea and you can start to tie him up for increasingly longer periods once he has settled. Stay with him when he is tied up.

From then on use every opportunity to practise – for example, tie him up when mucking or skipping out. If he fidgets when he's tied up, chances are he's just looking round to see what's going on. It's natural for youngsters to fidget – just like young children.

## LUNGEING

Lungeing can be a useful extension of leading practise but shouldn't be done with a horse before the age of three. You can get him used to being led around the school with a lunge line attached to a lunge cavesson, but only for about 10 minutes at a time. Use objects such as cones, plastic blocks and poles to make obstacle courses to lead him round, so he learns to trust you whatever he comes across.

*Lungeing can be useful for training youngsters but keep lessons short and relaxed*

When he's old enough, and is very good at leading, introduce him to lungeing. Begin by leading him around the school, then move away from him a metre at a time so you are still by his side, but further away. Try not to work him in a circle, as this is quite demanding on young limbs. Go large around a school or in large half circles, in walk.

Wear protective footwear, gloves and a hard hat just in case he gets frightened and jumps around.

# PROBLEM SOLVER

**Q** I have an unusual problem with my three-year-old Thoroughbred gelding. I first introduced him to a turnout rug last autumn and he seemed happy to wear it. However, a few days later, while he was turned out, he was bullied by a couple of other horses. They chased him and pulled the rug off his back, leaving it flapping around his chest. This sent him into a panic and he tore around the field until the rug fell off. Since then he has been afraid to go near his fieldmates while wearing a rug, and hangs around the gate instead. He panics if they try to chase him or canter past, and once he smashed through some fencing in a bid to get away from them. When he is not wearing his rug, he grazes happily with the other horses and he has no problem wearing a rug in the stable. What can I do?

**A** It is likely that when your horse wore a rug for the first time, he didn't fully realize how it would feel and sound at speed. However, as soon as the other horses bullied him into moving off, the rug started flapping. Then, when they pulled at the rug, it started to slip. The more he bolted, the more it slipped.

He now associates approaching horses with a flapping and slipping rug. They chase him into a trot or canter and the flapping gets worse, and each time this happens it adds to his phobia. In his mind, his rug is only a problem when other horses approach and chase him off, which is why he doesn't mind wearing a rug in the stable.

You need to deal with your horse's phobia in the same quiet, methodical way you would a human one. Phobias are, by nature, irrational, so desensitizing your horse to this problem will take time and patience.

Choose a small, safe area, roughly 20 x 20m (65 x 65ft). It is important that the surface is safe and non-slip, and the fencing is suitably high. A round pen is ideal or you can fence off half a manège. Choose an area that is safe and small enough to prevent your horse getting up too much speed. Make sure there are no horses nearby.

Rug up your horse, turn him loose in this small area and keep him moving. Let him trot and canter if he wants. Choose a cool day so he doesn't get too hot, and stay outside the area if there is a chance you could get kicked. Keep encouraging him to move. Once he has started to settle, stop the session. This exercise needs to be repeated until your horse is happy to move around the area in his rug.

The next step is to turn another horse loose in the manège or paddock with yours, keeping them separated by a fence. If, for example, you have fenced off half a 20 x 40m (65 x 130ft) manège, put the other horse in the other half. This way, they can sniff each other over the fence but your horse won't feel too threatened. Encourage both horses to move around, in trot if possible, as this is where your horse's phobia lies. He will eventually realize that his rug is flapping, and there's a horse nearby, but he is still alive and fine.

Once your horse is totally at ease with having a neighbouring horse trotting around near him, put both horses in the same, confined area. You can then introduce your horse to larger turnout areas. Keep him in a small paddock on his own, wearing his rug, with horses in an adjacent field at first. Then turn him out with one other horse and progress from there.

All this work will take some time, but these exercises will gradually desensitize your horse and help him learn to deal with his fears. Horses will get used to most things given time and patient handling.

*For most owners, a rug is a vital item of winter equipment, allowing their horse to be turned out comfortably while keeping him relatively mud-free for riding*

# PREPARATION FOR BACKING

**Opinions vary hugely when it comes to the question of how old a horse should be when he's backed. Most trainers think three-and-a-half to four years old is the right age as the horse is then mature and strong enough to cope with this next stage in his life. However, some prefer to back a horse at three, then turn him away for a few months. It really does depend on the individual horse as some mature earlier than others.**

## CAREFUL STAGES

It is difficult to put a timescale on backing because all horses are different. A quiet-natured, willing horse can progress much more quickly than a nervous type, which will need more repetitive work. For the average horse, it'll take about four weeks to complete the process of introducing a bridle, lungeing, introducing a roller and a saddle, long lining, backing (or 'sitting on'), walking and trotting in the arena under saddle and hacking out in company. Some horses may progress much quicker if they have been well handled and already know the voice commands on the lunge. Some may take longer, especially if they are nervous or bolshy.

As soon as in-hand exercises have become a regular part of your young horse's daily routine, you can move his training on. Now it is time to prepare him to accept the bridle. Thanks to the leading work, your youngster will have learned to trust in and comply with you, so should be happy to accept you introducing some basic tack.

It is important that this next stage is approached carefully, as a negative experience will influence the way your horse views being tacked up and handled generally. So, before you head off to the tack room, make sure your horse is happy to be touched all over. He will find bridling work particularly intrusive if he is unused to having his head and ears handled, and he may then learn to associate you – and his tack – with discomfort. So sound preparation work now will aid progress later.

### INTRODUCE THE FEEL

Put your horse in a headcollar and hold the rope instead of tying him up, to give him the freedom to move if he wants to. Using the flat of your hand or knuckles, gently rub around the top of your horse's neck, poll and forehead – avoid using your fingertips. (If your horse is headshy, see p.67.)

Another good tactic is to stand to the side of your horse's neck, cup your arm under his jaw and gently hold his face, just above the muzzle. Gently rock his head from side to side. Also, practise gently slipping your thumb or forefinger into the corner of his mouth to get him used to the feel. Some young horses can become nervous of having their mouths played with, so be patient.

## BRIDLING

Introducing the bridle is done in several stages. Work methodically through each stage, allowing your horse time to get used to the idea before moving on. This work may take one day or several days. Initially you will need a headcollar, a jointed snaffle and two pieces of string. Then you can progress to a bridle. Use just the headpiece, cheek pieces and snaffle; don't worry about the reins at this stage. Adjust the bridle so it is too big at first (so you don't have to scrape the headpiece over the horse's ears) and put on a headcollar underneath.

**1** *Make sure your horse is happy to have his neck, head and ears rubbed.*

**2** *Tie the string to the bit rings. It will be used to attach the bit to the headcollar – it needs to be long enough to allow the bit to sit quite low inside the horse's mouth.*

**3** *Tie the bit ring to one side of the headcollar.*

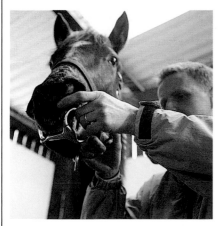

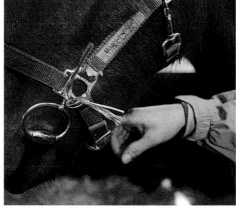

**4** *Gently open the horse's mouth with the thumb of your right hand and slip the bit into his mouth.*

**5** *Attach the other bit ring onto the other side of the headcollar. Most horses react surprisingly well to the feel of the bit, so leave him in his stable or a small pen for 30 minutes to play around with it.*

**6** *The next stage is to introduce a bridle. Hold the headpiece between finger and thumb, so the bridle falls open in front of the horse's face. Holding the bit in your left hand, put your thumb through the snaffle ring into the corner of your horse's mouth to encourage him to open it for the bit.*

**7** *Slip the headpiece over his ears and adjust his forelock and mane so that it sits comfortably.*

When you take off the bridle, take care not to let the bit bang against your horse's teeth. Removing the bridle should be two movements: first, bring the headpiece over the ears and drop the bit slightly. Second, hold the bridle there for a few seconds until the horse opens his mouth, then remove it completely.

Repeat this exercise regularly until you reach the stage where your horse feels the bit and opens his mouth. Remember, when it comes to your horse's training, think 'everything in moderation'. There are no set rules as to how much or how little your horse should be doing, so gauge his reactions and proceed accordingly.

Once your horse has had time to get used to the feel of the bit, you can begin to lead him while he is wearing the bridle. Keep the headcollar on underneath the bridle and lead off the headcollar. You can then progress to leading your horse like this over poles and through puddles, and so on.

## LET HIM CHOOSE

*It is important to fit the bit low in the horse's mouth at first as this allows him to choose whether to put his tongue over or under it. It is more comfortable for horses to carry the bit on top of their tongue, so there's no need to force him to do this. Give him the option of having a trial to see what he finds most comfortable by leaving him in the stable for 30 minutes with some hay – he'll soon choose to carry the bit on top of the tongue to enable him to eat. The height of the bit can be adjusted later.*

*You must watch your horse at all times while he is wearing a bit in his stable or pen.*

*Don't use a Fulmer snaffle as the cheek pieces are likely to get caught on something.*

# SADDLING

When introducing a saddle for the first time, work your horse in a headcollar and long rope in a quiet, safe area with a good surface. Throughout the saddling process be calm, confident and up front about what you are doing and make sure your horse is aware of everything that's happening. Don't creep around, hoping he won't notice what you are doing. Remember, all this stuff is new to him. It's your responsibility to set up the situation so it's easy for him to get things right. You can do this by choosing a time when the yard is quiet and there isn't too much wind to blow the pad around, and remaining calm and business-like – all common sense things that will help no end. How sceptical your horse will be of this strange 'alien' on his back depends on his personality. If a horse has been well handled in the past, he will usually be quite happy with it after some initial wariness.

*1 Start by placing a saddle pad on your horse's back and leading him round to get him used to the feel of it. It helps if he is already familiar with wearing a rug as this will have got him used to carrying something on his back.*

*2 Next, pop the saddle on (make sure the stirrups are either securely run up or removed and lay the girth over the seat of the saddle). Position the saddle far enough forward so that it could slip back slightly and the girth would still be in roughly the right place – however, don't do up the girth at this stage. If your horse wants to move, let him, but use the rope to direct him around you so he doesn't gain any distance from you. When he stands, thank him with a rub on the neck. This way, he will soon learn that moving is a waste of his time and standing still is much more pleasant. Gently push him away if he gets in your space, but don't make an issue of any 'naughty' behaviour. Instead, calmly deal with it.*

*3 The next stage is to quietly do up the girth. The first few steps a horse takes after he is girthed up for the first time will usually involve a buck or two – so unclip the rope and let him go loose. If he wants to have a buck, the safest place for him to do it is on his own away from you (though always watch him). It's important to have the saddle girthed up tightly enough from the start so it doesn't slip. Once your horse has had his mad 10 minutes and settled down again, you can clip the rope back on and lead him round.*

## ADDING THE BRIDLE

Presuming you have already introduced your horse to the bit and bridle (pp.38–39), you can bridle him while he's wearing a saddle. Put the bridle on over his headcollar and pop the reins over his head. Most horses are happy to allow this. If yours is worried, unbuckle them and put them around his neck. Cross the reins in front of the saddle and tuck them behind the stirrup leathers to simulate where a rider's hands would be.

You can let your horse wander around loose like this in your small paddock or arena, under observation, as long as there's nothing he can catch himself on. Doing this gives him a chance to stretch his neck, mouth the bit and get used to the feel of all his tack.

As with all aspects of training, there are no set rules as to how fast your horse should progress. Always gauge his reactions and proceed accordingly. With all the foundation work in place, it is possible to have a horse wearing a saddle and bridle by the end of the first session, but this work is not about how fast you can do something but how well it is done.

*You know that you are on the right track when your horse happily accepts the saddle and bridle and walks calmly around the school*

## PROBLEM SOLVER

**Q** I am preparing to break in my three-year-old Welsh Cob. I would like to know what it means when people say they turn away young horses after being broken. Does this mean that once he's accepted me as his rider, I have to turn him out and not ride for a while? If this is the case, how long does turning away last?

**A** Horses may be backed and ridden at an early age but they still have a lot of physical maturing and growing to do. They will not have a full set of permanent teeth until they are five, for example. The other point to consider is that a lot is being asked of them mentally. This is why many people believe a period of adjustment in the field is beneficial after a horse has been introduced to the basics of being ridden.

Whatever you decide to do, don't rush this stage of his development. Once you have backed him, start hacking out quietly with another horse as your companion. Then you may feel that it is best to turn your horse away for a rest, both mentally and physically. He will certainly appreciate the time to digest all that you have taught him. It may suit you to give him the winter off and work him during the summer months, but the rest period can be at any time of year. Once your horse has turned four, the more serious training work can begin.

*At three years old a horse still has plenty of growing and maturing to do. If he is given time to do this, it should enable him to avoid problems in later life*

41

# WORKING UNDER SADDLE

Saddling and bridling are big steps in a horse's training, but provided you have worked slowly and methodically, he should accept them reasonably quickly and will soon be ready to move on to the next step, which is long lining or lungeing (or both), depending on your preference. This stage allows your horse to get used to the feel of moving in his tack at walk and trot. Start off by doing this in a small area, such as a school or pen, for three or four days. (For more information about the techniques involved in lungeing and long lining, see pp.50–56 and 57–59.)

## LONG LINING OR LUNGEING

Take your time when putting on the lunge line or long lines – some horses react to the feel and sight of them behind them and need time to realize that they are not dangerous. Ask your horse to move forward gently and work him in walk to begin with. Unless you are very adept at long lining and lungeing, it is useful to have someone at his head to begin with to help explain what is wanted. Go through the basics of what he will be required to do when ridden: start, stop, turn. Keep the sessions short and upbeat and reward good work with rests.

*Long lining gives a youngster space and time to get used to the feel of the tack on his back. It also increases his experience of being asked to perform manoeuvres by his handler*

Long lines are more effective for teaching your horse to associate a rein movement with a turn or stop. Work in a small paddock or school, with someone walking by his head at first. To stop, ask your horse to walk towards the fence. The second he gets there and starts to slow, apply a feel on the long lines. The person at his head can do the same to back this up. The same goes for turns: when the horse reaches the edge of the arena and turns, apply a rein movement the second he turns so he can connect the two. Soon he will learn to associate the feel in the mouth with going left or right or stopping.

*Lunge or long line your horse with the stirrups up at first and then let them down. Tie both stirrup irons together under the horse's belly with an old stirrup leather*

Long lining is a great way to take your youngster out and about but make sure his steering and brakes are firmly in place in a small area before you move on to working him in a larger space, such as a paddock or quiet, traffic-free farm track.

# CASE STUDY: DOING IT WITH STYLE

Sam Booth bought Thoroughbred mare Style Council (or Cilla), when she was rising three. An experienced rider, Sam enjoys eventing and was keen to have a youngster to bring on.

*'I did a lot of work on the ground initially with Cilla, using Michael Peace's methods to teach her to lead properly and learn some manners so she was controllable on the ground. I spent the first summer establishing the basics. I did groundwork, introduced her to the bit, got her used to wearing a rug and lunged her. Then, at the end of the summer, I took two weeks off work so I could concentrate on backing her.'*

*'Once Cilla was used to the feel of the saddle on the lunge, I leaned over her back and was led round the arena. I gradually progressed from there, and in two weeks I was able to get on and ride her round the arena, then around the farm – first with an older horse for company, then on our own.'*

*'Cilla had a three-month break after this first taste of ridden work, then I brought her back into work. We spent the next year doing flatwork and more road work (in company at first). I took her to a couple of local shows in-hand so she could get used to the atmosphere, but mostly just allowed her to progress in her own time. The following year we did our first Preliminary dressage test and Cilla behaved impeccably.'*

*'This year I have introduced Cilla to the clippers and farrier and she had her first set of front shoes on in July. Since March we have competed in several affiliated Preliminary dressage classes and I was very proud when she qualified for the Area Festival in August (we didn't get placed but scored 58.5%).'*

Sam has had lessons with Jeanette Brakewell to work on Cilla's balance and collection and they've done a bit of jumping. It is early days with the jumping and she intends to spend more time on it once their flatwork has come along.

*By following a sensible backing programme and taking her time, Sam has produced a horse that she has every reason to be proud of*

*'My aim originally was to compete Cilla in a young event horse class as a four-year-old. However, when it came to it, I felt the amount of pressure I would have had to put on her would have been too much too soon. For the classes, horses have to be competent over a 1m (3ft) show jumping course and capable of doing an intro-level dressage test, and I didn't think she'd be able to cope. Instead, we've concentrated on our dressage because I think taking it slowly is key.'*

*'My plan now is to progress to affiliated Novice tests, work on our jumping and aim to do an eventing introductory class by the end of next year.'*

# INTRODUCING THE RIDER

Remember, riding a young horse for the first time can be dangerous, so only attempt it if you have the experience and ability to handle every possible scenario. If you've done the preparatory work properly, and ride lightly and in balance, your horse should handle having you on his back without too many fireworks. Always wear the correct protective clothing when dealing with young horses, including a hard hat, gloves and boots.

Once your horse is long lining or lungeing happily in his tack and has learnt the basics of turning and stopping, you can start his ridden work. Work in a safe, enclosed area with a helper. Methods used to back a horse vary and if you are unsure of how to proceed you must ask an experienced person for help. Some people initially simply lie sideways over the saddle then drop down again, to give the horse a chance to feel their weight. Trainer Michael Peace has had experience with many youngsters and his preferred technique is to have a leg up and put his left foot in the stirrup. Lying across the saddle like this he asks the person on the ground to have the horse move one step away from them then one step towards them. This left/right action gets the horse's legs moving and allows him to feel the rider's weight. It also enables him to see his rider with his left then his right eye. As long as Michael feels that the horse is happy, he then gently lowers himself into the saddle and asks the person on the ground to repeat the stepping away and back exercise. Over a period of one or more sessions you can gradually progress to taking a few steps around the arena on your own, and steadily increase the variety of manoeuvres you are asking for, always ensuring that your youngster understands his job and responds happily.

As the work your youngster does increases, it is vitally important that you keep an eye on his tack and make sure it is comfortable and fits well. Young horses change shape very quickly, especially as they mature and muscle up, and a saddle that is too tight will both restrict this development and make him reluctant to respond to your requests.

## Basic skills

When you begin work on backing your horse, there are three basics that he needs to learn – they can be put into a few words, but cover a wide range of skills.
1 Start, stop and steer.
2 Trust and confidence. If you run into difficulties, or meet a 'scary monster' in the hedge, your horse must have the confidence to trust your instructions to continue past.
3 Voice commands. Your voice commands should always be encouraging, clear and simple: eg 'walk-on' and 'whoa'.

*Hold yourself over the saddle while your helper reassures the youngster*

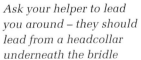
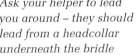

*Ask your helper to lead you around – they should lead from a headcollar underneath the bridle*

*Take a few steps on your own, gradually building up the work*

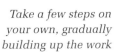

## PROBLEM SOLVER

**Q** I've just started riding my four-year-old. Everything is fine except that he won't let me mount from a mounting block. I've tried getting other people to hold him. What can I do?

**A** Your horse is at the start of his career, which means that you should treat everything that you do with him as 'teaching'. Therefore, when you bring him out of the stable don't think of the next bit as a hassle, think of it as a training session.

To work on mounting it is easiest to use a moveable mounting block. Place it beside him and see what he does. If he moves off move the block next to him until he accepts it sitting beside him. Once he's standing still, climb on top of it. If he moves away step down and move the block towards him again. Repeat this until he'll stand still with you on the block next to him. If he stands still then reward his good behaviour – pat him all over just as you would a youngster who had never been sat on before. Never use a loud voice if he doesn't do what you want.

Next put your foot in the stirrup and if he moves follow him and repeat this until he stands. Once on-board ride away but at the end of the session go back to the block. He'll be tired and may stand much sooner. Mount and dismount several times, rewarding good behaviour. Do this regularly until he learns to stand calmly. (There is more about working on mounting on pp.68–69.)

*A young horse needs to be told if he is doing something wrong, otherwise he won't know. If he moves when you mount, teach him how to stand still*

## PROBLEM SOLVER

**Q** My four-year-old bolts back to the other horses when I school him in the field so, in the absence of an enclosed arena, we're hacking out. He is doing well, but he carries his head very low and leans on me. What can I do?

**A** Schooling your horse in a field full of horses is not a good idea. As you've found out, when he doesn't understand you he'll run to his friends for reassurance – a sure sign that he doesn't trust you yet. It is crucial you find somewhere enclosed to train him. Hacking is not safe until you've established some basic training.

All young horses carry their heads low and lean on the reins at first because they don't have the strength in their muscles to hold themselves in self-carriage. A young horse will look for support on the reins and one way you can counteract this is to match his pressure with the strength of your position: keeping your legs on and sitting up tall, so your muscle tone matches the rein contact. Only when your rein, leg aids and torso match will your horse learn to balance within the 'framework' you give him.

Once he becomes stronger in his back, you'll be able to soften the reins so he learns to balance with his weight more on his hind legs, lightening and lifting his forehand. This doesn't mean throwing away the contact , but easing it so it feels softer. Young horses benefit from lunge work, allowing them to stretch down to the ground, as though they're grazing. Leading exercises using poles and obstacles to walk over and round add variety and develop your horse's concentration. For example, ask him to walk over a pole on the ground, then progress to trotting over it. Remember to keep all tack and equipment as simple as possible.

*Vary your youngster's work to give him the opportunity to develop the correct muscles to carry you*

# BASIC MANNERS

It would be wonderful if every horse was beautifully trained and did exactly what he was asked to do without fuss or worry. The sad fact of equestrian life is that an awful lot of horses simply haven't had sufficient training in all the skills that they need to work with people or have been worried by something to the extent that they have never really accepted doing it, both of which can eventually lead to difficulties. This section focuses on a variety of methods of working with your horse that help to increase your mutual understanding and trust, and dealing with common problems.

# PRODUCING THE PERFECT HORSE

Even though most of us love our horses, few of us would say they were perfect. Perhaps they are great to hack out or do wonderful dressage tests but aren't so good in other ways. Good examples of problem areas are not being quiet for the farrier, taking hours to load into a trailer or horsebox, or not going in at all, being unwilling to stand still to be mounted and being scared of the clippers. While many owners might dismiss these saying 'That's horses for you', the truth is that with time and effort most horses will accept most things, as long as they are introduced in the right way and explained clearly. The way to work towards the perfect horse is to work through any 'problems', not avoid them. Start by teaching your horse general skills such as long lining and lungeing, then go on to specifics, such as helping a poor loader or catching a horse that really doesn't want to be caught – niggly habits that can be frustrating and difficult to resolve.

*A willing responsive and calm horse is a pleasure to own and ride*

## SUCCESSFUL TRAINING

• *Whenever you are training a horse, the trick is knowing when to praise and when to hassle. It's all in the timing. Watch your horse's facial expressions and read his body language. The eyes give away a lot – they soften the second a horse decides to think and co-operate. Learn to read these subtle signals and you'll be more effective in your training.*

• *A horse will often try everything he has ever learnt to throw you off guard or evade the situation, so it's up to you to teach him that his repertoire of tricks won't work.*

• *However evasive and tricky your horse's behaviour, you should never ever lose your temper.*

• *It's best if a horse can learn the basic skills when he's young, but it's important that he understands them whatever his age. However, it may take an older horse longer to break the habits of a lifetime, so be patient. Allow plenty of time and don't let any training situation degenerate into a battle of wills.*

• *If a horse is genuinely worried or scared by something you are asking him to do, you've got to make it easy for him. Set up each situation so it becomes clear to him that what you are asking will be beneficial for him. Break everything down into stages and reward each step.*

• *Look for ways to reward good behaviour and try to prevent things going wrong before they actually do so. That way, he will have a positive experience, rather than a negative one.*

• *Before you try to retrain undesirable behaviour always consider whether it might have a physical cause – make sure your horse is comfortable in his mouth, back, neck, legs and feet.*

# CASE STUDY: **RACY RACEHORSE**

A couple of years ago, Jodie Grey bought a five-year-old ex-racehorse. *'If I'm honest, he was too much for me, but I was keen to persevere with him. Initially I really struggled with his spookiness – and his desire to gallop every time we hit grass. I fell off numerous times. In the end I realized I had to take him right back to basics to educate him for every-day riding.'*

Jodie sought the advice of a good trainer and was told that there was every possibility of her new acquisition turning out to be a useful riding horse, but that it would take dedication and time. In addition, the process would be on-going as he was by nature a highly strung and hot-blooded horse and so would always need careful handling. To start him on the right track, she was advised to provide plenty of turnout in the company of other horses and feed a high-forage diet.

Trainer Charles Wilson offered her further advice:
*'I have had a good response to re-schooling using natural horsemanship. The work begins on the ground, where you can watch your horse's body language and gauge his mental state.'*

*'Start by teaching your horse to yield in halt. This sounds basic – and it is. When a horse is fleeing danger he'll keep his body straight and tense. When he's coming out of this mode, he'll yield his quarters away to turn and look at the danger. This turns off his flight response and allows him to think again – and this is what you are replicating when you ask him to yield in halt. Using a headcollar or halter, stand by your horse's side with a loose leadrope. From halt, gently ask for a crossing of the hind legs with your free hand in the position where your leg would be were you on his back. This hindquarter yield should be done calmly, with the leg nearest to you moving across the other. If he shuffles, this means he's tense. Keep repeating the request – it may take many attempts before he gets it right.'*

Jodie says:
*'The next step was to ask for the yield in walk, using it as a transition down to halt. I asked for the yield from touch – aiming, in the end, to get it just by pointing at his quarters. We continued in this way and eventually we could go through the different paces on the lunge and I could still yield him right back to halt. There are other yields, such as backing up and forehand yields. All proved excellent in training him to listen to me.'*

*'When he was working well in a school environment, I started to take him out into a large field and go through the exercises there. His energy was higher than in the school, but he learnt that I was still in control – grass doesn't mean gallop.'*

*'Although we still have some way to go, I have been able to ride him again. When he gets tense and ready to flee, I use the yields to bring him back down to earth again.'*

*Re-educating any horse is a time-consuming and rewarding task – although racehorses will always remember that they used to race, they can become useful general riding horses*

# LUNGEING

There's more to lungeing your horse than just going round in circles. It's a great addition to your weekly exercise regime. Used once or twice a week, it can help your horse become more supple and responsive. So, if you've never used groundwork to the full before, now's the time to start.

Lungeing is an extremely useful tool. Correctly done, it allows you to teach your horse all sorts of new movements, build up his muscles correctly, exercise him without having to ride, supple him up, take the freshness out of him and do polework. In fact, anything you can do from the saddle can be done on the lunge. And what's more, 20 to 30 minutes' lungeing is equivalent to one hour's riding.

Lungeing is also useful because it gives you an opportunity to observe your horse from the ground – something you may not be able to do very often. You will be able to assess his muscle development, his general way of going and how he is carrying himself. Although a school with a prepared surface is great, you don't need one – a corner of a paddock will do as long as it's level and the ground conditions allow it.

## Equipment

• You have two options: use a lunge cavesson – over the bridle if you want to progress to working on the bit – or simply use a bridle, which simulates more closely the feel the horse would get with a rider on board. If you use a cavesson over the bridle, remove the bridle noseband so the cavesson sits comfortably over your horse's nose. Attach the lunge line to the centre ring, as this enables you to change direction without having to detach the line first.

• Your horse must always wear boots – brushing boots ideally, plus overreach boots if he has a tendency to overreach.

• He may also wear a lungeing roller or saddle to which you may attach side reins (see p.54). Rollers are useful because they are purpose-built for the job and have various rings attached – great if you want to use a training aid. For extra comfort, always use a pad under the roller.

*A cavesson on its own is the best choice for a young horse or if you are new to lungeing as you won't interfere with the horse's mouth*

• You will need to wear gloves, stout footwear and a hard hat for your own safety. You will also need a lunge line and whip, of course.

*Horse and handler suitably equipped for safe lungeing*

## HOW TO DO IT

When working on the lunge ensure the horse is going forward. Many people become concerned if their horse gets excited and goes too fast, and focus on trying to slow him down. As long as the situation doesn't get dangerous, allow him to go forward so he takes a better contact; he will gradually learn that it is easier to go more slowly. If he tries to fall in then point the whip towards his shoulder and use the command 'out' to train him to stay out on the contact. Again he might get a little excited but stick to your guns and he'll soon settle.

Lungeing is an art and done properly it can help most horses, whatever their problems, but if done badly and with the wrong equipment, it can damage ligaments and muscles. Seek help if you doubt your abilities.

You are likely to have problems lungeing if you horse doesn't know how to lead (see Problem Solver, p.53), so address any leading problems before you attempt to lunge (see also pp.27–33).

### MAKE A TRIANGLE

Your position is everything when lungeing – just like it is in riding. If you don't position yourself correctly you won't be effective and your horse could become confused. Think about you, your horse, the lunge line and the whip forming a triangle. You are one point of the triangle and the whip and line are two sides. You should be standing opposite your horse's roller or saddle. If you get in front of his shoulder or nose he may think you want him to slow down or stop and he could turn in towards you. By standing in the triangle shape you are in the best position to send your horse forwards – at the same time being in his line of vision so he can see your body language and movements.

*Your horse, your lunge line and lunge whip form a triangle with you at the apex*

### COMMANDS AND CONTROLS

You will need to use voice commands to communicate with your horse. Keep them simple so you don't confuse him. 'Walk on', 'trot on', 'canter' and 'whoa' are the norm. As your horse will respond to the tone of your voice, change it for different commands. For instance, if you want him to move from walk to trot, use a higher pitch of voice. If you want him to slow down, lower the pitch. Some people also find 'purring' a useful command – higher pitched for upward transitions and vice versa.

Use the whip to support your voice aids. Hold it so it's pointing towards your horse's hindquarters and so it follows him around the circle – this is the driving position. The whip isn't used to hit your horse, but to encourage forward movement. However, if he's being lazy or disobedient it can be useful to flick him with the whip or snap it behind him to remind him to listen. If your horse is scared of the whip hold it further away from him until he gets used to it. If necessary, you can turn the whip away from him altogether, by tucking it under your arm if he's running on or getting out of control. This is the non-driving position and is also used when you are asking your horse to stop. You can point the whip at your horse's shoulder to encourage him to keep away from you and on the circle; or point it slightly in front of him to help him to stop.

# A SAMPLE SESSION

This is a session devised for a horse that is new to lungeing and tends to come in towards the handler. It can be adapted to suit your purposes – for more information, see Planning a lungeing session, p.54.

*1 Begin your lungeing session by going for a walk around the arena. If you are going to use side reins, do not attach them to the bit at this stage. Simply lead your horse with your lunge line, carrying a long schooling whip rather than a lunge whip. An old lunge whip with the lash cut off, leaving about a foot of lash on the end, will do. This makes it easier to lead your horse without falling over the lash and also easier to give him a tap on the thigh if you need to.*

*2 When your horse walks and halts calmly and quietly with you by his side, move away from him slightly to take up your lungeing position and hold the whip so it points at his hocks. You should be facing his shoulder, with the lunge line in the hand nearest his head.*

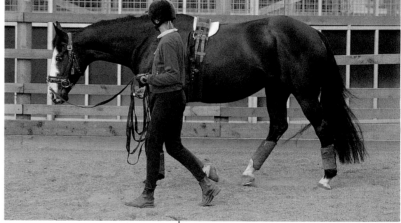

Look ahead at all times and make sure that you walk tall, with authority and a calm attitude, and remain next to your horse's shoulder, not in front of his nose.

Practise transitions from halt to walk, making sure that your horse responds immediately to your requests. A quick tug on the line, and a clear voice command to 'whoa', may be necessary at first. If he responds well, praise him. Ideally, he should walk and stop when you do.

If he does not want to move away from you, change your whip around so the handle end is pointing towards the girth. Give him a small push away from you. For a ridden horse, this simulates him moving away from your inside leg when you are on board. If he is familiar with leg yield and/or shoulder-in he should understand what you mean.

*3 Once he moves away, bring your whip around towards his hocks again. Let the line out and ask him to trot on a small circle about 12m (40ft) in diameter. After one or two circuits, decrease the size of the circle with small tugs on the line to ask him to walk again. Use your voice to let him know what you want.*
*Go for another walk around the arena, then repeat the trot on a circle. Keep him in a slow, controlled trot. Remember to work equally on both reins.*

**4** *If your horse is happy with what he is being asked to do, you can attach both side reins so his nose is just in front of the vertical if he is a novice horse (or more or less vertical with an advanced horse), and repeat the same leading/lungeing routine. This is probably enough for the first session. Next time you can work more on the circle. Once he is responding well, and making good transitions between walk and trot, let the line out so he is on a larger circle for trot/canter work – depending on his level of skill.*

*Lunge for a minimum of 10 minutes and a maximum of half an hour. Finish your session by removing the side reins to allow your horse to stretch down, loosen off and relax*

## PROBLEM SOLVER

**Q** I have an eight-year-old Welsh Cob x Arab gelding who is difficult to lunge. He charges at whoever is lungeing him unless someone leads him. I'm worried he has had a bad experience in the past and don't know how to help him. I have no problems with riding him.

**A** Lungeing should purely be an extension of leading your horse. When you lead him does he walk freely forwards while you remain at his shoulder? If not this must be sorted first. If necessary carry a schooling whip when you lead him so you can encourage him forwards. This must be achievable from both sides. (For leading work, see pp.27–33.)

If the horse will lead correctly, putting him on the lunge is simply a matter of allowing him to circle away from you. You must remain facing his shoulder and he must remain walking forwards. If he tries to come in at you or turn in it is because you are getting too far in front of his shoulder. He's using the opportunity to swing his quarters out so he can come in towards you.

To begin with it may be necessary for you to walk a 15m (50ft) circle while your horse walks a 20m (65ft) circle. Gradually reduce the size of your circle and the amount you walk until you can stay in the middle while your horse walks on a large circle around you.

# PLANNING A LUNGEING SESSION

Lungeing is strenuous exercise for your horse, so plan ahead to make sure he gets the most out of each session. An ideal session for an averagely fit horse is:

• Five minutes on each rein (with no side reins or other training aid in place). This will encourage him to stretch down and warm up his muscles. If he's stretching properly he'll look like he's seeking grass. Walk for about three minutes, then trot for two before changing the rein. If he is balanced enough to canter and stretch, do a minute of this too.

• Attach your side reins or training aid and work for 15–20 minutes in walk, trot and canter. Change the rein every few minutes to help prevent him getting bored.

• Do lots of transitions and vary the pace within the gait

• Increase and decrease the size of your circle. This will help with your horse's suppleness and balance.

• Remove all training aids and let your horse stretch for five minutes to cool down and relax his muscles.

# ADVANCED LUNGE WORK

Once you have mastered the art of lungeing, depending on your horse's level of training, you can move on to trying more advanced movements and jumping, too. Turn on the forehand, leg yielding, shoulder-in, travers, passage and piaffe can all be done from the ground. Teaching these moves from the ground gives the horse the freedom of movement he needs to work out exactly how they should be done without also having to balance the weight of a rider. Once mastered in this way these movements are easily transferable to ridden work.

Turn on the forehand (p.126) is an easy introduction to this type of work. For this, your horse should be wearing a bridle under the cavesson. Use a long schooling whip instead of a lunge whip and work off the cavesson. Stand in front of your horse, holding the rein close to the cavesson. Ask him to walk forwards, with you walking backwards. Slow to almost a standstill and ask him to step around you, encouraging him to cross his hind leg by tapping gently on his cannon or hock with the whip. While he is moving around you, walk backwards slightly to encourage him to move forwards and cross his hind legs in front of each other rather than behind. Only expect a few steps at a time. This is a great suppling exercise and one that your horse shouldn't find too difficult.

*Lateral movements such as shoulder-in (left) and travers (right) can be practised on the lunge*

## Side reins

The most common training aids used during lungeing are side reins. These give the horse the feel of the reins to guide and balance him, and help him to work in a correct outline on the lunge. This, in turn, helps to make sure he is using the correct muscles and not getting into any bad habits.

• Side reins must be fitted correctly otherwise they can do more harm than good. They attach to the D-ring on the side of the roller, or around the girth straps if you are using a saddle.

• Before you attach the reins to the bit, adjust them so you leave a hand's width between the end of the side reins and the bit ring (photo above) to give you the correct length once they're attached. This will give the horse the right amount of feel on the reins.

• Remember, if your horse is not used to wearing side reins, start with them loose and tighten them gradually, as some horses may react badly to them at first.

Never be tempted to overtighten the side reins in order to force your horse into the 'right' outline. While pulling in his head might make him look the part, in reality a good outline is only achieved by activity in the horse's hindquarters and the support of his back through his stomach muscles; and restricting his head carriage discourages both of these.

## JUMPING ON THE LUNGE

Lungeing your horse over fences can be a useful way to teach him to jump, introduce jumps he may find scary, or increase the height of his fences without the burden of a rider on board. It's also a chance to assess his jumping ability.

When jumping on the lunge, it is very important that your horse is wearing protective boots. Equipment-wise, you need just a cavesson, lunge line and whip – no training aids should be used. For safety, it is essential that you use low plastic wings or blocks instead of normal jump wings in order to prevent the lunge line getting tangled up. It's also a good idea to use guide rails to draw your horse in to the fence and help prevent him running out.

Start with polework. Use one pole at first to make sure you can keep your horse balanced and straight. Then increase the number of poles you use and fan them out on the circle. Lunge near the poles and gradually move towards them until they form part of the circle.

Once your horse can tackle polework confidently, start with a cross pole at about 45cm (18in), and ask him to jump it calmly. Using a placing pole about 2.4m (8ft) in front of the fence will help on the approach. Circle near the jump and, when you are ready, position yourself close to the jump and ask him to go over it. You must move with your horse so you don't hamper his movement.

Once he is jumping confidently you can raise the jump, make a spread, use fillers and set up a double, and so on.

As with all lunge work, always work from both reins to prevent your horse becoming one-sided or refusing to jump one way. Remember this is hard work – always pay attention to your horse so that you don't risk overfacing him.

*Jumping on the lunge gives your horse a chance to improve his technique without the weight and possible interference of a rider*

# LUNGEING WITH TWO LINES

Double lungeing is a great way to get your horse using his hind legs as the lunge line behind him helps him step under more actively. The nearside line can be used to create an accurate bend. As you progress, you'll be able to take more pressure on the outside line which, in turn, will activate the hind legs even more – this will support his weight better and prepare him for more collected work. With practice, you'll be able to control your horse enough to get him to change direction without stopping him, which helps steering and suppleness.

Lungeing with two lines recreates the act of riding more effectively than lungeing with just one line. This is because you have a lunge line attached to each bit ring and can use them like reins, just as you would if you were sitting on board. Remember, your hands always need to be light and soft. Until you get used to double lungeing, use a cavesson so you're not interfering with your horse's mouth. It's easy to get in a muddle using two lunge lines, so you may need to practise before you attempt anything too complicated. If possible, practise on a horse that is used to double lungeing.

*Lungeing with two lines takes a little bit of practice but opens up more training possibilities for you and your horse*

## The set up

To set up the lines for double lunging you need a roller.

• Run one line through the offside D-ring and clip it to the offside bit ring. Bring it over the horse's back, near the roller.

• Run the other line through the near side D-ring on the roller and up to the nearside bit ring. You can use a saddle with the stirrups run down and secured under the horse's belly and the lines run through the stirrups, but this means the lines are lower and the feel on the horse's mouth will be different to the feel he would get if you were riding him.

• If necessary, use a long schooling whip rather than a lunge whip as it's easier to control.

• Slip the offside line down your horse's back until it drops around his back end. If he has not been double lunged before, you need to get him used to the feel of this line behind him. Ask someone to hold him for this. In halt, only holding the offside line, move it gently so that it touches his quarters. If he objects, take the line away. Continue to do this until your horse will accept the lunge line behind him without any reaction – it may take a number of sessions. Once he will stand quietly with the line behind him it's time to get him moving.

*Probably the most difficult thing for your horse to get used to is the fact that the outside line rests around his back end, which can feel ticklish or threatening. Give him time to get used to the feeling*

# LONG LINING MASTERCLASS

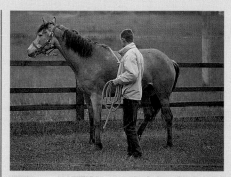

Long lining is basically double lungeing, but you stand behind the horse (or slightly to the side) at a safe distance. Devotees of long lining believe it has many advantages over lungeing in that it relies less on circling, which means that it can be used to teach straightness as well as lateral movements and rein back. For a young horse circling is hard work and long lining is a great way to teach the basic steering, starting and stopping aids without too much emphasis on circles.

Long lining can be used to introduce a young horse to the world without the risks involved with being on his back. It helps to develop a horse's topline, whatever his age, by keeping the weight off his back and enabling you to ask him to round. And, in advanced work, long lining is used to teach a horse collected lateral exercises.

## THE CLASS

If your horse has never been long lined before it's best to work him in a circle at first, which is much the same as lungeing with two lines. You can progress to long lining from behind when your horse has got the idea. A round pen is ideal as it guides the horse in a natural circle. If you don't have access to a round pen, section off an area of the manège. This will enable you to use the outside fence to guide the horse round. Don't start by long lining in a wide open space as your horse might try to get away from you. Always wear a hat, gloves and sturdy boots for long lining.

**1** *With a young horse that's never been long lined before, the first thing you need to do is let him get used to the equipment. With the youngster in a headcollar only, make a loop with the line, pass it over his neck and then stroke it along his back and quarters. If he spooks, move with him and try again. Keep everything calm and take each stage at a time. It's important that you keep it matter of fact and workmanlike. Once he is happy with the feel of the rope on his back, gradually slip it around his quarters. Teach him that he doesn't have to panic, and give him time to think about what's happening.*

**2** *The next step is to tack up. Cross the reins and tuck them under the stirrup leathers. Make sure the reins are loose enough to allow a natural head carriage without the horse getting pulled in his mouth. The reins should be even (the buckle must be in the middle), and cross over where the rider's hands would be.*

**3** *Run down the stirrups and use a spare stirrup leather to hold them together under the horse's belly. This will stop them banging around.*

**4** *Before you attach the long lines, make sure they are tangle-free. Standing on the horse's nearside, slide the first rein over the saddle until the clip touches the ground.*

**5** *The second rein goes through the nearside stirrup iron and clips onto the bit. Then thread the first rein through the offside stirrup and clip it onto the offside bit ring.*

## MOVING OFF

If your horse is not used to long lining, your aim at this stage is to simply allow him to settle into a rhythm and move around the outside of the pen, or section of the manège. Most horses will move forwards on their own and settle into it quickly. If your horse doesn't settle, try to give him as much room as possible. Never try to slow a horse down – if he is tense this will merely result in more tension. Instead, allow him to go as fast as he wants and make your actions faster to compensate. Once he starts to relax and slow down you can slow down too.

Like all groundwork, it is essential that the handler is sensitive to the horse – be careful not to pull on the lines, for example; you must remember you have your horse's mouth at the other end. If you pull on the lines it is easy to turn the experience into a negative one for the horse. If you feel confident enough, try lots of changes of direction to slow a speedy horse without having to physically restrain him. This will force him to think about what he's doing and, after five or 10 minutes, he should become more settled.

### GETTING TO GRIPS WITH LONG LINING

• *Position yourself behind your horse's shoulder at a 45-degree angle to him. This will help to open up the space in front of him and close down the space behind, which is a good way to encourage forward movement.*

• *Don't hassle the horse with the outside line as this could inadvertently pull him towards the outside fence.*

• *As well as line action, use space to get the horse moving. Decrease the distance between you and the horse and hassle him forwards if he's being lazy, then increase the distance when he's moving well.*

• *Once your horse has settled into a rhythm you can start to ask him to do things such as a change of pace – but don't rush it.*

• *Keep your lines tidy. The key to long lining is being able to lengthen and shorten the lines easily. I find it easier to let the ends trail on the floor as this gives me more freedom to shorten and lengthen them. Experiment, but don't get tangled up.*

• *Move your horse around on the long lines until he gives you his attention, then start to teach him stopping and starting or turns.*

• *When turning a horse on long lines, shorten the rein that is to become the inside rein and lengthen the one that is to become the outside rein. This turns the horse away from you.*

• *End on a high note while the horse is still feeling fresh and eager to learn.*

*Ask your horse to move off gently. Most horses move forward of their own accord*

Don't worry if he sets a fast speed. Go with him as far as possible, keeping everything calm and low key – this work is hard and he should soon slow down

With a more experienced horse, and when you are well practised at long lining, you can venture further afield

# DIFFICULT CASES

Horses that absolutely refuse to let you anywhere near them require a different approach. Feed your horse every day in a small, enclosed pen within the field. You can make a pen using electric fencing.

Make sure the entrance is inviting and wide to encourage him to go in and be ready to close up the entrance behind him as he enters. Leave your horse in the pen for a short time after he has eaten, then let him go. Never shout or attempt to chase him into the pen – let him wander in to get his feed. Stand quietly on the outside of the pen while he's eating.

After a week or 10 days of this routine, carefully enter the pen and give your horse a friendly rub on the neck. Then let him out of the pen. Progress until you reach the stage where your horse comes into the pen every day. Sometimes he gets fed, sometimes he gets fed and handled and, occasionally, he is led out of the field. It will take time until the pen work becomes an accepted part of his routine, so remain patient and keep at it.

## PROBLEM SOLVER

**Q** I own a 16hh ID x TB gelding that has a tendency to pull away when I'm turning him out. This usually happens as I turn to close the gate and it can be really unnerving. In a few weeks I am moving him to a new yard and I'm worried he will become even more of a handful, especially as he gets excited in unusual surroundings.

**A** The sheer anticipation of going out for a day's recreation can make horses headstrong. First, always make sure you wear gloves and a hard hat when turning him out, because you are in a potentially dangerous position.

You need to take your horse's attention away from the fact that he is about to be let free and also get him to do as you ask. Food (carrots or pony nuts, etc) can help with this.

On the way to the field, stop at various points and give your horse a tidbit. Each time, make sure he walks straight and calmly and halts nicely. Reward only good behaviour.

Initially, you may need the help of a friend to open and close the gate for you so you can concentrate on your training. Always turn your horse to face the gate and give yourself plenty of room to step backwards once he is released. Give a tidbit before release and again after, if he is still with you. Leave a leather or turnout headcollar on initially so you can quietly and slowly unclip the leadrope without fuss. The tidbit helps to keep your horse's interest on you rather than dashing off to the grass. In time, the tidbits can be reduced. As with all training, do everything consistently, methodically, calmly and safely.

Try to turn out your horse when the others in the field are quietly grazing. Spend a few sessions catching him then turning him towards the gate and releasing him. He won't be expecting this, which should mean he won't spring away. Practise leading work (see pp.27–33) and stopping and reversing, so you know you have the right technique and your horse understands what you require.

*A horse that pulls on the end of a leadrope or springs off when you release him is dangerous – it is important to school him out of the habit*

# HANDLING A HORSE'S LEGS AND FEET

Throughout his history the horse has survived by running away from danger. Even now, after centuries of domestication, his first method of defence is to run. Within a short time of being born foals are on their feet, learning the art of moving, in case they do have to literally run for their lives. Think of horses grazing, for the very first time, in a field alongside a railway line. As the first train thunders past, they will inevitably gallop off and then, when they have put a safe distance between themselves and the train, they stop, wheel round and stand snorting, smelling the air, listening and watching. As they become more exposed to the trains, they learn that they are not in danger and continue grazing.

## FLIGHT INSTINCT

It is easy to see that from the horse's point of view, the worst thing that can happen to him is to lose the ability to run away. Therefore, he feels a great need to have command of his feet and legs, which is why he finds it hard to surrender them to a human. By picking up and holding a horse's foot you are effectively immobilizing him. Even though our domesticated horses very rarely face deadly danger, they are still programmed for survival. A wild horse lives inside every domestic horse – it's just that with patient and correct schooling we can show our 'wild' horse that by behaving in certain ways he will have a less traumatic life in our world. Having his feet picked up is just one of the lessons he has to learn.

## WHAT'S GONE WRONG?

There are two main reasons why some horses have more of a problem with this lesson than others: poor teaching and pain.

As it's unnatural for horses to surrender their feet they have to be schooled to do so. Most horses are taught this lesson at a young age and if this initial schooling is done badly it can have a lasting and negative effect. Many older horses that have problems with having their feet handled or shod have had bad experiences of one sort or another and sometimes the horse just knows that he can get away with being difficult. A horse that has just moved to a new yard or has a new owner may also be reluctant to pick his feet up, simply because he doesn't yet feel safe in his environment.

Older horses may be arthritic or just generally stiff, and so find having their feet picked up uncomfortable. This is especially so if the handler forgets to consider the horse's age and condition and tries to get the foot too high or hold it up for long periods. A horse may also have had an injury that results in discomfort if the foot is lifted too high. In such cases, accommodate the horse by lifting the foot only as far as is comfortable. You may find that exercises such as leg circling, stretches, massage

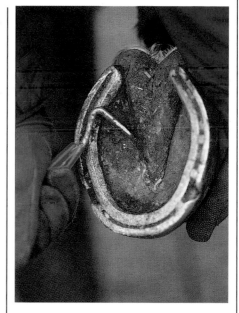

*Ideally you should pick out your horse's feet twice a day. Ensure you clean along the lateral and central clefts of the frog and always use the hoofpick from heel to toe*

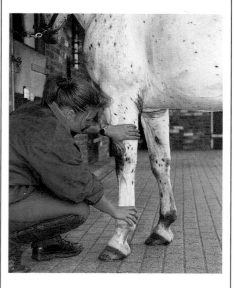

*Leg exercises or simply gentle massaging or grooming will help your horse become used to having his legs handled*

or physiotherapy help. If your horse suffers from shivering, he may be reluctant to keep his foot in the air for very long. Keeping the foot low to the ground helps in these cases. Shivering is an uncommon nervous disease that gets progressively worse – in advanced cases the horse may find it very difficult to pick up his hind feet.

## MAKING A START

It is never too early to teach a youngster to pick his feet up, nor too late to retrain a horse that has a problem. First and foremost, make sure your relationship is good and that your horse is relaxed with you. He will only give you his feet if he trusts you. You can easily lose his trust – for instance if he is struggling to balance himself and you try to hold on to his foot while he is desperate to put it down.

Have your horse in a headcollar and use a long rope. Make sure he is standing in balance, with his weight distributed evenly. All you are asking for in the first lesson is for the horse to lift his foot when you ask him. This may initially be for just a few seconds. This is fine – you can build up the time later.

### What's in a method?

The method of picking up hind feet described here differs from that taught in many riding schools, but is used by a number of trainers with great success. If the horse brings his leg up sharply your arm blocks the movement (see step 2) – if your arm is along the inside of the horse's leg as shown below there is nothing to stop the horse's leg or foot coming into contact with you.

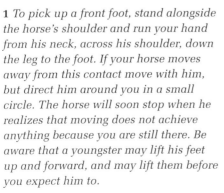

**1** *To pick up a front foot, stand alongside the horse's shoulder and run your hand from his neck, across his shoulder, down the leg to the foot. If your horse moves away from this contact move with him, but direct him around you in a small circle. The horse will soon stop when he realizes that moving does not achieve anything because you are still there. Be aware that a youngster may lift his feet up and forward, and may lift them before you expect him to.*

**2** *For the hind feet, position yourself closer to the midline of your horse. Run your hand from the top of the quarters down the outside of the hind leg. Again, the aim initially is to get the horse just to lift his foot. As the foot comes off the ground, draw it forward slightly to help the horse balance.*

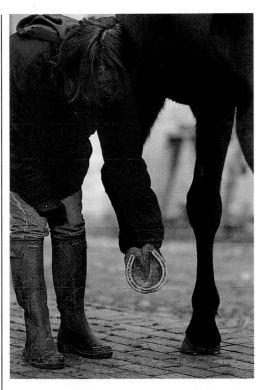

**3** *Once your horse will lift each foot off the ground on a leg cue, start to take hold of the foot, remembering to support its weight. Be careful not to lift the foot too high as this can be unbalancing, and ensure there is enough slack in the leadrope for him to be able to use his head and neck to balance. Gradually build up the time that the foot is held up so that eventually you can pick it all out in one go.*

**4** *Once he is confident with you holding his feet, introduce some of the moves necessary for when a horse is shod, such as using a hammer around the hoof, taking the foot forward for clenching up or holding the fetlock between your legs like a farrier would.*

## GETTING IT RIGHT

*If you are unsure of how your horse will react when you touch his hind feet you can ask him to lift his foot by using a rope or lunge line. This avoids your head being in a dangerous place when he lifts his foot and enables you to be in closer control of his movement via the headcollar and leadrope. You should always wear a hard hat when doing this sort of work.*

*Slip the lunge line behind the fetlock and, with a firm hold on both ends, take up the slack and apply a steady pressure, immediately releasing the pressure when the horse lifts his foot.*

## PROBLEM SOLVER

**Q** My gelding hates being sprayed with a hosepipe. He loves rolling in big patches of mud, so I always need to give him a bath before shows, but I have had to resort to using a bucket and sponge as he pulls back and breaks loose when I try to hose him. What can I do?

**A** Lots of horses don't like the hosepipe but, with time and careful handling, most learn to tolerate it. First, hold your horse in-hand rather than tying him up, as this may make him feel trapped. Choose a time when the yard is quiet and make sure the area you are working in is safe and secure.

The best type of hosepipe to use in this situation is one that allows you to regulate the flow with your finger. Start low – at your horse's forefeet – and let the water dribble out onto his hooves. If he is very wary, you can let the water dribble out near his feet, not actually onto them.

Don't try to restrain him. If he moves, quietly move with him, keeping the hose low and close to him. Eventually, he will realize that attempting to move away from the hose doesn't achieve anything and he will stand still. Once he is standing still, run the hose gently over his hooves, then praise him and take the hose away. As soon as he realizes that the hose is not going to harm him in any way, he will start to relax.

Regular, positive training sessions like this will slowly improve your horse's confidence. Gauge his progress and slowly build up his exposure to the hose, hosing further up his leg and onto his shoulder. Remember, this is a confidence-building exercise, so don't push him so far that he feels the need to totally freak out. At the same time, make it clear that this is something he has to deal with, so be sympathetic but businesslike.

Horses are often very touchy about having their back legs hosed, so save any tricky areas like this until later in your horse's training. Continue to use a bucket and sponge for these areas until your horse is more confident with the hose.

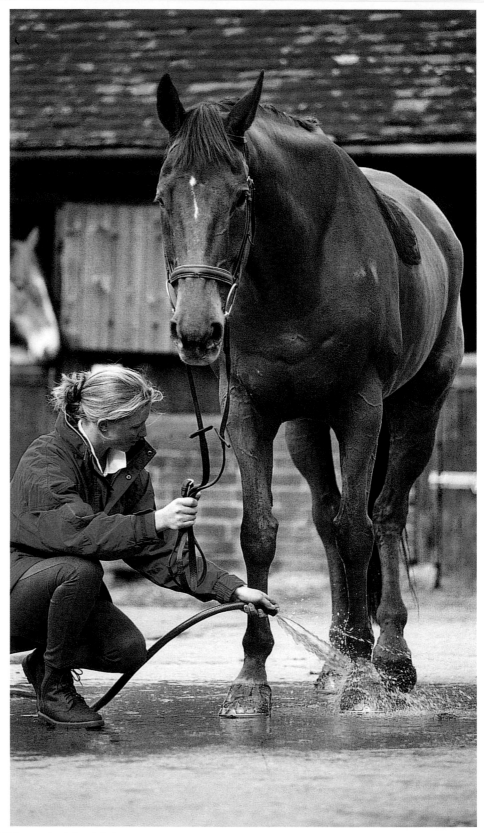

*Most horses will accept a hose once they are shown that it will not harm them*

# HELPING A HEADSHY HORSE

**Horses are instinctively protective of their faces and soon become headshy if they are handled inconsiderately. As we have to touch their faces to carry out even the most basic of care routines, it is important to help a horse overcome headshyness.**

## START SIMPLY

With your horse in his stable, choose a relaxed moment and put on his headcollar. Stand quietly to the side or in front of him. (Standing in front is easier for the horse if he's very phobic, as you will be in his line of vision.) Hold the leadrope just short enough to be able bring his attention back to you if he gets distracted, but don't try to restrain him with it as he will merely pull against you.

For the first few days get into the routine of gently rubbing your horse's ears, moving down to his forehead only. The idea is to put the thought into his mind that if he allows you to touch his head, nothing bad will happen. Start with your hand high on his ears or poll and move down – that way, psychologically for him, things can only get better. Don't put so much pressure on him that he feels he needs to back off, but don't creep around either. Instead, make sure all your movements are quiet, gentle and firm. At first he is likely to try to evade your touch and move away, so drift after him and persist.

Once your horse is happy to allow you to rub around his ears and forehead, you can progress to stroking other parts of his face. As your horse's training progresses you can start to groom his face too, using a soft body brush or cloth.

## KEYS TO SUCCESS

Keep each training session short. When your horse develops a soft eye and drops his head, he has started to relax; he is accepting what you are doing and is considering his actions, so this is the time to end the session and come back to him later. Gauge your progress carefully and always use common sense.

It will take a great deal of time and patience for your horse to learn to deal with his fears and you will only be able to progress in tiny stages.

Keep a note of where you were yesterday, or the day before, so you can thank your horse for his achievements, no matter how small. Every time you (or someone else on the yard) handle your horse, continue his training. Be considerate when putting on a headcollar or bridle and take care not to worry him.

*Be gentle but firm and your horse will soon relax and accept your attentions*

*Eventually he should be happy for you to rub his face anytime, even when he is free to move away. Don't dispense with the headcollar for this work until you are sure he will stay with you*

# MOUNTING

It's surprising how many of us run into difficulties before we even make it into the saddle. In an ideal situation your horse stands patiently while you hop aboard from a handily placed mounting block. In reality, however, horses prance about, feet fail to reach stirrups and riders land heavily in the saddle.

Always make sure you can get on easily before you leave the safety of the yard. When you think about it, being able to mount easily is your insurance – it means, should you fall or have to dismount for any reason on a hack, you can get back on safely.

## BRINGING HIM ALONGSIDE

When it comes to getting on from a mounting block or fence, a horse that is wary of being mounted will often avoid the situation by swinging his quarters round to stand at a 90-degree angle to you. Your natural instinct may be to jump off the block, re-position the horse and try again but, by doing this, you are rewarding him for swinging out. He will soon learn that he can get you doing all the work.

You need to turn the situation around. If your horse continually twists round to face you, stay put. Use your right hand to put pressure on his nearside rein and guide him round to the right in an arc around you. As you pull his head round, his quarters will naturally follow so he is level with the mounting block.

As soon as your horse is on the right line – even if he's not quite close enough for you to get on – give him a rub on the neck to say thanks. Let him stay in that position for five or six seconds to give him time to think about what he's doing. It doesn't matter how far away the horse is, it's the position that counts.

Now, ask for a forward movement. If your horse takes a step in the right direction, give him another rub on the neck and let him stand for a few seconds. If he swings his quarters out again, simply repeat the process calmly and quietly. Don't allow him to stand in the wrong position for a second, as this will send confusing signals. If he's wrong, keep him moving and keep hassling until he's right. Then, as soon as he's in the correct position, reward him with a rub on the neck and let him relax.

You must be very clear in your actions so that the horse learns the difference between right and wrong. His

*Ask your horse to stand alongside the mounting block without swinging his quarters away*

*If he is not quite close enough ask him to move forward a step at a time*

punishment for getting it wrong is not being allowed to stand still. When he's right, he gets a rest and a thank you. Give your horse every opportunity to offer you something you can reward, and praise him the second he tries to co-operate.

## GETTING ON BOARD

Once you have reached the stage where your horse is standing alongside the block in the correct position, don't try to rush things and leap on board straight away. Instead, divide the mounting process into the following stages:

• Fiddle with the reins and gently move the saddle from side to side. Now lean over the pommel, but keep your feet on the block. The instant your horse goes to twist away, repeat the first exercise to get him standing level with the block. Then begin the mounting process again.

• Once your horse is happy to stand as you lean over the pommel, reward him by stepping back. By rewarding him for standing, as opposed to correcting him after he's moved or done something wrong, it will become a more positive exercise and he'll learn faster.

*Lean over him to give him to opportunity to get used to the idea of you getting on board*

• The next step is to put one foot in the stirrup and gently lower yourself into the saddle. Don't do this until the horse is comfortable with you leaning over the pommel. If he moves once you've got your foot in the stirrup, get on anyway. Not doing so would be rewarding his behaviour.

## MOVING OFF

If your horse moves off the second you've either put a foot in the stirrup or sat in the saddle, things can get dangerous, so you need to school him out of the habit. First, gather up the reins before you mount up so you're in control. (You should do this every time you prepare to mount, whatever the situation.) The instant you are in the saddle, expect the horse to move off and be prepared to draw him round in a tight circle. Don't squeeze with your legs or ask him to move off in any way, merely use the reins to direct his movement back round on himself. The instant he stands, give him a rub on the neck and stop hassling. He will soon learn that moving off is uncomfortable, but standing still is pleasant.

*Swinging the quarters away is particularly common if you need to mount from a fence. Work in the same way as you would with a mounting block to bring his quarters back to the fence again*

# CLIPPING MASTERCLASS

Clipping has become the norm for the vast majority of horses and ponies who are in work over winter. Many a sweaty, hairy equine is transformed into a sleek, smart animal thanks to a neat trace or blanket clip, but not all horses appreciate their seasonal visit from the hairdresser. Clipping problems are common and range from a mild dislike of the clippers' noise, vibration or dragging cables to violent, potentially dangerous behaviour, such as pulling away or continuously moving around. Try to see things from your horse's point of view. Horses are instinctively protective of their bodies, particularly the areas that enable them to sense, and flee from, danger. They have a right to be wary of a noisy, vibrating machine touching these areas but, with careful handling, they will learn to tolerate being clipped.

With the right approach, you can teach an older horse to get over his phobias and educate a young horse to accept clippers for the first time – the principles are the same.

## THE CLASS

The first thing to do is check that your horse respects your space and maintains a steady distance from you of 0.5–1m (2–3ft). This is a basic exercise that you should repeat every time you handle your horse from the ground, especially when leading. Ask him to move back if he's crowding you; don't move away if he pushes into your space, as he is likely to follow. Once your horse is standing a respectful distance away, gently pull his head towards you so you've got his attention.

Don't tie up your horse to be clipped. A nervous horse will fight against the restriction, so work with the horse in hand, using a long rope for extra control. Choose a safe, open space so your horse doesn't feel enclosed and trapped. As you turn on the clippers for the first time you will often see a horse glance round, looking for an emergency exit should he need it. If your horse does this and he sees there's room to escape it will put his mind at rest.

Plan each clipping session to make everything as easy as possible for the horse.
• Make sure you allow plenty of time so nothing is rushed and don't attempt to clip your horse if you are already in a bad or impatient mood.
• Bear in mind your body language. If your horse has developed a strong dislike of the clippers, you need to communicate the message that you are the person who is going to help him get over his phobia. It is vital that you have an effective relationship with your horse before you attempt to do this sort of work with him. He needs to trust you.

*First check that your horse respects your space*

*1 A horse's eyes are set on the side of his head to give an almost all-round field of vision (known as monocular vision). However, if something catches the corner of his eye he will turn to look at it with both eyes to get a clearer view (binocular vision). So, when you introduce a horse to clippers, position yourself out in front of him rather than at his shoulder. This way he can use his binocular vision to see exactly what's going on and will feel more in control of the situation. You can move round to his side once you know he is able to deal with it.*

**2** *Hold the clippers in the hand that's furthest away from the horse but don't switch them on until he is settled. Once the clippers are running, keep them still and at a distance. Most horses respond to the noise by pricking their ears and flaring their nostrils. They may glance round looking for a get-out route. After 30 seconds, let the horse investigate the clippers. Turn them off first – if they're still running and he gets a scare, he'll pull back and it will become a negative experience. Turn the clippers on and off, keeping them at a distance, gradually increasing your horse's exposure to them to reinforce a positive message. If you switch the clippers off and your horse thinks 'where did that noise go?' that will grab his attention.*

**3** *Once your horse accepts the noise of the clippers, start to move them gently. Then begin to co-ordinate a rub on the neck with movement of the clippers so the horse begins to connect the two movements. Hold the running clippers and touch the horse with the back of your hand so he can't feel the vibration. A nice easy place to start is in front of the horse's shoulder.*

**4** *Gradually introduce the vibration of the clippers by running them along the horse's shoulder, avoiding any contact with the blade. Extend this work to all over his body and remember to cover both sides equally. Just because a horse has learned to accept something on one side of his body, it doesn't mean he will on the other. Once your horse is happy with this, you can begin to clip him but go for a small bib clip to start with.*

**5** *Horses are often sceptical about clippers touching their face due to the noise, vibration and proximity of the senses they need in order to survive. The same goes for the legs, which are also essential for a horse's survival. Make sure your horse is happy about having his body clipped before you attempt any problem areas. Put the clippers on their slowest speed to reduce the noise and vibration and, if available, use a cordless pair so there are no cables.*

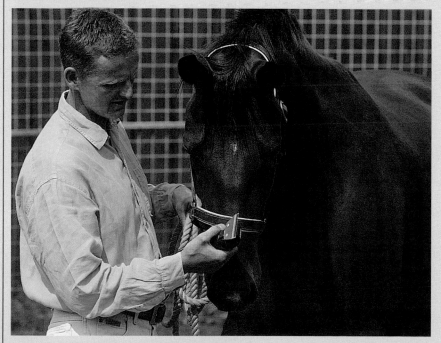

**6** *Apply the same principles you used when introducing the clippers to the rest of the horse's body. Turn on the clippers and rest the back of your hand on the horse's skin, then let the clippers touch the horse but don't actually use them. Remember to take one stage at a time and be aware of anything that may trigger a negative response – such as the clipper cord, vibration or noise.*

## TROUBLESHOOTING

It is important to get the timing right and to keep your cool if things seem not to be going according to plan. For example, if your horse gets a scare from the clippers and you immediately turn them off, you are inadvertently rewarding the wrong behaviour. Instead, if your horse moves away, keep the clippers running and drift after him, but don't chase. If your horse wants to move, let him, but go with him so he soon realizes that moving has no benefit.

If a horse freaks out or pulls back, it's because you have gone too far. Your aim should be to avoid any negative response so make sure your horse accepts each stage happily before you move on to the next.

---

### CLIPPING GOOD SENSE

• *Keep the clippers flat and take care to avoid digging the corner of the blades into the horse.*

• *Take your time and handle the clippers carefully. Working too fast can result in the clippers catching a fold of skin.*

• *Blunt or hot blades drag the hair out rather than clipping it smoothly. Keep the blades sharp and regularly test their temperature.*

• *Always clip against the direction of the hair.*

• *Brush the horse's coat well beforehand as dirt will blunt the blades.*

• *Keep the clippers clean and well oiled and make sure the air vents don't get clogged with hair.*

• *Make sure all cables are kept well out of the horse's way. Extension leads must be fully extended to prevent overheating.*

• *Keep the clipper oil and brushes close to hand, but not so close that the horse could tread on them.*

---

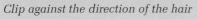

*Clip against the direction of the hair*

*Watch your horse to ensure he remains relaxed. Don't be tempted to continue on regardless of how he is feeling*

---

## PROBLEM SOLVER

**Q** My gelding is very difficult to clip – nothing seems to calm him down. I've tried using a twitch, using ACP gel or clipping other horses in front of him, but as soon as the clippers start to buzz he goes mad. The only thing that helps is having him sedated, but I'm not keen on this option. What can I do?

**A** This is a difficult problem to overcome. Although you have concerns about sedation, this is the best method you have found and you may need to continue using it for a while. You could consider asking your vet to administer a little less sedation each time your horse is clipped until he is having the smallest dose possible.

Follow the advice given on pp.70–71 to start helping your horse overcome his fear. The main problem you have is time to practise because clipping is only done three or four times a year. However, during the summer you regularly remind him about clippers by using a small pair of electric clippers to trim him or even just run them over his coat without any intention of removing the hair. Many horses are more laid-back in the warm weather and it could be that your horse will find it easier to accept clippers in the summer. Good work, done regularly, will help you when you need to clip him for real.

If possible use a pair of cordless clippers; they are your safest option as you don't have to worry about the lead when you're clipping. They are very quiet and some of them are powerful enough to use on the horse's coat to give him a small clip like a bib and belly or even a low trace clip.

# LOADING AND TRAVELLING

**Horses that won't load are a real pain. Even if you don't compete, it's likely that you'll have to box your horse at some point – such as making an urgent trip to the vet. If he won't get on board straight away then you're in for a fight. So it's important to get your loading problems sorted before you need to transport him.**

## WHAT'S THE PROBLEM?

Sometimes it just doesn't make sense. Your horse will load one day but not the next, or perhaps he'll load on the way to a show, but not on the way back. So what makes the difference? We now know a lot more about horses and their natural behaviour than we did years ago, so it's easy to see why they don't want to walk into a small, dark, moving box. Gone are the days when it was acceptable to use brooms or whips to get them on board – today, people are looking for more humane methods. Trying to work out why your horse won't load may be the key to unlocking his problems.

*Trailers are noisy, bouncy, narrow things that a self-respecting horse would never go near, given a choice. He needs to trust you to load happily and you must be careful not to betray this trust*

• **A bad experience** Sometimes it's a vicious circle: a horse won't load, so eventually people get aggressive, forcing him in. The next time he's asked to load he's even less likely to co-operate, and so they get aggressive with him again, and the problem just worsens.

• **A scary journey** If a horse experiences a bad journey due to the driver going too fast, braking late or cornering wildly, he won't be so keen to repeat the experience.

• **Negative thoughts** Horses can soon work out that going on a journey means hard work for them – perhaps involving a competition or lesson. If your horse makes this connection, he may refuse to load as a protest. If your horse is always easier to load on the way home than on the way out, this could be your problem.

• **Size matters** It's common to see big horses squeezed into small trailers or lorries. If the horse hasn't got enough room to balance, and isn't able to move around a bit, then he won't be keen on loading in the first place. He needs space to spread his legs and use his neck for extra balance, and enough head clearance so that he's not in danger of banging it and injuring himself.

• **Movement** Horses want to feel safe and don't like standing on ground that moves or bounces. So try to imagine how your horse must feel when he stands on a ramp that bounces slightly or is very steep. He will quite naturally assume the ground is not safe to stand on.

• **Noise** Lorries and trailers can be very noisy, and this can startle and scare horses. There's often metal clanking, branches brushing the outside and road noise so bear this in mind and give your horse time to get used to it.

• **Trust** Your horse has to trust you implicitly to follow you up the ramp. If he doesn't have faith in you to do the right thing then he won't want to listen.

### OVERCOMING LOADING PROBLEMS

Loading can be made straightforward using the principles of positive and negative reinforcement (not to be confused with punishment). Negative reinforcement means 'taking something away' when the horse gets it right – in this case removing pressure from around the horse's nose. The pressure will be applied using a halter. Garry Bosworth, an associate of Intelligent Horsemanship, uses a Dually halter (designed by Monty Roberts) and a long rope. (It's important to know how this kind of halter works and to practise using it effectively and safely before trying it out on a difficult loader.) This method of loading works by taking away the decision-making from the horse, so that the handler is viewed as the leader. In order to load your horse successfully, he must respect you and your space, and be obedient to your commands. The more leader-like you are (in horse terms) the more he will learn to trust you.

*Groundwork teaches your horse to follow you and to pay attention to what you are asking him to do*

## HOW TO LOAD A HORSE

Loading practice should be done when you have plenty of time and nowhere to go. Put aside a few hours each week to work on loading and be prepared to spend as much time as it takes. You can be sure that if you have somewhere else to go, your horse will sense the urgency in what you are doing, and this is not conducive to learning. Practise loading until your horse walks happily in and out of the trailer, and will stand quietly inside with the ramp down and up.

• Begin each session by getting your horse to walk with you calmly in-hand – asking him to stay just behind your shoulder and stop when you stop. If he doesn't stop, back him up a few paces, using a light pressure on the halter. Repeat this a few times until your horse begins to respect your space. (If you have problems with basic leading work, revise this with your horse before you begin loading, see pp.30–33.)

• Change direction, both quickly and slowly, and expect your horse to follow. Avoid using the rope to pull him around, you want him to follow of his own accord. Use lots of backing up and praise (rubbing your horse on the head or shoulder to encourage him to listen to you). This work will also teach him the principles of pressure and release.

• When your horse is responding well to the groundwork walk him over to the trailer or lorry. It is important to walk with determination and not to allow him to stop at the bottom of the ramp. A poor loader will probably do just this and the best way to deal with this behaviour is to keep him moving. Using the rope, move him from side to side a

*Your horse must know how to back up, and respond to your cues for backing up in order to learn to load*

little – stopping him from planting his feet firmly. Then put a little pressure on the halter, and ask him to move forward. Keep asking until he puts one, or both, front feet onto the ramp, immediately release the pressure, and then back him off the ramp as a reward.

*For some horses even putting just two feet on the ramp is a tremendous step in the right direction. Be generous with your praise*

• Gradually increase the number of steps onto the ramp and into the trailer, each time backing your horse off and giving him a short break as a reward when he has done as you ask. Eventually he should walk happily up the ramp, but it might take a few sessions. Be prepared for this: you want to build on good experiences rather than make each session a battle to achieve the final goal.

## HELP YOUR HORSE

There are lots of simple things you can do to help make loading in a lorry or a trailer less of an ordeal for your horse.

• Park on a slight downhill slope to reduce the steepness of the ramp, and next to a wall or hedge, to reduce possible escape routes. Also, park somewhere quiet to minimize outside distractions.

• Open the front ramp or jockey door on a trailer to let in as much light as possible.

• Load on soft ground if possible to help reduce the risk of injury if your horse slips.

• Lead your horse confidently on to the lorry or trailer. Never stand facing him as this is quite threatening and may stop him from walking forward.

• Use confident, competent helpers and let them know what you want them to do.

• Practise loading regularly, even if you just walk your horse on, through, and off the trailer on the way to the field.

• Stay calm and keep your temper. The angrier you become, the less likely your horse is to do what you are asking.

*Open up your trailer to make it light, spacious and inviting when you first start loading practice*

*Both you and your horse will feel a great sense of achievement when he finally walks into the trailer calmly and easily*

75

## THINGS TO REMEMBER ...

• Make your horse box or trailer the best place to be in the world! After doing some groundwork your horse should want to be with you – and be happy to follow you in.

• Include backing up in your groundwork, it is an essential movement to teach your horse in preparation for loading.

• Use body language – make yourself 'large' and look the horse in the eye to get him to stop or focus on you.

• If using a trailer, take out the partitions and breast bar until your horse is loading well. Then gradually put the trailer together again as he gains in confidence.

• Use a long line instead of a leadrope as you'll have more control with this.

• Don't let anything behind your horse distract him. If his attention is drawn to other activities, gently bring it back to you and the job in hand.

• Wear sturdy boots, a hard hat and gloves when training your horse to load.

• Make travelling as comfortable as possible for your horse. Make sure he is properly kitted out to help avoid injury. Your horse's travel boots must fit well, and it's important that he's used to wearing them before you load. Some people use brushing boots instead of travel boots (if their horse doesn't like wearing travel boots). He may also need a rug, depending on the weather.

### AVOIDING PROBLEMS

• *A common loading mistake is to achieve a step in the right direction and then desperately try to cling onto this 'success' by tugging on the leadrope. Your horse may have taken one step forward, but as soon as he feels any tension on the rope he will merely pull back again and may take four or five steps in the wrong direction.*

• *Another common mistake is to hold the horse tight under the chin and attempt to drag him up the ramp. He will simply throw his head in the air, tug back and pull you off your feet.*

• *Use the rope to keep the horse's attention focused on you and the direction he should be heading in, but don't pull on it or crowd him. If he has ground to a halt and is staring in the opposite direction, nudge his head back towards you.*

• *To encourage forward movement, squeeze and release the rope. You can also wiggle the rope to move the horse from side to side and cue a movement from his front feet.*

• *Praise every movement – be it sideways or forwards – with a stroke on the neck and keep the situation calm, friendly and positive. Keep up the tempo so your horse doesn't fall asleep and after a while he will start to offer a couple of steps forward.*

• *If he backs himself up, let him, then position him at the foot of the ramp and start again.*

*It is possible to train your horse to load happily, every time*

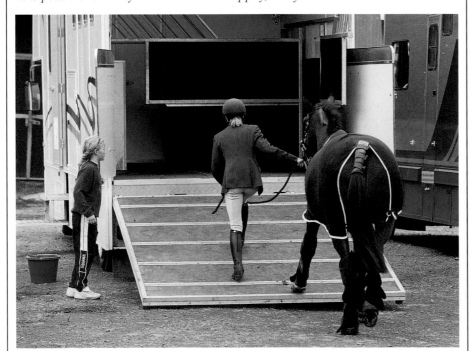

## PROBLEM SOLVER

**Q** My Thoroughbred mare loads into a trailer without hesitation. However, once in, she becomes agitated and bargy, attempting to rear and kick when I tie her and put the ramp up. She settles straight away if I load my other horse in with her. How can I help her?

**A** To understand your horse's behaviour, look at how she views travelling. It's good that she loads fine, but she obviously finds the confines of the trailer very claustrophobic. Instinctively, horses dislike small areas – their natural environment is wide, open spaces where they can flee danger. In a small, enclosed space they feel there is no escape and so can become very agitated. When another horse is with them they often become calmer, and so cope with the situation. You can tackle this problem in several ways:

First, you need to get your mare used to many different small spaces. Start by gradually getting her used to more familiar small spaces – and being tied up in them if possible. Whenever your mare goes down a narrow passageway or through a tight space, such as the stable door, see if she will stop and stand quietly. Reward her by stroking or even giving her a feed. Don't coax her with feed however, as she will just get greedy. Any use of feed must be strictly controlled – only use it for reward, and expect her to do more to earn the feed as the tasks get harder.

Get your horse used to standing near cars, tractors, horse boxes and so on, all with their engines running – be very careful not to endanger yourself when you do this. Do this gradually and reward each small step in the right direction. You can use your car and trailer for some of this training, then she won't only associate the trailer with going places.

*Have a friend help you if you are experiencing difficulties with loading. They can give you moral support as well as being there to open and close the ramp and so on*

Next, stand in the trailer with your horse as somebody else closes the ramp – it doesn't have to be all the way up. Use your common sense – do not risk being inside the trailer if it is not safe; if you don't trust your horse to react well, continue to work on things that she is happy with before you ask someone to put up the ramp. For safety's sake, the person putting up the ramp must stand to one side as they lift it up, and be ready to let it down again gently if necessary. Stroke and reassure your horse, and repeat this exercise until she stands calmly when you tie her up. Always finish on a good note – otherwise she might start trying to train you to lower the ramp when she panics.

You must do this training using common sense and caution. Only increase the difficulty for your horse very slowly.

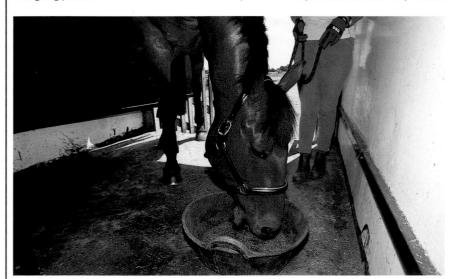

*Horses are quick to make the association between a place and a meal. Use this to your advantage by giving your horse a meal in the trailer*

# STANDING STILL

Standing quietly and calmly should be easy for your horse. So why do some horses find it so difficult? The answer is partly because teaching a horse to stand correctly is often neglected in his education – maybe because it doesn't seem terribly exciting or interesting. Yet it's important that your horse can stand properly, for convenience, ease of handling and safety. And it is something we frequently ask our horses to do, but it's also something we're often not very successful at achieving. The other part of the answer is that although it seems like such a simple thing to ask of your horse, in fact it can be very challenging.

There are many exercises that can help this situation – and which can be just as absorbing and educational for you as they are for the horse, as you'll find it necessary to develop your own powers of observation and co-ordination to teach them to him. The exercises described here are part of the repertoire used by highly respected TTEAM practitioner Sarah Fisher.

## WHY IT'S DIFFICULT TO STAND STILL

A horse that finds it hard to stand still isn't purposely trying to be awkward or resistant; more often than not the problem's linked to poor balance. A horse requires as high a degree of balance and co-ordination to stand still as he does to move. Try it yourself: stand in a good posture, feet parallel to each other and spaced comfortably apart, with your head, shoulders and hips in line directly above them (use a mirror or a friend to help you get properly aligned). It's easy and almost effortless to stay motionless once you've got it right; but now try moving one foot forwards and inwards slightly, and you'll notice how much more difficult it is to keep still. There is an increase in muscular effort needed to hold that position, and before long it will become uncomfortable and you'll want to move.

Horses with poor balance often find life tricky when tied up because they find standing still difficult and like to move around to regain their stability. When their movements are restricted by the leadrope, it causes them to become even more unbalanced, and they'll often struggle to try to free themselves. Spending a bit of time teaching your horse how to stand in a better balance will make it easier for him to stand quietly when you want (or need) him to.

## HALTING CAN BE DIFFICULT TOO

It's a reflex action for a horse to pull back when he feels pressure on the top of his poll, and if the muscles in this area are tight, he'll be even more sensitive and likely to be reactive. This can cause difficulties when asking your horse to halt in-hand. Some horses get into a real panic about it – hanging back, running backwards or even rearing, until the pressure is released either through their own efforts, or the intervention of the handler.

Your horse primarily uses his neck for balance, but he also relies upon his eyes (visual balance) and inner ear (vestibular balance) for stability and positional awareness. As the ears and eyes can be affected by tension in the upper part of the neck, muscle restriction around the upper cervical vertebrae in the neck will have a dramatic effect on the horse's ability to establish true self-carriage in movement, as well as when standing still. In addition, tension in the neck affects spatial awareness, the ability to learn, and can cause problems with depth perception and changes in light. This can make it hard for horses when moving into or out of trailers, boxes and stables. They may be inclined to be spooky, and exhibit concern about bright objects. Pushy behaviour or crowding when being handled can also often be attributed to tension in some part of the neck.

Signs of tension in the neck include:
• Incorrect muscling of the neck, either over-bulking or under-development
• A tight or non-existent topline
• You may notice your horse's mane 'jumping' as he lowers or raises his head
• Any changes in the way the mane lies often correspond to areas where tension is present (swirls can also cause the mane to change direction)
• Pushy behaviour when being handled

# LEG CIRCLING

Spending just a few minutes a day doing this simple exercise while grooming or picking out your horse's feet can help improve his balance, relax his shoulder, neck and back muscles and relieve tension in the quarters, making it easier for him to distribute his weight evenly.

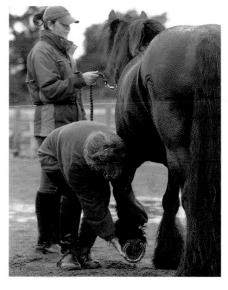

**1** *Stroke down the back of your horse's fore leg with one hand, and then ask him to pick up his foot by squeezing the back of his leg between knee and fetlock with your finger and thumb.*

**2** *Support the fetlock joint with your inside hand and cradle the hoof with your outside hand. Keep your thumb over the hoof wall or shoe, and cup the front of the hoof with your fingers. Avoid flexing the fetlock joint too much. Keep your hip and knee joints flexed and rest your outside elbow on your outside thigh. Gently circle the hoof the same number of times in both directions, just above the point on the ground where it was resting. Create the movement by circling your body, not just your hands.*

**3** *Circle the hoof at gradually decreasing distances from the ground until your horse's toe is finally resting on the ground. If he is very stiff or unbalanced he may not be able to do this – in which case just get as close to it as you can.*

---

## TTEAM TIPS

• *Try to remain calm and relaxed whenever you ask your horse to stand still. If you get tense, anxious or forceful, you won't succeed.*

• *Make sure you praise each small improvement your horse shows and don't scold him if he can't maintain the halt for very long at first. Allow him to walk on a few steps, then ask him to halt and stand quietly again. Gradually you should notice that he's finding it easier to stand for progressively longer periods.*

**4** *Repeat the exercise with the other fore leg, then with both back legs. Support the cannon bone with your inside hand, and don't lift the feet higher, or make the circles bigger, than the horse is comfortable with. Make sure the leg is circled under the horse, not out to the side, and be particularly careful with very stiff horses, or those that are elderly and may be arthritic.*

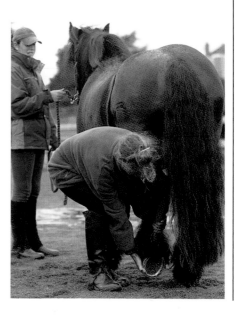

## WHY DO I WANT MY HORSE TO STAND STILL?

There are many occasions when it's helpful to have a horse that'll stand still rather than constantly shifting around. These include:
• Tying up
• Picking out feet or shoeing
• Grooming and bathing
• Tacking up
• Clipping
• Vet inspection or treatment
• Mounting and dismounting
• Tightening the girth
• Opening or closing gates
• During competition – in a dressage test or the show ring
• Waiting to cross at road junctions
• Travelling
If you fall off – it's nice to have a horse that will not only stop, but stand waiting quietly for you while you recover yourself!

Apart from the obvious advantages, improving your horse's balance so he finds it easier to stand can have other benefits. By releasing tension in his body and teaching him how to distribute his weight more evenly over his fore and hind legs, you'll enable him to develop increased elevation and freedom of movement under saddle. And he'll become more receptive to handler/rider requests.

Posture also influences self-control and self-confidence; a horse that is physically out of balance will tend to be more reactive and emotional than one that is in a state of equilibrium. Improving a horse's balance can therefore not only improve his performance, but also his behaviour.

## BODY WRAP

A body wrap may look peculiar, but it can help your horse to integrate his whole body and become more balanced and co-ordinated. The elasticity of the bandages enables a gentle contact with the body to be maintained during in-hand work. It can also have a calming effect (similar to swaddling for fretful babies!) with nervous or spooky horses. You can use ordinary 10cm (4in) elasticated exercise bandages – if you're using old ones, make sure there is still plenty of stretch left in them.

*1 Ask a friend to hold your horse while you put one bandage around his neck. Tie it in place around the base of the neck using a quick-release knot. Ask your horse to walk forward a few steps, halt and move on again so he gets the feel of the wrap around the front of his shoulders. Once he is happy, move on to step 2.*

**2** *Tie the end of a second bandage on to one side of the neck wrap. Carefully bring the wrap along your horse's side, around his hindquarters, and under his tail. Don't tie it in place, but hold the end in your hand while your friend asks your horse to walk forwards a few steps and then halt again. The feel of the wrap around his quarters may cause your horse to move off briskly initially. If necessary, hold the wrap a little more loosely until he's more confident about this new sensation. Make sure you stay on the same side as the person leading the horse. Most horses get accustomed to the wrap quickly; if yours continues to react badly to it, he may have a deeper physical problem.*

## Problem areas

As well as poor posture and balance, other factors can affect a horse's ability to stand still. These include:
• Arthritis
• Back problems
• Tension through the neck
• A lack of (or incorrect) muscle development
• Age
• Conformation
• Discomfort while grooming or tacking up (or the anticipation of discomfort)
• Poorly fitting tack
• Anxiety about being clipped/bathed/shod/handled
• How he is being held or led
• Poor shoeing

Some of these issues may require further investigation, and will need to be remedied appropriately with assistance from a vet, saddler, farrier or other equine professional.

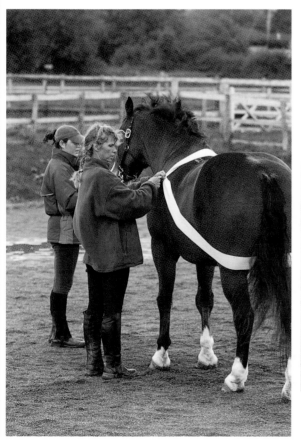

**3** *Once your horse is happy, attach the end of the second bandage to the neck wrap with another quick-release knot, about 38cm (15in) from the first knot. Draw back the neck wrap so that it sits just behind the withers and forms a 'bridge' over the back. The bandages should be snug, but not tight; check that the second bandage doesn't slip down the back legs when your horse moves.*

**4** *Practise walking and asking for halt again with the wrap secured completely – you can see here how the finished body wrap should look.*

## THE CATERPILLAR

This exercise can be done while the horse is standing still or on the move. It helps to reduce soft tissue tension around the neck vertebrae, enabling him to lengthen and release through his neck, and assisting him to establish self-carriage.

Working on your horse's nearside, support his head by hooking your fingers lightly on the headcollar noseband. Alternatively, hold the leadrope up by his headcollar with your left hand. Place your right hand on the base of his neck, your thumb on or near his jugular groove and your fingers cupped on the top ridge of the neck vertebrae. Slide the heel of your hand up the line of vertebrae to your horse's ear applying slight pressure.

Repeat, but this time move your hand like a caterpillar, inching your way up the neck to the ears.

Finally, add the action of opening and closing your thumb and fingers as your hands travel up the neck. Experiment with the pressure you use as it will vary from horse to horse. Repeat this four to five times before switching sides.

## WANDWORK

The 'wand' is a 1.2m (4ft) long stiff dressage whip with a hard button on the handle. It is used as an extension of your arm to touch your horse all over his body, while remaining at a safe distance if necessary, as well as to cue actions. Horses that dislike having their legs touched are often bad at standing still; teaching them to accept having their legs handled can help them overcome a tendency to be fidgety or spooky. Using the wand to stroke the neck, chest and legs can also have an amazing calming and relaxing effect, and will encourage lowering of the head and neck, making it easier for your horse to balance.

Working on the nearside of your horse, hold the leadrope in one hand – this can be close to the headcollar if necessary. Facing your horse, hold the wand in your other hand like a sword. Keep your hand relaxed. If your horse shows concern about the wand, hold it so just a short section of handle protrudes from the top of your hand and use the button to stroke the underside of his neck and the front of his chest until he begins to lose his fear.

Start by stroking the front of your horse's chest with the wand. Use a series of slow, graceful, downward and slightly forward sweeps, following the contours of his body. The pressure should be positive and firm enough to make contact without tickling, but not so strong as to cause discomfort.

If your horse is not showing any anxiety, use the wand to stroke the whole underside of his neck, progressing slowly and steadily downwards to the front of his chest again. Continue to work down your horse's front legs, right down to the ends of his hooves.

# TAMING THE TIGER

Taming the Tiger can be used to help stop bad habits, such as running backwards or leaning against the rope. Most horses that pull back when tied up are tight and sore in the poll area, mid-neck, and base of the neck, so do the Caterpillar and Wandwork first. Alleviating tension and encouraging lowering of the head and neck will break the flight instinct and help your horse relax, so that you both start in a receptive and calm frame of mind. Practise on a quiet horse first to develop your co-ordination before trying this exercise with a more difficult horse. Initially use a corner of the yard or the stable, to create a natural boundary behind your horse that limits the extent to which he can move backwards.

**1** *Position your horse beside the wall where the tie ring is fixed. Either use a TTEAM lead (shown), or clip a leadrope to the side ring of the headcollar noseband closest to you. Thread one end of another length of rope through the bottom ring of the headcollar, below the jaw. A piece of climbing rope about 6mm (¼in) diameter is ideal as its rounded shape allows it to slide easily through the headcollar and tie rings.*

**2** *Pass one end of this second rope through the tie ring on the wall.*

**3** *Bring the same end back to the headcollar, tying it to the ring at the side of the noseband closest to the wall, using a quick-release knot.*

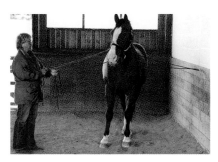

**4** *Softly hold the leadrope in one hand, and the second rope in the other, creating a light contact with your horse's head. If he walks forward, use the leadrope to gently ask him to stand. If he moves sideways, signal on the second rope. Don't restrain him by pulling on the ropes as this will cause him to pull back – just give gentle feel-and-ease signals when necessary. Don't signal on both ropes simultaneously, or their actions will contradict each other. If you gently signal on one, you must give a little with the other. When your horse stands quietly, slacken both ropes slightly.*

**5** *Once you're used to holding and signalling on the ropes with two hands, hold them both in one hand. Keep them separated by holding the leadrope between first finger and thumb, and the second rope between the first and second fingers. This leaves you one hand free to hold a wand, which you can then use to stroke the underside of your horse's neck and front of chest and legs, as in the wandwork exercise. If he tries to move backwards, let the rope slide and step sideways so you remain opposite him. Use a gentle 'come forward' signal on the leadrope to encourage him to step forwards back into position.*

## Test your know-how

**How should you tie up your horse so he finds it easy to stand still?**

• Clip the leadrope to the side ring of the head-collar noseband, rather than the one under the jaw; this reduces pressure on the poll.

• Give him a little slack – don't tie him up so short that it restricts his ability to use his head and neck to balance.

• Check the height of the tie ring: too high and it will cause him to stand with his head high and back dropped, making it hard to balance.

# NATURAL HORSEMANSHIP GAMES

American horseman Pat Parelli's philosophy of love, language and leadership is well known among Parelli students, but what does it really mean? We've all heard people described as 'having a way with horses' or being 'a born horseman'. But Pat Parelli, founder of Parelli Natural Horsemanship, believes that, with his systematic approach to horsemanship, having a feel for horses is something that can be learned by everyone. His groundwork training can help in all areas of horsemanship, including competing.

*Pat Parelli is world-famous for his groundwork training*

## KNOW YOUR HORSE

Parelli's training is based on allowing the horse to learn naturally using trust, rather than by controlling him. He believes that this encourages a horse to work with dignity and exuberance.

So how do we earn our horses' trust? Communication is the key – learning the language of the horse and understanding his nature. Horses are prey animals and survive by being aware. In the wild a mare has limited time in which to form a strong bond with her foal. When a foal is born the dam will first lick him all over, then urge him to get up – biting if necessary to get the foal to respond out of respect and fear. She will play a dominance game with her body and this is how the foal's education continues as he is prepared for life within the herd. Horses are natural followers and are looking for natural leaders. To develop this bond a mare communicates with her foal in seven ways. These are:

1 Rhythmic motion (for example, the mare's tail swishing over the foal)
2 Moving away from pressure
3 Rhythmic pressure
4 Moving in straight lines forwards and backwards
5 Circles
6 Sideways motion
7 Squeezing between objects (to escape from danger)

## SEVEN GAMES

Parelli has developed seven games (see opposite) based on these steps. They are designed to enable you to build this same bond, using a language the horse understands. You and your horse need to learn the seven games in sequence and you must both have learned and understood each one before moving on to the next. Every response from the horse, however small to begin with, is rewarded. And each exercise is built up over time.

*'Games played in a sequence make sense to the horse,'* says Pat. *'Horses love certainty and if you are consistent you will get results.'*

## WHY DO THE GAMES WORK?

Body language and your body position are what influence your horse most. Before you even get on your horse's back, you must make sure you have a language and a way to communicate. It's your responsibility to become your horse's leader and teach him to be calmer, smarter, braver, more athletic, trust your judgement, negotiate obstacles, go sideways and backwards with ease, yield to and from pressure and try whatever you ask him to without any resistance.

The seven games help you achieve this because you 'win' them, thereby becoming the alpha or leader in your herd of two.

## LEARNING THE GAMES

The first three games are like building blocks for the rest; the final four are 'purpose' games and are more complex. The games are designed to be played on the ground first and then in the saddle. If you can't play them on the ground then you're going to have a problem when you try to ride your horse. Make sure you follow the phases, where indicated.

### Equipment

- A rope halter.
- A 4m (12ft) line. This needs to have 'life' and 'feel', which means it needs to be soft, supple, reactive and be weighty, but not too heavy.
- A 1.2m (4ft) stick. Known by Parelli students as the carro stick, this is not a whip and is not designed for punishment – it should be an extension of your arm to prove to your horse that you are taller and longer than him.
- A 2m (6ft) length of string. This is tied onto the end of the carrot stick, which enables you to play the friendly game at a safe distance when starting.

**1 The friendly game** *proves to your horse that you're friendly, trustworthy and not a predator. You need to gain his confidence and be able to touch him with a friendly 'feel' everywhere on his body. If he becomes defensive when you touch him in a particular place, he's still a bit worried by you. By using an approach and retreat technique, you'll be gaining permission to touch every place on his body without forcing him to accept it. You can advance to tossing ropes, plastic bags or coats or anything you can think of, near him, to get him braver, more confident and less sceptical. Be sure he is on a slack rope, not being held tight or tied up.*

**2 The porcupine game** *is called 'porcupine' as a reminder that the horse should not lean against a point of pressure but learn to move away from it. Learning this prepares him to understand how to respond to the rein, the bit or the leg, and it's applied with a steady feel, not intermittent poking. The steady pressure starts soft and increases slowly until the horse responds. When he moves away, the steady pressure must be instantly released.*

*This pressure is applied in four phases – press the hair, then the skin, then the muscle, then the bone. Each phase gets stronger, and there's no release until the horse responds – teaching the horse that he made the right move by responding. If he responds at phase 1, then go no further. If it takes him up to phase 4, be prepared to persist until he tries to find comfort by moving away from the feel. Reward the slightest effort with instant release, a rub and a smile. Teach this game all over his body.*

**3 The driving game** *will teach your horse to respond to implied pressure – you suggest he moves and he does so without you touching him. In the beginning you may need to stand at close range. As you progress you'll be able to affect him from greater distances, until it seems like invisible communication. Again, four phases are important – in phase 1 tap the air, phase 2 lightly tap the horse with your fingertips, in phase 3 use insistent tapping with your fingers, while phase 4 is slapping with flat hands. The rhythm must not falter, or change. As soon as the horse responds even a little bit, relax your arms, smile and rub him. It doesn't take long for a horse to learn how to move away at phase 1. Learn to drive your horse in different directions – backwards, moving the front end and moving the hindquarters (hold the neck bent towards you for this).*

**4 The yoyo game** *sends the horse backwards away from you, then brings him towards you in a straight line. Its object is to get backwards and forwards movements equal and light. Use four phases and the 'hinges' in your finger, wrist, elbow and shoulder. Start phase 1 by just wiggling your index finger at the horse. Phase 2 – wiggle your wrist so it affects the rope only slightly. Phase 3 – bend at the elbow and shake the rope using your lower arm. In phase 4 straighten your elbow and shake your whole arm and watch how much more the rope moves. Only escalate the phases until you get a response. The instant your horse moves backwards, stop. Keep both your horse's eyes on you; if he turns his head you'll lose the back up and the straightness. Pay attention to the details and make corrections before he goes off-course.*

*Play slowly at first, on flat ground. As he gets better, ask for more – play on uneven ground, at a faster pace, over a pole, or on a longer rope.*

*This game helps him to respect your space when leading, to develop suspension and self-carriage, improve his stop, develop a slide stop and come to you.*

**5 The circling game** *develops a horse mentally, emotionally and physically. It consists of three parts: the send, the allow and the bring back. You do all of it without moving your feet. To send your horse, lead his nose in the direction you want. If he doesn't follow the rope, lift the rope's tail and swing it towards his neck. Once he's travelling around you, smile and pass the rope behind your back, 'allowing' him to take responsibility for maintaining gait and direction. Do between two and four laps. If he stops, turn and face him with a concentrated look, redirect his nose onto the circle and start again. When he goes, smile! To bring him back to you, turn and face him for phase 1. For phase 2, start reeling the rope in until you have enough tail in the rope to lift it. Phase 3 – swing the rope towards his hindquarters. In phase 4, touch the hindquarters until he has swung them away and faced you. Again, stop and smile at any moment your horse makes the right response. Then bring him all the way in to you and rub him as a reward.*

*Disengagement of the hindquarters (swinging them away from you) is how you teach a horse to be easily controlled.*

**6 The sideways game** *teaches your horse to go sideways equally right and left, with ease. The two important areas on your horse for this game are the neck to nose area (zone 1), and the hindquarters (zone 4). You need to play the driving game in zone 1 then zone 4. Send zone 1, then zone 4, then 1, then 4, etc. until the horse straightens out and moves laterally sideways. Allow a loose rope and a little distance for the horse to get moving but not so much distance between you that he could turn away and kick you. Start slowly and go to the right then come back to the left; use a fence or rail to help prevent forward movement while the horse is learning.*

*This game is important for developing suspension, lead changes, spins and balance in your horse.*

## HOW TO PLAY WELL

• *Develop the right attitude.*

• *Develop your knowledge.*

• *Use the right tools for the job.*

• *Improve your technique and your timing.*

• *Make sure you have the time to complete the task.*

• *Be imaginative if it doesn't work first time.*

• *Don't act like a predator and blame the horse, the tools or the knowledge. Accept that you may not be asking in quite the right way for your horse to understand you.*

• *Remember: this is horse language. Horses are experts at it, of course, and some will test you more than others.*

**7 The squeeze game** *Horses are claustrophobic. The squeeze game teaches your horse to become braver and calmer and to squeeze through narrow spots easily. Start with a large gap between you and a fence, wall, or even a barrel. Ask your horse to go through the space while you stand still. In the beginning, it may help if you walk backwards and parallel to the fence to help your horse squeeze through – walking backwards works well because it helps draw the horse towards you. For phase 1, direct your horse's nose into the gap. In phase 2 lift the tail of the rope; phase 3 swing the rope a few revolutions and in phase 4 touch the horse behind the withers once. Now stop and begin again until the horse tries to move forward into the gap. As soon as he does, release the pressure, relax and smile – pretty soon your horse will make it all the way through. Stand still and allow the rope to slide through your hand as he passes by you so he feels total release – you want to avoid him feeling a jerk backwards on the rope. As your horse becomes more confident, make the space smaller and smaller until it's just 1m (3ft) wide, like the stall of a horse trailer.*

*Use the principle of the squeeze game to teach your horse to jump fences and to go into a trailer.*

# DEVELOPING FEEL

Natural horsemanship can help you overcome your training problems, boost your ridden performance and empower your horse to move as freely as nature intended.

Many common equestrian problems stem from the horse not having fully developed mentally, emotionally or physically. We need to work through any problems he may have in those areas before we can progress in his training. The three exercises described here will make you more aware of your horse's emotions as well as improving your focus and feel. They will help you understand your horse's state of mind: does he trust you or is he defensive or anxious? Look at his body language – and remember that he will be looking at yours all the time! A trusting horse stays relaxed in his mind and body and enjoys your company. The exercises also develop his understanding and co-operation, and introduce him to movements that soften and supple him.

*Walk down beside your horse with your hand on his back, watching his body language as you go*

## TASK ONE – BEING AWARE OF EACH OTHER

Hold your horse loosely in a halter and 4m (12ft) rope and see if he is happy to let you walk down his sides to his hindquarters with your hand gently on his back. Do this on both sides. Next, stroke him firmly following the lay of his hair, using long, rhythmic movements. Start on the neck and slowly move back. If he remains relaxed you will be able to stroke from croup to hock in one movement while holding the leadrope loosely.

Ideally, your horse will remain relaxed and still, with his eye and ear directed towards you, allowing you to stroke him anywhere. Unwanted responses include: showing anxiety and being unable to stand still as you move further down his sides; defensive postures such as head turned away, shoulder pushing against you, tail swishing, ears back; or a totally withdrawn, dull attitude where he does not even seem to notice your presence.

To help your horse give the correct response you must be relaxed in your movements and appear unconcerned. An anxious horse has to become used to you and know there is nothing to fear, so persist in stroking him, even if to start with it is only on a safe place like the shoulder. As he becomes more trusting you will be able to move further down his body without him moving away. If he feels threatened, he may try to move you backwards with his shoulder to tell you to leave him alone. Stand your ground and defend your space with a quick bump with your hand if necessary. If you have a dull and unresponsive horse, persist with the stroke – he will come to enjoy your touch.

## TASK TWO – RESPONSE AND REWARD

You are now going to move your horse's hindquarters with a light feel of your hand on his side. If he moves from that light pressure, reward him by releasing the pressure and stroking him until he stops moving. If nothing has happened, reapply the pressure slightly more strongly until he moves. A dull horse may even have to have a short bump on his quarters from your hand to begin with but always make sure you reward every effort by stroking him. As he learns what to do, use less pressure. Eventually, he will be happy to move away from the lightest of touches.

Make sure you are relaxed, and then stand by your horse's girth area. Take a slight feel on the rope; not a pull, just enough to slightly turn his head. This lets him know you are about to ask him to do something. Bring a sense of purpose to your own body and focus on where you want the quarters to go. Apply light finger pressure to a point a few centimetres behind where your leg would be if you were riding.

*Teach your horse to follow your feel and move away from a light touch, so he will become a responsive ride. Horses can become dull through riders kicking their sides – only the lightest squeeze is needed*

## TASK THREE – FINDING YOUR BALANCE

As riders, we have to train ourselves not to pull back with the reins or use them to aid our own balance. If we do, the horse's mouth becomes less responsive or he learns to lean on the bit to try to avoid discomfort. One of the best ways to teach ourselves balance is to ride on a completely loose rein. With the bridle on, and in a safe place (manège or similar), hold your reins at the buckle end in one hand. Stretch your arm further forwards than usual, so the reins are looped, then go for a walk around the arena. It doesn't matter where the horse goes, just keep him walking and concentrate on your balance. You will find you still have a connection with the horse's mouth.

Does his walk become freer? Is his head lower and is there more swing to his body? If his head gets down to the ground, don't worry – he is exploring his new freedom! It may take a while to happen, especially if he is used to being held together. This exercise allows your horse to relax through his spine and encourages him to carry his head and neck less stiffly.

Practise this often, and always use it before and after a schooling session to loosen the muscles. Work at it until you feel you can sit in balance without needing the reins as a prop. It may seem like a basic exercise, but it is of great benefit to both of you, especially when you progress to doing it at faster gaits. It will give you the beginnings of a much lighter feel on the reins.

*Your horse will learn to move more freely when you aren't using the reins as a prop*

# SCHOOLING ON THE FLAT

Among the main aims of schooling a horse are to train him to be calm, willing, responsive and obedient. Correct training also enables the horse to do his work to the best of his ability, without mental stress or physical strain.

Horses come in all shapes and sizes and they all have different temperaments and abilities – the work we do with them has to be tailored to match. The exercises that are featured in this section will help you work through most schooling areas. However, if you do find yourself struggling in a particular area consider having a few lessons. A good trainer will be armed with a whole host of exercises, all designed to achieve specific goals. Well-structured and effective lessons will enable you to identify your horse's strongest and weakest points and help you build a harmonious and successful relationship.

# FINDING THE WORKING PACE

Every horse has his own natural rhythm and working pace, and in recognizing and making use of this, the rider contributes to the horse's mental and physical wellbeing, as well as ensuring the horse can work to the best of his ability. It is well worth spending a few minutes at the beginning of every schooling session establishing a working rhythm. You will recognize it as the horse drawing forward willingly and his hoof beats having the regularity of a metronome.

Drawing forward willingly means having plenty of impulsion without a desire to get faster and faster, and it feels rather like being on a ship that has wind in its sails. You as the rider must be willing and able to travel with the horse but, just like the mast of the ship, remain central and balanced at all times, so that the horse can keep moving forward with confidence.

*Travel in balance with your horse and allow him the freedom to move in his natural working rhythm*

## MAKING THE MOST OF YOUR HORSE'S PACE

Some horses are enthusiastic in their work, and may need a half-halt from time to time to maintain the working pace. Those who are on the lazy side will need to be encouraged forward. Avoid these two common problems:
• Riders who find the horse's natural rhythm too much to handle often defend themselves against the movement by hanging on to the mouth. If the rider compromises the rhythm in this way, the horse soon becomes frustrated, which leads to physical discomfort and often rebellion.
• Riders who feel the horse's stride is too long often hold him back, and, in order to shorten the stride, ride slower than the horse's natural rhythm, leading to a similarly discordant result. Of course, if the horse is over-striding you need to correct that, but there is a big difference between taking half-halts to re-balance him and constantly pulling against his front end in order to stop him going any faster.

### FEEL THE RHYTHM

If you find your horse's natural movement too much to cope with, invest in some lunge lessons so you can learn to absorb it more easily. An alternative is to have some lessons on a horse with an easier way of moving, so you become capable of handling the movement in stages. You may also need to do some work on your physical fitness – there is, after all, a distinct difference between being riding fit and the level of fitness required to school a horse effectively.

It can take the less experienced rider a little time to discover what the horse's natural working pace is. It helps if you go into your schooling session with the intention of finding a good rhythm, just like you would when you get on the dance floor. As with dancing, counting to yourself can help, especially in the trot. Saying, 'One, two, one, two' out loud can help you hear if the horse is rushing away, or if he is dragging his feet.

## GOOD FOUNDATIONS

The working pace is the foundation from which you can advance your schooling. Once it is established, you can start to work on collecting and extending the horse, which will improve his flexibility, but remember to check back on the working pace from time to time throughout the schooling session. Make rhythm your key word. Whether working on the flat, jumping or even just hacking, check in with yourself and your horse that you are keeping an even rhythm and are working in the horse's natural pace. When the horse is allowed to move in his natural rhythm, with the rider balanced on top of him, he will relax, gain trust in the rider and be more attentive. He is happy because he is allowed to be himself, and this makes him a more willing partner for you.

*Give your horse a chance to stretch out and relax at regular intervals throughout each schooling session*

### STARTING A SCHOOLING SESSION ON THE RIGHT NOTE

*It is important to spend time walking at the beginning of a session, partly to aid in the warm-up (see pp.94–95) but also to assess your horse's mental and physical well-being. Give him a long rein, let him walk out freely, and then observe his way of going.*

• *If he is relaxed, he will stretch his head and neck down.*

• *If he is short in his neck, and his footfalls are irregular or hurried, it shows that he is uptight.*

• *If your horse comes out fresh, do not try to force him to walk, as you will end up with an agitated and wound-up animal. He needs to burn up some energy in a straightforward way in trot and canter before being asked to walk.*

• *If the horse has lowered his head and neck, but you can hear his feet dragging, it is an indication that he is hanging back. In this case, it is up to you to decide if this is because he is lazy, and needs waking up, or because he is genuinely feeling off-colour.*

*The way your horse goes during this period of assessment will help you decide the best way to proceed with your session. Don't forget that you can return to walk on a long rein a couple of times during your schooling to reward your horse when he has worked hard and to give him time to recover.*

# WARM UP BEFORE WORK

Spending time warming up your horse is so important, but is an area that is often neglected. By warming him up correctly you will make it easier for him to carry out more difficult movements later on in a schooling session. He needs time to loosen up, so his muscles are warm and flexible and ready for further work. How long you need to warm up will vary, as it depends on the individual horse, but if you ask him to work in an outline too soon his muscles will get tired and the quality of work will suffer. The warm up will also help your horse become more relaxed mentally, so when you ask for more demanding work he will be happy and able to do it easily.

*Often a horse will come into the school rather tense and offering outlines that you are not looking for at this stage of the session. Rather than trying to correct this directly it is best to do exercises that will help him relax and stretch out*

## EXERCISE 1

Begin by walking round on each rein and then go into trot. Encourage your horse to stretch his head and neck down and out. Keep the trot tempo slow. Do a few transitions from walk to trot and back again to test that he is listening to your aids.

## EXERCISE 2

A good exercise to help your horse relax and encourage him to stretch is to ride a 20m (65ft) circle, gradually making it smaller into a 10m (30ft) circle. Then leg yield back out onto a 20m circle. It's much easier to ride a fresh horse on a circle and not around the edge of the school. Keeping him on a curve helps him concentrate and not be so spooky. Start riding this exercise at one end of the school, then repeat the exercise riding circles around the school. Your horse should begin to stretch and become more relaxed. You are aiming for the top of the neck and underside of the head to form a upside down 'U' shape not the 'V' shape which is all too often seen.

Change the rein and repeat the exercise.

*As you warm up, the tempo of the trot will improve. Your horse should begin reaching forward with his head and neck, and his back muscles will become looser. Keep riding him forwards to encourage him to take the contact down*

# EXERCISE 3

The next stage of the warm-up is to make transitions on the 20m (65ft) circle from trot to walk and back to trot keeping the neck stretch you have achieved. In walk make sure that your elbows are soft so you don't restrict your horse's movement: as the horse's head nods and his neck goes forward you need to take that forward movement through your elbow joint. You can now begin to make transitions from trot to canter, still on a circle. Keep your elbows behind your hands so there is a straight line from your elbows to the bit and your thumbs are on top of the rein.

Repeat this on the other rein.

*Once your horse is warm, move up to canter work, making trot to canter transitions in balance and with a good rhythm*

## ENDING A SESSION

To finish, walk on a long rein to stretch and cool off.

*Always allow some time at the end of the session to cool off. Use this time to think about the good things that you have just achieved together and what you might benefit from doing differently next time*

## PROBLEM SOLVER

**Q** My Warmblood mare was turned out for two years before I bought her. I would like to school her and eventually try jumping but she gets lazy, refuses to move forward and is domineering. She's very dependent on other horses and becomes annoyed when I tell her off. My trainer says a professional should re-train her. What do you think?

**A** Your horse seems to be high up in the herd, which would explain her dominant character. The more time she spends with other horses, the more herd-orientated she becomes, but she has to realize that you are also part of the herd. You need to be a higher rank than her for respect to develop between you.

It may be an idea to stable her at night, train her in the morning then put her in the field as a reward for good work. If she doesn't behave, return her to her stable for thinking time – have a short training session later in the day doing something you know she can do, and then she can go in the field. You'll have to keep a strict routine for about a month until you've established that you are the boss.

Vary the type of work you do with her. School her each day, either after lungeing or before hacking. Twice a day for a short period of time would be better than one long, stressful session. Try to make the work fun and imaginative using ground poles, obstacles or small jumps. If she enjoys hacking, then introduce schooling exercises when you're out so training is not limited to the school.

It's important that you ride her yourself to establish a rapport. If she goes in the school to be trained by a stranger she'll most likely resent this. Ask your trainer to help you ride her, rather than getting him to ride her.

Be firm but fair. If you're too soft she'll take advantage but if you're too strict she'll fight back.

*Short fun schooling sessions are more productive than long stressful ones. Always end a session on a good note*

# WALK

Many riders underestimate the value of cultivating a good walk in the horse. We are often in a hurry to move on to trot and canter, and sometimes the weather dictates that it is simply too cold to walk for very long. However, a sound walk provides the foundation for excellence in the horse's other paces, and is also the best pace for the horse and rider to work in when learning a new exercise or improving a weakness.

## YOUR ROLE IN WALK

The rider's seat has a great deal of influence over the quality of the horse's walk. The type of movement a horse makes in the walk means that the saddle moves around more than in any other pace, so the rider needs to develop a seat that follows this movement in a calm and easy fashion. You can begin to appreciate the amount of movement underneath you by walking your horse on a long rein and closing your eyes for a few moments. You will feel the horse's back dipping and rising under each of your seat bones as he steps under with each hind leg.

You can encourage the horse's walk further by pushing and relaxing with your legs in the rhythm of the walk. Make sure you do not swing around unnecessarily, as this will disturb his balance; instead, focus on matching his natural movement.

### HAVE YOU GOT THE RIGHT FEELING?

Allow your seat bones to go with the movement of your horse in walk while growing tall in your upper body. A good way to identify this 'growing' feeling is to ride in walk with one arm stretched up above your head. Make sure your arm is parallel with your ear, not behind or in front of it, and stretch your fingertips up while keeping your shoulder down and relaxed. You will get the feeling of your upper body becoming quiet as your seat bones follow the movement. Maintain this feeling when you put your hands in a normal position and you will often experience the horse letting go in his body and his walk becoming freer.

### Test your know-how

**How many beats are there in walk and how many types of walk are there?**
Walk is a four-time movement, so the horse always has at least one hoof on the ground.

There are four types of walk – collected, medium, extended and free walk on a long rein. In each your horse should display good ground cover and an active movement. This activity comes from his hindquarters, although ground cover in the collected walk is shorter (see p.99).

## IMPROVING YOUR HORSE'S WALK

Some horses have a naturally better walk than others, but many have a walk that has become shortened or stilted, usually because the rider has interfered with the mouth too much at the same time as pushing strongly with the legs or seat.

The best way to begin re-establishing a horse's walk is to go back to riding in a natural way. Ask your horse to walk in a positive, unhurried manner on a long rein. Once the pace is established, relax your legs and become more vertical in your upper body. After a few attempts the horse will react by slowing down his rhythm, and you can then pick up the reins and ask him to give in his jaw. If he does soften, you will find that the quality in his walk remains.

There are also horses that, due to tension, habitually hurry or break into a jog. The solution to this is patience and many light checks with the rein that tell the horse to slow down a little. As soon as your horse responds to your checks, relax your hand and allow him to walk forward. You will need to ask him to slow down again after a few strides, but always remember to soften the hand afterwards. When dealing with a horse that runs away in walk, aim for progress by degrees, rather than expecting him to slow down with a single aid. If your horse seems to be hotheaded make sure you are not contributing to his tension. It is easy for the rider to be influenced by the horse and to start moving around excessively. Instead, sit quietly and breathe deeply while carrying out this exercise.

## ACCEPTING THE BIT

One of the most pleasurable feelings for a rider is picking up the reins and having the horse in the bridle instantly. You can train your horse to do this by walking on a long rein, then picking up the contact and asking him to go on the bit. As you pick up the reins, take care to maintain the same rhythm the horse had when he was on a long rein, and make sure you don't restrict his neck. As soon as he gives in his jaw, give him a long rein and a pat. Let him walk for about 15m (50ft) before picking up the reins and repeating the exercise. You will find that the horse becomes more receptive to going on the bit immediately, because he knows he will be rewarded for his submission. When you see an improvement, move on to something new.

*A good walk is purposeful and rhythmical. The horse moves his head and neck up and down in a relaxed way in the rhythm of his footfalls, and gives the sensation of being fluid throughout his body. His tail will also move slightly from side to side, which indicates that he is relaxed through his spine*

---

### CHECKLIST FOR WALK

• *Is your horse's walk following a regular four-time beat? Riding on a hard surface, such as a road, can help you hear whether or not his movement is rhythmical.*

• *Is your seat following the horse's walk in a natural way?*

• *Does the horse accept the bit easily in the walk?*

• *Is he overtracking (see box, p.98)?*

• *Does his walk on the bit have the same quality as the walk on a long rein?*

---

# Walks within walk

When you have progressed beyond the basics in your schooling, you can begin to work on the variations within each pace. These play a large part in achieving responsiveness and suppleness in your horse and are important in dressage competitions.

In any dressage test, walk receives a high percentage of the marks so don't be tempted to look at it as a rest period rather than one of the three gaits. Medium walk and free walk on a long rein are the most common types of walk asked for in Prelim and Novice tests. Higher-level dressage sees the introduction of collected and extended walk. These types of walk are given as many marks as one-time changes and canter pirouettes when done well, so it's important to get them right.

## FREE WALK

In free walk, your horse's head carriage will be at its lowest – and longest of all the walks. His frame will lengthen as he overtracks fully and takes longer steps.

Free walk is your horse's natural walk. However, even though his walk feels relaxed, you still need to keep it active and rhythmical. Make sure he's working through his hindquarters, that he stretches through his back and has free, ground-covering steps. Hold your reins as long as possible and keep a good leg contact, pushing your horse forward. This will encourage him to stretch his head and neck down. Remember, free walk on a long rein should be purposeful and 'marching'.

Even though free walk is one of the easiest walks to master, it can still create problems – and the main reasons for losing marks in a free walk include:
• An inconsistent movement
• Your horse wandering off the track
• Head shaking
• A broken rhythm (moving into another gait).

## MEDIUM WALK

In medium walk, your horse's head carriage will be lower and his neck slightly more extended than in collected walk (opposite, bottom) and his nose should be vertical (a slight fault in the photo, opposite, top). His frame will be collected, but slightly longer than in collected walk. He will step

### Test your know-how

**What is the difference between overtracking and tracking up?**
When the horse is walking well he will overtrack, which means that the hind foot passes over the print left by the forefoot on the same side. Your horse should fully overtrack in all types of walk, except collected. In collected walk your horse's frame is at its shortest so he shouldn't overtrack. Instead he should step into his front footprints, which is tracking up.

out more and should overtrack as his movement is longer. His back will lift, thanks to the engagement of his hindquarters.

When you ride medium walk, your reins should be slightly longer than in collected walk, but your horse should still work on the bit.

Medium walk can be used as an introduction to collected walk. Ideally, you need to keep the correct contact and control, so you can make smooth transitions to collected or extended walk.

Medium walk can become lethargic if your horse loses his rhythm and energy. He'll amble along and you won't be able to feel a regular four-beat rhythm due to a lack of engagement in the hindquarters. Exercises like shoulder-in (pp.132–135), leg yield (pp.128–129) and polework (pp.120–125) can clarify your horse's rhythm. They help to engage his hindquarters and add interest to his work.

## EXTENDED WALK

In extended walk, your horse's frame will be longer than in medium walk as he lengthens his stride. His strides will lengthen as he 'steps out' into extended walk and he should overtrack more because of this extended stride. His neck will lengthen and his head carriage will become lower than in medium walk. His back should be relaxed.

Extended walk is used in many Elementary tests, and judges look to see that your horse covers as much ground as possible (without rushing). It's important that your position remains balanced, even though your horse's frame changes. Maintain the longest possible rein contact. Remember that your horse's movement should feel like purposeful marching.

## COLLECTED WALK

To achieve a collected walk, ride in an upright position, holding your horse's energy between your hand and leg. Your horse's frame will be at its shortest in this walk as his energy is compressed, and his steps will cover less ground than in any of the other walks. His head carriage will be higher because he's working from his hindquarters – you are asking him to intensify his energy and maintain an active, upwards movement.

You need a good rein contact so you collect and compress your horse's energy between your hand and leg – so use half-halts (pp.114–115) to steady his rhythm.

A good collected walk has activity and rhythm.

Collected walk can have its problems – namely, a lack of activity and trouble losing the four-time beat. If this is a problem for you, take a contact and make sure your horse is walking forwards. Push him forward, so he's in front of your leg and doesn't 'bunch up' against it. He should track up, not overtrack.

# TROT

A good trot is active and springy, with the horse loose through his body. The regularity of the horse's rhythm reflects his balance, and a well-balanced horse will take even, regular strides. Accentuating this good natural rhythm, and increasing the engagement (activity) of his hindquarters, will lead to a better balance and a more brilliant trot. In a really flamboyant trot, the horse will look as if he's hardly touching the ground.

## YOUR ROLE IN RISING TROT

As in all the paces, your position as a rider can either enhance or detract from your horse's natural movement. Horses are usually naturally balanced and it's often the influence of the rider that causes a horse to go out of balance and take irregular steps. Take particular care to have a light touch in rising trot. If you're heavy with your seat, and land with a thud in the saddle every other stride, your horse will soon tighten, drop his back and become unwilling to go forward because of the discomfort.

The most important point for achieving a light rising trot is for your hips, knees and ankles to act like shock absorbers for the up-and-down movement of the trot. The top half of your body should be carried with your shoulders fractionally ahead of your hips, and with a sense of travelling with the horse.

Another tip is to try to connect, mentally, with the horse's hind legs as he trots. It's relatively easy to pick up the one-two beat, particularly in rising trot, and then to softly join that rhythm with your legs, to encourage activity in the horse's hind legs. Squeeze both legs together as you sit and release as you rise.

Your hands are also worth a mention. It's a common mistake for riders to move their hands up and down as they rise and sit – but if you allow yourself to do this you'll catch your horse in the mouth. Instead, your hands should stay as still as possible, but they must not be fixed or rigid.

**Test your know-how**

**How many beats are there in trot?**
Trot is a two-beat movement, so the horse moves his legs in diagonal pairs, and there's a moment of suspension between each beat, when all his feet are off the ground.

Maintain an even contact while the up-and-down movement of your body is absorbed by a slight opening and closing of your elbows.

Also, take care to rise on the correct diagonal – that is, come out of the saddle as the outside fore leg and inside hind leg leave the ground. Although, technically, it doesn't matter which diagonal you're on when on a straight line, it's much easier for your horse to balance on a circle or through a turn if you're rising when his inside hind leg is leaving the ground. It gives him the space to step underneath his body and balance his weight. Also, changing diagonals every time you change the rein means that you change the side of the horse that's bearing the load – and so give his muscles a chance to develop evenly.

If your joints are stiff, you're going to find it difficult to absorb the movement in rising trot so ride with extra short stirrups for a while. The increased bend in your joints will help them become springier, and more able to accommodate the horse's movement.

## IMPROVING YOUR HORSE'S TROT

There are different types of trot. The most commonly used is working trot – where all the horse's basic work takes place. In collected trot the horse shortens the outline he had in working trot, and takes higher, shorter steps. In the medium and extended paces the horse lengthens his outline and his stride becomes longer, covering more ground with each stride.

At a basic level, your horse's trot will be improved by accentuating the rhythm. Do this by taking half-halts to re-balance him, and then moving him forward again. Half-halts will engage your horse's quarters, allowing him to increase the amount of suspension in his stride – which leads to improved rhythm.

To maintain suspension the horse needs active hindquarters, and this is why strengthening the hindquarters is one of the main aims of schooling. The stronger your horse's hindquarters become, the more he'll be able to engage, making him capable of bigger and better extended paces.

If you want a good trot, especially in the medium paces, it's always a good idea to use exercises to engage your horse's hindquarters first. These include transitions, half-halts, circles and turns of various sizes, and simple sideways movements. (For more about half-halts, see pp.114–115, circles and turns, pp.118–119 and lateral work, pp.126–135.)

*In trot you're always looking to be in balance with your horse and flow with his movement, so he can give the best of his natural ability. The trot will be enhanced by defining his rhythm and increasing the engagement of the hindquarters, and is also the pace in which you can best work on your horse's flexibility and suppleness, helping to make him fit, healthy and obedient*

---

### CHECKLIST FOR TROT

- *Are my hips, knees and ankles working as shock absorbers?*

- *Is my rising trot light and travelling with the horse?*

- *Have I mentally connected with the horse's hind legs?*

- *Is the horse's rhythm regular?*

- *Am I doing work that will further engage the horse's hind legs?*

## SITTING TROT

Many riders grimace at the thought of sitting trot, and too often that look of pain is mirrored by the horse's tense back and his head held high as he tries to avoid the uncomfortable bouncing of the rider in the saddle. A good sitting trot, on the other hand, is a joy to watch and experience – the horse and rider look as one, and the rider feels a closer connection with what's happening beneath her.

The growing tall feeling and following seat that you've developed in walk (see p.96) offers a good foundation for sitting trot, although the movement of the trot is followed in a slightly different way. As well as the hips, knees and ankles acting as shock absorbers in rising trot, in sitting trot the lower back also becomes vital in absorbing the horse's movement. These areas need to be supple without collapsing.

In order to complete the seat in sitting trot, you also need to continue carrying your upper body in an elegant way, maintaining a broad open chest and balancing your head levelly over your neck.

## WORK ON YOUR BODY

Many people are tight in their hips, making it difficult to sit to the trot and causing them defend themselves against the horse's movement. As the hip joint is a ball-and-socket arrangement, it potentially has a tremendous range of movement. Try the releasing your hips exercise to help release it and then try levelling your pelvis, so that you can accommodate the horse with your seat. Do these exercises at halt.

**Releasing your hips**

*Use your palm to find the point at the top of your outer thigh where a bone sticks out. Keeping your hand flat on this area, make small circular movements with your whole leg. If your leg is very stiff, you might need someone to lift it for you the first few times. This bone fits in the hip socket. Keeping your hand on it helps you connect to the sensation of that joint undoing itself.*

**Finding the level pelvis**

*1 Sit in the middle of the saddle, then tip forward, sticking your bottom out, so that your pubic bone is pressing against the pommel. Hold that for a few seconds so you can register what it feels like.*

*2 Now go the other way, tucking your tailbone underneath you in an exaggerated manner. Think about feeling the tailbone pressing onto the saddle.*

*3 Now return to a position in between these two, and make small adjustments until you feel your weight is evenly distributed throughout your seat. Take a mental snapshot of this feeling, and check with it to ensure that you're still in the right place when you're doing sitting trot.*

## PROBLEM SOLVER

**Q** I have a problem with sitting trot. My German Warmblood has good strides but his back doesn't seem to swing in trot as it should and I find it very hard to sit to. My hands bounce up and down too. What can I do?

**A** For your horse to work correctly with a softly swinging back, it is vital that you have a toned upper body in order to control your reactions to him. Lack of body tone causes instability, making it difficult to co-ordinate your back movement with your horse's, which may result in your hands becoming unsteady.

Make sure your position is correct. Rather than trying to sit heavily on your horse – which will block his back muscles and not allow him to work correctly – make sure you are sitting up and supporting yourself with your stomach and back muscles. Keep your hips upright and allow your legs to hang down against your horse's sides, using enough muscle tone to keep your legs in position. Loose legs render your leg aids ineffective.

You should be able to feel your horse's sides with your legs so that you can adjust your leg pressure accordingly to give instant, effective leg aids.

If you have full control over your upper body, you should be able to stabilize your upper arms against your sides, with them hanging vertically. Maintaining tone in your upper arms will help you to keep control over your forearms, which should form a straight line from your elbows to the bit. A controlled arm position enables you to keep your hands steady. It can help to visualize keeping the bit still and level in the horse's mouth, rather than holding on to the horse. Be aware of the strength in your stomach muscles at all times.

Once you are sure your aids are correct, if the problem is still there, it may be worth getting your horse's back checked thoroughly by a vet or equine chiropractor.

*You need to be fit and supple to be able to sit easily in trot. Focus on moving softly with your horse's movement*

# CANTER

**A well-balanced and adjustable canter is essential for any horse, particularly a jumper. You can recognize this type of canter when you see it because the horse will be light on his feet, have his hocks underneath him and have lift in his shoulders, all of which creates a round canter stride.**

*A balanced canter is instantly recognizable – the horse brings his hocks well underneath him and lifts his shoulders as he springs forward*

## WORKING ON BALANCE

If you've introduced changes of pace to the horse in walk and trot, you can also use them in canter to develop his balance. As long as your horse already has good basic balance, you can further improve it by collecting him and then moving him forward for a few strides on a straight line. Straightening the horse before you collect him is important as this enables him to get the full benefit of his hind legs coming underneath him, thus allowing him the maximum possible elevation of the shoulders. It's from this forward riding after the collection that the horse gets his lift and energy.

Horses that are unbalanced in canter demonstrate it in various ways:
• Getting faster and faster
• Getting heavy in the hand
• Going disunited or changing leg
• Breaking into trot.

In these cases the horse will benefit from cantering for short periods only. For example, you could try trotting on a line at least 10m (30ft) inside the track. As you near the short side, take a small half-halt (pp.114–115), turn back to the track and strike off to canter. The turn will help the horse to make a neat strike-off. Canter roughly halfway round a 20m (65ft) circle, before turning into the middle of the circle and making a transition to walk. Then change the rein and repeat.

**Test your know-how**

**How many beats are there in canter?**
Canter has three beats, followed by a moment of suspension, so the rider should be able to count one, two, three, and then be silent for a beat.

## STRIKING OFF

Many riders, in their desire to get into canter, lean forward and load the horse's shoulder just at the point when he should be lifting it in order to jump into canter. An easy way to correct this is to turn your head and look to the outside as you apply the aids for canter. This centralizes the upper body and allows your inside hip to come forward just as the horse brings his inside hind leg forward underneath him.

This exercise is particularly good if the horse persistently strikes off on the wrong leg, a mistake that is nearly always due to rider error. It also counteracts the habit of having a sneaky look down to check if the horse is on the correct lead. Instead, you will feel the strike-off through your seatbones and it will become a calmer and more elegant experience.

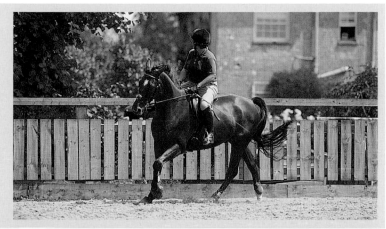

Asking the horse to canter for a short amount of time in a confined space like this encourages him to keep himself together.

As the canter improves, you can reduce the size of the half-circle in order for him to step under more in the strike-off. Gradually, as he gets stronger, he will be able to stay in a balanced canter for longer periods.

Remember, however, to collect the horse again while he still has lift in his canter (rather than waiting until he's floundering) in order to preserve its quality.

## CANTER STRIKE-OFF

A neat strike-off is the foundation for a well-balanced canter. A messy strike-off, when the horse rushes from trot into an elongated canter, is difficult to recover from. These rough transitions are sometimes due to rider error and sometimes the horse is confused.

In order to create a neat strike-off, it can help to take a small half-halt just before you apply the aids for canter. It's a bit like changing gear when you want to drive your car uphill, and will set up the horse to respond better when you apply your strike-off aids. If, despite taking a half-halt, the horse still rushes into an elongated canter, or strikes off on the wrong leg, it may well be that you are losing your balance at the crucial moment of transition (see Striking off box, above).

## CANTERING A YOUNGSTER

With a youngster, cantering is best introduced on hacks. Once he has established some balance and understands what you are asking of him, you can begin canter work in the school.

Start by riding a big circle at one end of the school as the three sides will lend him support. You will need more pace in the trot than normal – use your voice sharply over a number of strides to get him moving on in trot. You can practise this on the lunge.

As you pass over the centre line and are trotting towards the corner, ask for canter. The school sides will encourage your horse to back off so you should get a canter that isn't too on the forehand. You will need an active inside leg on the girth – but don't use your outside leg behind the girth as a canter aid at this point. Horses often find it quite disturbing to be poked in this area and it will probably result in a negative reaction.

*With a youngster, try a few canters while out hacking before trying to canter in the school, which is much harder work for him*

Remember, your aids mean nothing to a young horse until he learns what they are for – you need to coax your horse into his first few canters so he doesn't get stressed. Always ask for canter in the same place initially as horses learn a lot through repetition.

### FUNNEL EXERCISE

If your horse is confused about the strike-off, you can use this exercise to clarify the transition. Place two poles in a funnel shape, about 6m (20ft) apart at the narrow end, and 12m (40ft) apart at the wide end. On the left rein, trot around the end of one pole and go through the middle of the funnel. Change your bend to the right, turn right as you go through the narrow part and strike-off to right canter. The shift of weight caused by the change of bend will position the horse so that he finds it easy to canter, and the poles will help you pick a neat line.

If your horse struggles in the canter, just canter for short periods – maybe 10 or 12 strides – before coming back to trot or walk, and repeating the exercise in the opposite direction.

## MAINTAINING CANTER

A common mistake to make in canter is to press harder and harder with the legs to maintain it, so the rider ends up working more than the horse. What eventually happens is that the horse gets to the point of no return, where he is getting longer and longer and on his forehand – so he breaks into trot, which is exactly what the rider was trying to avoid in the first place.

Your horse needs to learn that once you have put him in a pace, he needs to stay there until you tell him otherwise.

'Re-start' is an exercise used by Olympic dressage rider and trainer Richard Davison. It involves cantering a circle and, once you have the pace well established, asking the horse to trot for two to three strides before going straight back into canter. Practise this through many repetitions and see if you can get to the point where you only trot for one stride. Your horse will start to anticipate the trot and canter re-start to the point where he won't need much leg to get him cantering again. Eventually, he won't want to break into trot at all. By asking him to canter as soon as he is trotting he will learn that breaking into trot isn't a very good evasion.

Use this exercise whenever your horse is feeling sluggish, keeps breaking into trot or is on the forehand in canter. Leg yield in trot (see pp.128–129) is good for suppling up your horse, which will improve his canter.

## RIDE IT RIGHT

If you're sitting in the saddle in canter, you should follow the rocking motion of the gait, which enhances the action of the horse's hind legs and so encourages engagement of the hindquarters. One way you can attain this seat is to imagine you're gently polishing the saddle with your bottom – a gliding feel.

Pay attention to your self-carriage. Circling your inside arm forwards, up and back is a good way to open up the chest area and get length through the spine, while also encouraging the following seat. First try this exercise in walk and trot, in a safe, enclosed area. Be sure your horse is familiar with the exercise before moving on to canter. Holding the reins in the outside hand, and keeping your inside arm perfectly straight, circle it around and back in an even tempo several times. Put your hand back on the reins and try to retain the 'open' feel.

You can also ride the canter with your seat out of the saddle and your shoulders inclined forward. Your weight is balanced over your lower leg, which should lie at the girth. While the lower leg stays stable, you should still have flexibility in your hip, knee and ankle joints in order to absorb the horse's movement. Have your stirrups at least two holes shorter than your flatwork length.

*Repeatedly asking your horse to do a couple of strides in trot and then go back into canter will increase his responsiveness and help to prevent him from seeing dropping into trot as an easy option*

## THE JUMPING SEAT

To jump, you must be happy with your seat in and out of the saddle and also be able to move in balance from one position to the other. A good way to achieve this is to practise standing and sitting for a specific number of strides, say four of each. Once you've established the canter, count to yourself: 'Sit, two, three, four; stand, two, three, four,' and change your position accordingly. Be prepared to shorten your reins when you come out of the saddle so you can maintain an even contact. Be diligent with sticking to the number you've picked, as this will promote an improved rhythm in you and the horse.

# CANTERS WITHIN CANTER

Just as with walk and trot, canter has several variations of pace. These range from the working canter, which is the canter that most horses will do naturally, to the collected canter – a pace that requires great balance and athleticism on the part of the horse. Once he can do collected canter he can learn advanced dressage movements such as canter pirouette.

## WORKING CANTER

In a good working canter the horse's inside hind leg should swing through and underneath his body in a strong, rhythmical way. If you look at a cantering horse from the ground you should see a triangle made by his hind legs. If the inside hind leg looks like it's working in an up-and-down motion and not forwards, then the horse isn't working through.

As the inside hind leg leaves the ground (if you are unsure when this is, glance at the outside shoulder as this will lift at the same time), use your inside leg to encourage the hind leg to reach more forward. Ask someone to watch from the ground to see if you are getting a nice open triangle shape.

To achieve a good, active canter the rider needs an upright, still position. A lot of riders let their bottom leave the saddle too much in the canter. This has the effect of hollowing and unbalancing the horse. You need a sense of vertical balance and your hip joints must be loose enough to follow the horse throughout all phases of the canter. The horse's back pitches up, down and forwards – it's a bit like riding a wave, and you mustn't lose the contact of your seat bones with the saddle. You will be amazed at the difference it makes to your horse.

## COUNTER CANTER

Counter canter is simply cantering on the wrong leg on purpose. It is a useful exercise for gaining extra co-ordination, suppleness and engagement. It is also useful to help straighten your horse.

Three steps to help you perfect your counter canter:

**1** In canter, ride 5m (15ft) loops along the long side of the school.
**2** In canter, ride half a circle at the short end of the school, returning to the track on the long side and maintaining the counter canter for as long as you can.
**3** Counter canter all the way round one corner, then two corners, then three and so on.

Keep your horse slightly bent to the outside (towards the leading leg) during counter canter and watch that he stays tracking straight.

A common mistake is to let the quarters drift out – especially on a circle – and to overbend the horse's neck.

**Test your know-how**

**Why is the moment of suspension in canter so important?**
The moment of suspension, when all four legs are off the ground, is the jewel in the crown of canter. It is during this phase of canter that the horse can move sidewards, do half pass, flying changes and so on.

## MEDIUM CANTER

Medium canter is first asked for in Novice dressage tests, so it's worth getting to grips with it early on if you can. To ride medium canter think of the feeling you get when an aeroplane takes off. You want the rush and the sense of being lifted off the ground, but without actually losing control of the horse. Think of your horse's withers being up in front of you – this is what you are aiming for. Too many riders end up with the quarters high and the withers downhill when they ride medium canter – a bit like a plane crash-landing – avoid this.

When riding medium canter you need to ask your horse to cover more ground, but don't push your hips so far forward that you tip backwards as this will unbalance him. You need to sit down and let your hips swing with the movement – leaning forward slightly will help, but don't do this too much or you will put your horse on his forehand.

To keep your horse round, think connection – the seat, leg and hand being one circuit. Just because your horse is moving onwards don't lose him out of the front end.

As you work on your medium canter, feel for the moment of suspension – this will become more pronounced as your canter develops. Again, it helps if you have someone on the ground (perhaps videoing you) to assess how you are doing.

> **What makes a good canter?**
>
> • Good uphill balance
> • Good reach of the inside hind leg
> • Supple topline, flexible jaw, poll, neck and back
> • A straight horse
> • Clean moment of suspension

## COLLECTED CANTER

Many riders think they are riding a collected canter when they are just riding a slow working canter. In collected canter the triangle made by the hind legs is less open than it is in working canter, but the horse takes more weight on the hind legs while still travelling forward. For true collection you must achieve this sitting-down effect; collection is not just shorter and slower. Your horse's neck will be raised and arched and he should feel light in your hand. In collection, balance is very important and will improve as the horse becomes stronger in his hind legs and can take more weight in his quarters.

To start collecting the canter, decrease your 20m (65ft) circle down to 10m (30ft) in trot and then canter. Using a circle this way will effectively collect your horse for you. Practise this until you understand what collection feels like, then try to get the same feel on larger circles – again ask someone on the ground to tell you what is going on. Don't try to collect your horse by pulling in the front end – this will simply kill the engine.

## EXTENDED CANTER

In extended canter you need to look for the same feeling you get with medium canter, but with the horse covering more ground – as much as possible, in fact, without losing his rhythm and balance. His outline lengthens as he lengthens his stride and his head and neck carriage become longer. Good impulsion is required before extending the canter, otherwise the horse will lose his balance. To achieve a good extended canter you need to have a tremendous amount of power coming through from the hindquarters.

# HALT

Having a horse that will stand still when required is invaluable. Whether you're crossing the road or asking for a square halt in a dressage test, it's important that your horse stands calmly. Plus, a horse that stands correctly will be easier (and safer) for you to mount, dismount and adjust your girth and stirrups on. Spending a little time working on this aspect of your horse's education can also significantly increase his abilities in other areas, helping him to develop balance, freedom of action and lightness of movement. Learning to halt correctly can even improve your horse's outline – as he becomes more responsive, able and willing to carry out your requests, your aids can be applied more subtly and smoothly. (The exercises described here are used by Sarah Fisher, the highest qualified TTEAM practitioner in the UK. If your horse finds standing still difficult even when you are not riding him, try the TTEAM exercises on pp.78–83 before working on ridden halt.)

*The benefits of a good halt go far beyond simply having a horse that is happy to stand still*

## IMPROVING YOUR STOPS

A horse's natural balance tends to be with 60 per cent of his body weight supported over his forehand. If he is not taught how to alter his balance when ridden this unequal weight distribution will put strain on his front legs and he will tend to work 'downhill', lack the ability to use his quarters efficiently, and be more likely to stumble and tire quickly. In addition, it will be hard for him to achieve upwards as well as downwards transitions and halts, and to remain still for any length of time when in halt.

Using a balance rein is a very effective way of teaching him how to transfer his weight backwards, through his body. He'll learn how to rock onto his hindquarters as he comes into a halt, instead of leaning onto your hands (which can cause him to become tight in his jaw and jammed through his neck), or braking with his front legs.

Learning how to halt properly will also make it easier for your horse to understand how to re-balance himself when you use a half-halt. A balance rein has another benefit – it makes you much more aware of what you're doing with your hands, helping you become more subtle and co-ordinated in your rein aids.

When asking for halt, using a verbal command as well as physical cues can be helpful. Keep your voice low-pitched and soothing, and draw out the syllables – using two words, rather than one: 'aaaand whoaaaa'. The 'aaaand' part of the command gives your horse warning that a request is about to

110

follow, so he has a chance to prepare himself for it. As you say 'aaaand,' slacken the tension on the leadrope, bridle or balance rein. As you say 'whoaaaa' close your fingers and give a gentle signal, followed by a slackening of the tension once again. It's vital to remember this release, as this is when your horse will come to a stop, whether you're riding or leading him.

## THE BALANCE REIN

1 *Introduce the balance rein from the ground first. (If you don't have a balance rein, as shown here, use a 2.2m/7ft length of 10mm/½in climbing rope, or improvize with a leadrope, cutting the clip off first.) Ask someone to lead your horse while you walk alongside, holding both ends of the rope (one in each hand) around the horse's neck. Make sure the balance rein hangs loosely as you move. When you want to halt, give a gentle upwards signal on it. Take care that you don't pull sideways as this can cause your horse to lose his balance.*

2 *Immediately after giving the upwards halt signal, release the tension so the balance rein hangs slack again. It is on the 'release' that your horse will slow or stop. Don't keep up a constant pull as this will encourage him to lean against it. If your horse doesn't take any notice of you, try using a firmer upwards halt (and release) signal. Your assistant can also cue him, using a wand (see p.82) if necessary.*

*Once you can halt using the balance rein alone, you're ready to move on to ridden work (see box for details). Ask your horse to walk forwards a few steps, keeping the balance rein slack. Then ask him to stop, using the ask-and-release signal on the balance rein, as before. Ride lots of transitions between walk and halt in this way. Each time you use the balance rein to stop, your horse will be learning how to lighten his forehand and improve his balance and his ability to stop promptly, correctly and efficiently. You'll also find his halts becoming squarer and straighter. Eventually you can introduce transitions from trot to walk.*

### Riding with the balance rein

Secure the ends of the balance rein so it forms a loop around your horse's neck, and position it so it lies beneath your bridle reins. Hold your reins as usual, and hold the balance rein so it passes between the second and third fingers of each hand.

Practise using the balance rein in a safe, enclosed area and have someone on the ground to help at first in case you get into difficulties.

## PROBLEM SOLVER

**Q** The horse I ride is wonderful in every way, but when I ask her to stop she throws her head in the air and opens her mouth. When I'm trying to get her on the bit she eventually accepts but her head isn't relaxed for long. I don't want to use gadgets on her but I would like to improve her way of going.

**A** Your questions are related, as they are all concerned with acceptance of the bridle and the rider's aids.

It would be beneficial to work your horse on the lunge in a pair of correctly fitted side reins. These can be very useful as they imitate the rider's hands. Work her through basic transitions (halt, walk and trot) until she will move freely forwards with no resistance to the contact and will happily accept it.

Repeat the same work under saddle. Keep working her forwards, at all times riding her from your leg to your hand. Keep your hands as still and as quiet as you can. Practise upward and downward transitions until they are quick, responsive and free from resistance. Most people get stuck in a

gear and neglect the importance of transition work, so remember to keep changing the pace up and down, even out hacking.

This will take time, a lot of repetition and much patience but if you stick with it I'm confident it will help you overcome your problem.

**Consider this**

If your horse finds it tricky to come to a halt this may be due to:
• A poorly fitting saddle
• Bitting/teeth problems
• An unbalanced rider
• Abrupt, rough or contradictory aids
• Back problems
• A high head carriage
Seek advice from your vet, saddler, equine dentist and riding instructor if you suspect that any of these may be either causing, or contributing to, the problem.

*Horses can pick up on the smallest of body signals – so be subtle. Strong or abrupt cues to slow down or halt will often have the opposite effect*

## ACHIEVING A BALANCED HALT

*Your posture and aids while mounted will have a big influence on how well, and easily, your horse comes to a halt – and the length of time he can remain standing still.*

**Don't...**

• *Lean backwards.*

• *Grip inwards or upwards with your legs and heels.*

• *Slouch.*

• *Use over-strong or jerky rein aids, or draw your hands backwards.*

**Do...**

• *Think about your horse moving forwards into halt, rather than coming back to it. Allowing the transition to be gradual initially will help with this.*

• *Try sitting lighter, rather than deeper; imagine that you are being gently lifted by a small wave passing under the saddle.*

• *Concentrate on staying with your horse's movement. Although you shouldn't actually tip forwards, it can help if you think of your chest floating forwards.*

• *Keep your shoulders, arms, wrists and fingers relaxed so rein signals are subtle.*

• *Check you're sitting straight – you may need someone to watch you from the ground to determine this.*

## GIVE IT TIME

When you ask your horse to do something, it can take a few seconds for the message to filter through from brain to body. The less well balanced he is, the longer it'll take him to respond to your request, especially if he's learning to do something in a new way. If your horse doesn't respond instantly when you ask him to halt, don't assume he's being naughty or disobedient. The temptation may be to repeat your request immediately, and more forcefully, but this is likely to make him more resistant. Instead, give him extra time to work out how to organize himself and make sure you pause between each request.

Also, bear in mind that your horse may be slow to respond if your signals aren't clear or interfere with his balance.

*A poor mounting technique may make your horse fidget so use a mounting block whenever possible and check that you aren't pulling on the reins, landing heavily in the saddle, sticking your toe in his ribs or doing anything else to cause him discomfort. When you have a horse that will stand still during and after mounting it makes all sorts of in-saddle adjustments so much easier and safer*

113

# HALF-HALT

A half-halt helps to re-balance a horse and prepare him for the movement you're about to ask him to do. While helping to improve and maintain a good rhythm – it will 'lift' your horse up and forwards into the next movement. It also allows you to check that he is listening, aware and ready for this movement, whatever it is. If you're learning to ride a half-halt, or teaching it to an inexperienced horse, you need to start by keeping your aids simple and direct.

*Close your leg around the horse for two or three strides*

## TEACHING HALF-HALT

The classic aids for a half-halt involve the seat, hands and leg. However, this can be confusing for a young horse at the beginning of his training, because he only knows that the hand means stop and the leg means go. Apply them at the same time and he will not know how to respond.

In order to introduce the half-halt, squeeze softly on the reins a couple of times as if to say 'Hey, hey!' Be sure to keep your upper body tall and still. If you don't get a satisfactory response try again a couple of strides later, being certain to reward a good response with a pat, and then allow the horse forward again. When you're teaching the half-halt, it is useful to repeat these aids in the same place in the school a few times. This way, because the horse knows the half-halt is coming, he will start to prepare himself and you can use a lighter cue.

When your horse is responding in an uncomplicated way to your hand, you can gradually introduce more seat aids, letting your upper body grow tall, and your weight drop down through your thighs. After a few repetitions with seat and hand, you should be able to lessen the amount of hand you use until it is just a nudge on the rein.

Once your horse has understood the meaning of the half-halt in walk, trot and canter, you can also start to add some leg aids. Immediately after applying the seat and hand, close your leg around the horse's sides, a bit like a comforting hug. Keep this up for just two or three strides before relaxing the hand and moving the horse forward.

### IS IT RIGHT?

*The measure of a successful half-halt is the improved rhythm after it, so look for a feeling of increased lift to your horse's stride. If you don't get that elevated feeling, or it isn't satisfactory, try asking for another half-halt to see whether that improves matters.*

*Squeeze softly on the reins to ask for a half-halt. Be ready to soften almost instantly*

## YOUR ROLE IN HALF-HALT

Half-halts only work if done correctly by both horse and rider. Think of the half-halt as a 'stop-and-go' action. The stop aid asks your horse to stop but as soon as he hesitates, go forward again. This helps him to push off from his hocks when he moves forward after the half-halt.

• Make sure your position is correct and that your aids are clear.

• Close both legs around the horse and sit up, staying firm through your stomach and lower back with your chest and shoulders square.

• Keep your elbows by your sides, with your hands closed around the reins, without gripping or pulling. This bracing action asks the horse to step under with his hind legs and lift his back.

• Don't tighten your backside as you'll dig your seat into his back and he'll dip away from you, sticking his nose out.

• As you brace using all your aids at once, be ready to soften your arms. This allows the reins to soften without them going loose, which may encourage your horse to raise his head.

## USING YOUR SEAT

A great way to learn how to use the seat for half-halt is to do an exercise called 'legs-away'. Lift both legs, from the hips, out and away from your horse's sides. Do this by 'lifting the bones' and keeping your top body vertical, rather than using momentum to throw your legs out. After two or three steps, let your legs come back around the horse.

The 'legs-away' technique allows an opening and broadening feeling to occur in your chest and stomach, while the seat still follows the movement of the horse. When you are happily taking your legs away, you can start co-ordinating it with closing your hand. Once you've taken your legs away and closed your hands for a couple of strides, you then soften your hand and let your legs come round the horse to gently push him forward. Eventually you can forget about taking your legs away and reduce the time between each element until they all occur within a second.

*Half-halt is used within paces to re-balance your horse and just before you alter a pace to warn him that you are about to ask for something different*

## PROBLEM SOLVER

**Q** I don't have a horse of my own but have riding lessons every week including the occasional private lesson when I can afford it. Over the past few months I had felt that my riding was improving, but I had a lesson recently and things didn't go so well. I'm having problems with half-halts and particularly with downward transitions to halt – the halts are not square. In my last lesson the horse resisted the contact and was stiff and tense throughout. Can you explain the timing for riding half-halts? I have been told this can make a big difference to how effective they are.

**A** The half-halt is a very useful, but sometimes misunderstood exercise. The timing of it really depends on why you are using it and what type of half-halt you are applying.

If you are using a half-halt within the pace to improve engagement of the hindquarters and ultimately collection, the aid should be applied when a hind leg is on the ground with the joints flexed – in other words when it is

carrying weight. This will momentarily increase this phase of the stride and encourage the horse to carry more weight behind. In the extension phase of the stride the rider's hands should immediately release, otherwise this may cause resistance in the horse's mouth.

The half-halt can also be used as a corrective aid to improve transitions and straighten the horse. However, to use them at the correct time for this the rider must have feel and sensitivity. This takes time to develop but riding experienced horses can help.

The problem you're having with your halts not being square is usually the result of a lack of engagement of the hindquarters during the transition. Correctly ridden half-halts may help with this. (See also Halt, pp.110–113.)

## Rein back

Use rein back to help your horse learn basic manners, become supple and make him more collected by bending the hind leg joints and quarters. When your horse is doing rein back correctly he will step backwards with diagonal legs moving together.

Teach your horse the rein back from the ground first. Make sure he is standing straight before you begin. Stand in front of him and give the command 'back'. As you do this gently nudge your horse in the chest to encourage him to move backwards. As soon as he moves back, stop nudging him and walk him forwards. You can also do this with a headcollar, by gently putting backwards pressure on the leadrope, which will put pressure on your horse's nose, and releasing this pressure as soon as he steps backwards.

Eventually you should be able to say 'back' and your horse will automatically move backwards. When you can do this, try it mounted. You might like to test him out first by asking for a step back with the reins while you are standing beside him. Make sure the site of rein pressure on his mouth is the same as it would be if you were in the saddle – that is you are not holding the reins too high or too low. He should drop his nose into this contact and shift backwards.

Once you are on board, again ensure your horse is standing straight. Shift the weight from your seat bones forward as if you're asking your horse to move forward. Keep your legs down and around your horse to keep him straight. Put your leg on to move forward but keep a steady contact on the reins. This tells the horse to move backwards instead of forwards. As soon as he starts to move, even if it's half a step, relax the aids as you are getting the desired response. Pat him and move forward.

Repeat the exercise over a period of time and gradually build up the number of steps taken backwards.

# DIRECT TRANSITIONS

Before riding direct transitions – from halt to trot or walk to canter and so on – you need your other transitions – halt to walk, walk to trot and so on – to work well. To do direct transitions you need your horse to be in self-carriage – not relying on your reins for support. You need to keep a steady contact, but be able to soften the reins at any moment without your horse falling apart.

Half-halts have the effect of collecting your horse and will bring him into self-carriage. He needs to work through his back correctly, which means he should look slightly arched from his ears to his tail, with his head low and his neck curved.

Before attempting direct transitions make sure your position is correct and your aids are clear.

## DOWNWARD TRANSITIONS

When you half-halt or make a downward transition – the feeling is the same – imagine you're lifting your horse's back underneath you by stretching up and keeping your legs on. The reins just remain in a steady contact with the bit.

If you're doing a normal downward transition from trot to walk the last three trot steps should be collected. This keeps the horse in balance and helps to make a smooth transition. Your horse's back should 'bounce' behind the saddle as the hind legs step under. If he falls against the reins, next time close your legs more firmly and keep your stomach and back muscles firmer to give him more support.

When trying direct transitions, use the half-halt to collect during the last three steps before the transition then move into the pace as before. In canter to walk, as you make the downward transition make sure your leg position returns to normal, with your legs level on each side of the horse, so he knows the canter has finished.

## UPWARD TRANSITIONS

To trot from halt you need a good halt. If your halt is balanced, a small leg aid, without pushing with your backside, should get you into trot. Your body must go into trot mode – co-ordinate your back movement exactly with that of your horse. Don't alter your rein contact.

To canter from walk, you need a collected walk. Sit on your inside seat bone, position your inside leg at the girth and outside leg slightly further back, keep the rein contact and sit up tall. Nudge clearly with your out-side leg to start canter. You must go into canter mode – following the movement of his back with-out collapsing at your waist. Use your inside leg at the girth in time with the lift of the canter stride to keep going.

*To achieve a walk to canter transition you need to have a forward-going but collected walk. This gives your horse's hindquarters the power they need to go into a rhythmic and balanced canter*

# CIRCLES

How often do you find yourself riding an egg-shaped circle? Are you aware what shape your circle is at all? Many riders get so preoccupied with an inside bend, or getting the horse on the bit, they forget to ride a correct circle. The irony is that when you pay attention to the line you are riding, the bend often sorts itself out, and the horse relaxes and softens because he is getting clear instructions from you.

## CUTTING IN AND FALLING OUT

It is almost guaranteed that if a horse cuts in on one part of the circle, he will fall out in the area that is directly opposite. Riders sometimes misinterpret this situation, thinking the horse is resisting when he cuts in and then that he is finally giving when he falls out, but in reality he is just resisting in a different way by escaping through the outside shoulder.

Luckily, you can use the fact that horses are creatures of habit to your advantage. The horse will keep cutting in and falling out in the same places on the circle until you do something about it, so you can catch the error before it happens, knowing full well when it will happen.

It is a good discipline to ride circles that are completely inside the outside track of the school as this enables you to study what is happening and make adjustments as necessary. If, for example, the horse starts to fall out as you come parallel to the entrance of the school, next time around, start to apply your outside aids 3–4m (10–13ft) before the point at which he started to lose his shoulder and fall out. It is vital that you apply the outside aids before he starts to fall out, otherwise the old habit will still be present and you will simply be limiting the damage rather than teaching your horse something positive.

Once you have successfully corrected one side of the circle, observe what is happening on the opposite side. The circle may already be evening out because of the work you have done, but it is more likely that you will need to apply inside aids and lead out with the outside hand (an open rein) to correct the cutting in.

Practise riding circles of varying sizes, taking into account your horse's fitness and level of schooling, and make sure you have decided what size your circle is going to be before you execute it. This way, you will have a much better chance of riding a beautiful round one. (If you continue to have trouble with circles, teach your horse turn on the forehand, pp.126–127, as it is an excellent way of improving his response to your leg aids.)

*Cutting in or falling out is a sure sign of resistance in the horse*

*After a few thoughtful corrections your horse will start to understand what you want and you will begin to achieve good round circles*

## LEG MASSAGE

*Whether you are using increased inside or outside leg, make sure you gently massage the horse with a leg that squeezes and relaxes, rather than one that is clamped on. If you clamp the leg on it becomes stiff and will feel like an iron rod to the horse, which is hardly something he will want to 'give' to.*

## PROBLEM SOLVER

**Q** When I'm schooling my horse and I turn a circle he seems to swing to the outside. My instructor says he is falling out through the shoulder, but I have no idea how to correct this. I have to perform a 20m (65ft) circle in my Preliminary dressage tests and keep losing marks because of this. What should I do?

**A** You need to control both the inside and outside of your horse when you turn.

First, check that you are sitting in the correct position – remaining tall in the saddle and sitting straight and level.

To ask your horse to circle or turn to the left, sit up on your left (inside) seat bone, pressing your left hipbone forward in the direction of your horse's left ear. You should feel the muscle down the left side of your torso go firm. This feeling, in conjunction with your left leg pressing against your horse's side, with your thigh, knee and calf against his body, will support him as he turns. Have your toe level with the girth, your ankle flexed so your heel is slightly lower than your toe. Don't ram your heel down, as your lower leg will shoot forward, blocking the turn by getting in the way of your horse's inside shoulder and making him fall out (take the weight onto his outside shoulder).

Position your outside (right in this instance) thigh further back than your inside thigh. Reach back into your outside stirrup to keep it in place, with your heel pressed down and backwards towards your horse's right hock. This anchors your outside leg in position, which helps you press it against your horse to ask him to turn, and secondly to prevent him falling out on the circles. If he falls out through his shoulder use your outside knee and thigh more firmly. Your calf prevents his haunches falling out.

Keeping your elbows by your sides, turn your upper body in the direction you wish to go. Soften your inside rein to allow your horse's inside back leg to step under his body to balance the turn. Your outside rein should feel firmer than your inside rein. Make sure your outside hand doesn't cross over his withers as this is another reason his outside shoulder might fall away.

Look between your horse's ears as you turn, with your chin in line with the middle of your body. Your horse should turn his head in line with the midline of his body. This is the only way to ride a balanced turn, with your horse evenly bent around your inside leg. If his neck is too far to the inside – that is his nose is further to the left than his inside shoulder – this will also make him fall out through his shoulder.

*Rein aids alone will not prevent a from horse falling out through his shoulder*

# POLEWORK MASTERCLASS

Riding straight lines and performing accurate circles is all you need to do to improve your horse's movement and these lines and circles can be done using some simple pole exercises. Improving your horse's movement also means refining the quality of your riding techniques. Think about making your lines really straight, and your turns and circles accurate. Being able to ride in a straight line and change direction with ease are vitally important as they give you greater control of your horse. Accurate steering will also make you safer out riding.

## THE CLASS

The school movements described here work on developing your horse's balance, rhythm and paces. They also help to fine-tune your own riding skills. Vary the exercises. Spend 10 minutes on each and then refresh the pace by going around the school in working trot or medium trot. Have frequent stretches on a long rein to rest your horse's muscles. Don't feel you have to do them all in one session. It is better to do a few really well than all of them badly.

### SCHOOL RULES

• *Straight lines can only be truly straight if you are sitting level in the saddle. Ensure that you are sitting tall and evenly on both seat bones (see box, p.123).*

• *Turn with your horse. If you have a tendency to lean in around corners, you will upset your horse's balance. Turn your upper body toward the direction in which you want to go, not just your head.*

• *Every turn is part of a circle. A serpentine is made up of half-circles and straight lines. A corner is a quarter-circle.*

• *Each change of direction involves at least one or two steps on a straight line to prepare for the next turn. This is how you keep your horse balanced.*

• *The inside aids are on the side the horse is bending to and the outside aids are on the side the horse is bending away from.*

• *The bend of the horse's body must be consistent in order to keep him balanced. Make sure he is flexing through his whole body and not just turning his head. The action of your outside leg helps to bring him around your inside leg and this should help with his balance.*

• *If your horse is straight, your transitions will improve.*

• *Are your horse's hind legs following his forehand, or are they drifting in or out on the turns? If the latter, use your legs to help him.*

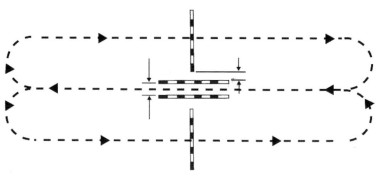

**1** *Lay out the poles as in the diagram. Begin by riding between the two adjacent poles in the centre. Continue straight forward and make a half-circle left when you reach the outside track. Walk straight towards the pole in front of you. Step over it and continue to the track. Half-circle left again up the centre line and go between the middle two poles. This time, half-circle right and step over the other pole. Aim to go over the centre of each side pole every time you cross it.*

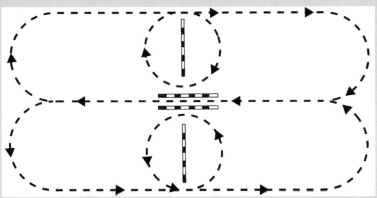

**2** *With the poles in the same formation as exercise one, ride between the centre poles. Half-circle left, and ride a circle around the side pole. Continue straight and then make a large half-circle left, aiming between the middle poles again. Repeat to the right. Make sure your circles around the side poles are the same size, and your turns towards the middle poles are the same shape as each other.*

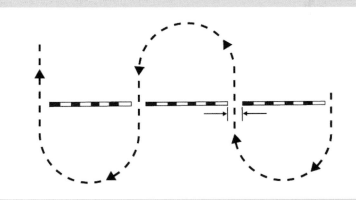

**3** *Position the poles in a straight line down the centre, 1m (3ft) apart as shown – you need to be able to ride through the gaps. This exercise will help to make your serpentines accurate. Serpentines are good flexibility exercises and should be an integral part of your training. Aim to ride directly between the poles as you cross the middle of the school. Maintain the bend through your horse's body as you ride each loop, then half-halt, positioning yourself and your horse for the next turn as you cross the centre line.*

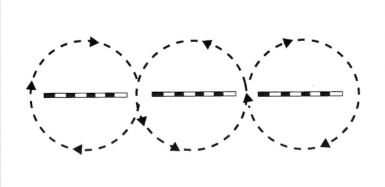

4 *Keeping the poles positioned as for exercise three, ride a circle around each pole before changing direction to go around the next pole. As you go through the gap to change direction, ride one step straight so that you can change your position and bend for the new circle.*

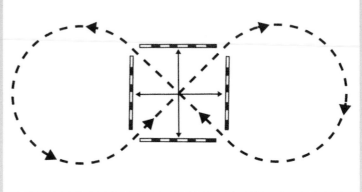

**5** *Set the poles in a 7m (23ft) wide square as shown. Riding between the gaps at the corners of the square, aim straight across the diagonal, turning left on a half-circle to return across the other diagonal between the other two gaps, then half-circling to the right.*

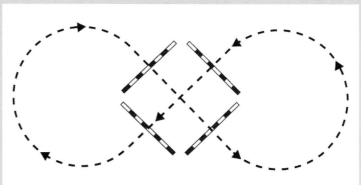

**6** *Again, with the poles in a 7m (23ft) wide square, ride over the centre of them, creating two diagonal lines, turning left and right respectively after each diagonal. Straighten yourself and your horse by sitting level as you come in line with each pole. If you aim straight, your horse will take an elevated step over the pole to aid the engagement of his hind legs.*

## WORKING HARDER

To increase the difficulty of all these exercises, add in a transition on each straight line. If you are riding exercises one and two, make a transition between the middle poles, from trot to walk and trot to halt. If you are riding them in canter, practise transitions from canter to trot, or canter to walk at the same middle point. If you have an advanced horse, try riding a flying change in the middle.

Exercises three and four benefit from a half-halt or a transition each time you go through the gaps between the poles, while you could do a transition as you cross the centre point of the square in exercises five and six.

## STRAIGHT LINES AND TURNS

For lines to be straight, the rider must be straight. Make sure your saddle is level and that your stirrups are even before you mount. Check that your body is not crooked – otherwise, your horse will not be able to work evenly on both sides of his body. This can result in uneven paces, leading to differences in muscle development on one side of his body, particularly his back muscles. This makes straight lines impossible.

While in halt, check your hands are an equal distance from the withers, and your legs are in the same position. Look down at your thighs and knees – the tips of your toes should just be visible. If you can see any more of your feet, they are too far forward.

(The problem solver on p.119 describes the best way to ride a good turn.)

*When asking your horse to bend left, sit tall in the saddle, keeping your pelvis upright. Avoid collapsing to the inside by keeping your ribcage level and in line with your hips*

## TROUBLESHOOTING

• If you turn in your shoulders too far, your horse will swing his haunches out.

• Trying to turn using too much inside rein does not allow the horse to step forward and under with his inside hind leg. He needs to do this to keep his balance.

• If you turn your shoulders to the outside, with your inside shoulder in advance of your outside shoulder, your horse will swing his haunches too far in.

• If you drift away from a pole when turning, make your outside aids (rein and leg) firmer.

• If your horse drifts around when he turns inward, you may be leaning in. Re-balance yourself by putting even weight in your stirrups. You should have a little more weight in your inside stirrup, but too much means your horse will fall in. Too much weight on the outside stirrup will cause your horse to fall out.

• Reward your horse with a softer contact as he begins to round his back and work into the bridle.

## MORE POLEWORK

Poles can also be used in a variety of ways to improve your horse's way of going. For example, asking your horse to step rhythmically and in balance over spaced poles can help all the paces, particularly walk and trot. They can encourage a horse to lift his feet so are good for horses with a lazy action, and they can also be used to improve a horse's outline by getting him to stretch down and out, rather than putting his head up.

### PACES WITH POLES

For improving extended walk set some poles 80cm (32in) apart; for collected walk set them 60–70cm (24–28in). You may need to experiment a bit with the distance, as every horse's stride is different. Place the poles further apart to encourage your horse to stretch out, in extended walk for example – this is helpful if your horse undertracks and you want him to walk out more.

*Poles are wonderful for improving your horse's walk*

*When positioned reasonably close together, poles can help teach your horse to carry himself in collected walk.*

**Use poles to…**
• Focus your horse's attention. If your horse tosses his head about, jogs or refuses to settle during a schooling session, it's probably because he's not relaxed. Polework can help to encourage him out of this.
• Encourage your horse to pick his feet up and carry himself.
• Regulate your horse's rhythm. Your horse has to even out his stride when he goes over poles and this will help to confirm the four-time beat of the walk or the two-time beat of the trot.

## IMPROVING OUTLINE

A horse that's been schooled incorrectly can develop the wrong neck muscles – usually too much muscle underneath the neck and not enough on top. This muscle underneath is what's used when the horse pulls and lifts his head in the air, and this stops him using his back and hind legs correctly, which can cause unbalanced paces.

Initially, go back to basics and work him on the lunge four times a week for a month. Start with 10 minutes and build up to 30 minutes. Your horse needs to relax and stretch down, so do work in walk and trot over single poles on the ground. This will encourage him to look at the poles and stretch the muscles of his topline. Don't fix your horse's neck in place as he'll resist. Even side reins are not a good idea as it's his whole body that needs remodelling rather than just the neck.

Polework while lungeing will also help your horse to use his joints more. Keep things calm and work in a steady walk or trot: a tense horse will use the wrong muscles, which is detrimental to what you are trying to achieve.

You will begin to see your horse's shape change – he will start to develop a slab of muscle on his back, and the top and central neck muscles will look more visible and his quarters more rounded. At this stage you can begin riding work. Copy the polework you did on the lunge and, once your horse can stretch down, start to work on a contact. Practise transitions, using half-halts to remain balanced.

Make your horse work with his hind legs underneath his pelvis, his back lifted and his neck arched forward and slightly down to the bit. When he can carry his neck in a lifted position, introduce canter. Expect it to take up to six months to really see a complete change in him.

*A horse that has a set of muscles like this needs re-schooling from the basics to develop a pleasing topline that will enable him to work correctly. Poles are a vital part of this work*

# TURN ON THE FOREHAND

Turn on the forehand is a basic, but important, lateral exercise. It can be taught early on in a horse's life – once he understands and responds to the aids for stop – but don't worry if your horse isn't a youngster, it's never too late for him to learn.

## WHY LEARN THE TURN?

Although it is hardly ever used in dressage tests, turn on the forehand is a very good training tool. It helps to teach the horse to understand the leg aid for stepping sideways. Lateral work generally has a very positive influence on the horse's education, testing his flexibility and obedience. It also helps to keep all parts of his body supple and develops athleticism, control and balance.

If you are having difficulty with circles, turn on the forehand can help by teaching your horse to respect the inside leg and move away from it, which means he is more likely to stay out on the circle and not be so prone to falling in.

Finally, turn on the forehand is an excellent hacking skill, useful in all sorts of situations, such as opening and closing gates, for instance.

## TEACHING THE MOVEMENT

When you start to teach turn on the forehand, use the school wall or fence as a prop. This will enable you to execute the movement without using too much hand. Choose an area that is not too close to the corners, as the horse will think that he hasn't got enough room to turn and may panic or become tense.

In walk, ride towards the edge of the school at a 90 degree angle. As you get to the fence ask the horse to move his quarters over. This is a straightforward way to teach him that the leg aid you are using means move over, as he can't go any further forward anyway. As he moves his quarters around, get him moving forwards as soon as his body is parallel with the school boundary. Aim to do the whole exercise in one smooth movement

It's always a positive step to have the horse thinking forward and doing turn on the forehand in this way encourages just that. Use half-halts to rebalance and slow him as you start the movement.

When he is managing to turn on the forehand using the side of the school for support, then move further away from it. Try turning on the three-quarter or centre line while still making sure the exercise is done as one movement. Only when the movement is fluid and the

horse is relaxed and working softly should you try it from halt.

To carry out a turn on the forehand, a gentle flexion is required towards the way you are turning, for instance if you are turning right, the horse's head should be slightly flexed that way. To turn right the rider's right leg moves back behind the girth and presses against the horse's side. The horse should move his quarters left away from this pressure. The horse's right hind should pass in front of the left as he steps sideways. His front legs walk a small circle. The rider's outside leg remains close to the girth ready to ask the horse to move forward the moment the turn is complete. If the horse resists moving sidewards, press your whip on his side to exaggerate the aid.

## TROUBLESHOOTING

• The most common problem when trying to carry out turn on the forehand is the horse moving backwards, or even, more rarely, rearing. This often happens if you try to introduce the exercise from halt. This is counterproductive because the horse won't know what you are asking him to do. Confusion sets in and this can result in him 'standing up' on his back legs or going backwards. If the horse does try to evade like this, ask him to walk forward positively. Using the sides of the school should prevent this problem occurring in the first place.

• The rider can sometimes make it difficult for the horse to turn correctly. By trying to pull the horse around the turn the horse will become overbent and fall out through his shoulder. To correct this, take up more contact on the outside rein and cross the hands slightly over the neck. Keep the inside rein open.

• Horses can become tense in the neck and resistant in the mouth when starting lateral work – this is a way of evading your aids and requests. If this happens, stop, give with the hand and then move off again.

• If you find that your horse is unable to make the turn or is getting anxious or tense, then always go back to basics. In this case just get the horse moving forward from walk to trot and then back again. Forget about the turn on the forehand until he is settled and working actively – maybe in another session.

### Test your know-how

**How far do you turn in turn on the forehand?**
A turn on the forehand may be 90, 180 or 360 degrees, although the latter is not practised often. When first starting the exercise, just ask for a quarter of a turn at a time.

*Ride towards the edge of the school at a 90 degree angle. As you get to the fence ask the horse to move his quarters over. Aim to do the whole exercise in one smooth movement*

# LEG YIELD

In leg yield the horse moves forwards and sideways at the same time, while giving very slight bend away from the direction in which he is travelling. He is on two tracks and his inside legs cross in front of the outside legs.

Leg yielding is a good exercise for teaching the horse how to step from the inside leg to the outside rein – important as this forms the basis of all his schooling. It also encourages the action of moving the inside legs over and across the outside legs – some horses are reluctant to do this. When first introducing leg yield to your schooling sessions, remember to make sure your horse is properly warmed up before you start so that he can use his muscles effectively without risk of damage. When leg yield is established, it can be used as part of the horse's warm-up routine at the beginning of schooling sessions or when warming up for a competition.

## TEACHING THE MOVEMENT

Leg yielding should only be attempted when turn on the forehand (see pp.126–127) has been mastered. Ideally, you should be able to ride a square with a quarter turn on the forehand at each corner, showing that you have good control of your horse when he is asked to move sideways. This also confirms that your horse understands the sideways driving aids.

When first attempting this exercise, do it in walk. Start down the long side of the school as this gives you longer to prepare and also time to straighten after the movement. Your horse will also naturally gravitate towards the school sides, which will help when moving him over. Don't expect too much to begin with. Leg yielding down half of the long side is plenty.

**Test your know-how**

**Why do we do lateral work?**
Lateral work is a fantastic way to test a horse's obedience and encourage him to use himself correctly – helping him to become more supple and athletic. It increases engagement and impulsion and helps with straightness and connection. It also increases the flexion of the haunches and freedom of the shoulder bringing a lasting improvement in the carrying power of the quarters. Trot and canter work also benefit from correctly ridden lateral movements.

In walk turn down the long side of the school about 5m (16ft) from the track. Walk a few strides, keeping the horse straight. Use a half-halt to make sure your horse is balanced, then start the movement. Do this by applying pressure with your inside leg behind the girth; your outside leg stays on the girth in a supportive action. Open the inside rein at the same time as holding the outside rein in a constant way closer to the horse's neck – this should stop him falling out through his shoulder and will create the necessary bend. Ideally, you should just be able to see his eye and the arch of the nostril on the inside. He should move over towards the track at the same time as actively going forwards. When you reach the track, straighten your horse and continue normally.

During the exercise, maintain the rhythm, pace and flow of the movement and the length of the horse's stride. He must stay almost parallel to the school sides with you encouraging activity so that his inside legs step over and across with a swinging action.

## ADVANCED MOVES

You will soon be able to progress to trot. When your horse is able to leg yield correctly in walk and trot down the long side of the school, then it is time to make things more difficult. Test him by leg yielding from the centre line to the track or from the track to the centre line and back to the track again, almost in a 'V' shape.

For more of a challenge try leg yielding on a circle. Start in walk or trot on a 10m (30ft) circle and using the inside leg, move the horse over until he is on a 20m (65ft) circle. Make sure he moves forwards actively at the same time as moving over and maintains the correct bend throughout. Circle at 20m and then leg yield back down to a 10m circle. This exercise is great for improving circles and accurate use of the inside leg.

## TROUBLESHOOTING

• Young or inexperienced horses may become confused when you ask for leg yield and could stop in their tracks. To encourage him to move on again use the schooling whip. Don't hit him, use it behind your inside leg in a 'pressing' way as a back up to your leg aid.
• If your horse 'runs sideways' from your legs, correct him by using your outside leg as a controlling aid, keeping it softly on the girth to support him.
• When learning to leg yield many horses try to take the forehand over, leaving the quarters trailing. Don't let the horse 'cheat' in this way as the whole point is to get even sideways movement from his whole body. Make sure you watch for this and learn to feel what the hindquarters are doing.
• Too much bend in the neck (right) is usually caused by the rider trying to 'pull' the horse over into the leg yield. To correct too much bend, open the inside hand and maintain a contact on the outside rein by crossing the outside hand over the neck slightly.
• Avoid drawing the inside leg too far back to give the aid. This is incorrect as it invites the hindquarters to move away but doesn't usually achieve any flexion beneath you.

### HELP YOUR HORSE

*If your horse doesn't understand what you're asking for, then use your inside leg quite a way back to indicate that something different is about to happen. Once he gets to grips with this, resume a normal leg position.*

# GOING STRAIGHT

When you are schooling your horse in lateral movements, it is important that he goes into them from being straight. It is vital that a horse goes on the line chosen by the rider, as an undirected horse will meander around. Straightness means schooling your horse so he goes physically straight, enabling him to make full use of the power created in his quarters. This is often considered to be the most challenging aspect of schooling, as horses, like people, naturally favour one side over the other and tend to travel with a slight curve in the body. It is a mark of truly successful schooling when you can ride your horse on a straight line and he goes evenly into both hands. (For more information about going straight, see pp.147–151.)

## DOWN THE CENTRE LINE

The easiest way to ride a straight line is to ride towards a specific marker. For example, when you ride down the centre line, focus on C just before you turn the corner at A. Once on the centre line, straighten the horse by applying your outside aids and, if necessary, use a leading inside hand (see box opposite) so the horse understands the direction in which he is meant to be moving.

As soon as he is lined up with C, ride forward a little more strongly so you underline the point that he is doing what you want. Keep your focus on C until you start to prepare for the next corner, so you can pick up and correct any deviations in the horse's straightness.

### EXERCISE

To check and improve your horse's straightness, plan a line 5m (16ft) inside the track on the long side of the school, and come through the turn with an inside bend. As soon as you are on the 5m line, change the bend to the outside for about five strides (right). Then, apply your straightening aids and ride directly forward. The theory behind this exercise is that to get something straight, you often have to push it in the opposite direction to the one it favours (think of a rolled up piece of paper – to get it flat you have to roll it in the opposite direction).

## RIDING ACROSS THE DIAGONAL

When you leave the track at the quarter marker, a horse's natural inclination is to hang towards the wall, so you must make a conscious effort to straighten him up as you turn onto the diagonal. Think of it like this: as you turn right off the track at M, apply your outside aids (in this case, your left leg and hand) and lead in with your right hand. Once straight, apply your forward aids. Be aware that most horses have a tendency to lean one way or the other just after you cross X, so be ready to apply the relevant aids to maintain the line.

It is your responsibility to keep the horse straight. If your horse's shoulder is falling out to the left, correct him by moving both your hands as a pair to the right and supporting with your left leg. Once he responds, ride him forward for a few strides with both legs.

## ARE YOU STRAIGHT?

Lopsidedness in the rider will affect the horse, so it is worth checking periodically that you are sitting level. Make sure that your stirrups are even. You can do this by checking them before you get on, or asking someone to have a look once you are on board. Ask someone to check that you are sitting level. Get them to check by standing directly in front and behind. Are your buttocks and shoulders level?

*To check the stirrups your horse must be standing square, and you should take your feet out of the stirrups*

### PROBLEM SOLVER

**Q** I ride a very green 15hh, four-year-old mare. The problem is I never know what to do when it comes to schooling her. We usually warm up in walk and trot for about 10 minutes, then do some canter work. But this gets a bit boring after a while, and I can feel my horse losing interest. I don't do any jumping with my mare but I don't want our schooling sessions to be boring. Any ideas?

**A** Schooling should be fun for you and your horse. You need to have a clear idea of your future riding aims. For example, what do you want the pair of you to be doing in a year's time? In addition, make sure you clearly understand the aims and objectives of schooling a horse on the flat – there is much more to be learnt than simply walk, trot and canter. The horse must work freely forwards from behind, with active use of the hindlimbs, a soft back, a relaxed neck, poll and jaw, and accepting a light, relaxed contact. Achieving this alone could take a couple of years.

Your work on the flat can be 20–30 minutes, two or three times a week. Use ground poles, turns, circles, transitions, serpentines, shallow loops and small amounts of lateral work. Introduce jumping to keep the work as varied as possible so your mare doesn't get stale and bored. You can do some schooling when you're out hacking, for example working on transitions. It may also be a good idea to have some lessons from an instructor – someone on the ground to give you that all-important help and guidance.

*Varied sessions will help a youngster retain interest in schooling*

### USING A LEADING REIN

*Straightening the horse often involves using a leading rein, but many riders feel inhibited about moving their hands away from the withers and prefer to move them backwards and down, which has a negative effect.*

*Practise moving your hand without influencing the horse as this will help when you use a leading rein in conjunction with your straightening aids. Walk on the inside track and move your left hand to the left three times, followed by your right hand to the right three times. Concentrate on making the movement easy and flowing.*

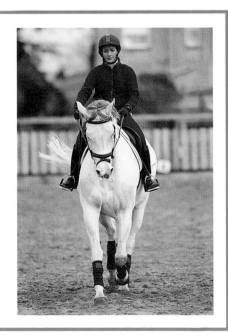

# SHOULDER-IN

When you've perfected turn on the forehand and your horse can do a nice leg yield and you are working on straightness – it's time to move on to shoulder-in. The aim of using shoulder-in as a schooling exercise is to achieve a more advanced level of collection, balance and lightness in the horse. Also, it's required in dressage tests from Elementary upwards, so it pays to get it right early on in the horse's education.

## WHY DO SHOULDER-IN?

Shoulder-in is one of the most important exercises a horse can learn as it's the main road to suppleness. The inventor of the movement, French master de la Guérinière, stated its importance as: 'It is the first and last lesson you must teach a horse.'

Shoulder-in is an excellent exercise to straighten the horse and make him level in the hand. It may seem strange that an exercise that requires bend will help with straightness, but in fact the continuous bending followed by straightening of the horse does just that (see also pp.130–131). Shoulder-in exercises all the major hind leg joints, and the suppleness and activity produced consequently gives more freedom to the horse's shoulder. It's great for developing muscle too.

## RIDING SHOULDER-IN

Although shoulder-in is primarily an exercise that's ridden in trot, a walk shoulder-in can be useful to straighten the horse if he has a tendency to fall onto either shoulder. Many riders also incorporate walk shoulder-in into their pre-competition warm-up routine to ensure that the horse is supple, straight and listening to them before going under the judge's eye.

Ideally, shoulder-in is performed at an angle of about 30 degrees to the direction in which the horse is moving. However, when you first start off, the degree of angle is not really important. What is important is that whatever angle you achieve, you must maintain it until you decide to straighten the horse again.

If you don't maintain it, you won't have control over the horse's shoulders, which is defeating the object.

In shoulder-in, the hind leg is encouraged to step further forward than usual and the hip and stifle joints are required to bend more. The horse takes more weight onto his hindquarters, which is why this exercise helps to improve collection.

### Test your know-how

**Can you describe shoulder-in?**
Shoulder-in has a clear definition: the horse is slightly bent round the inside of the rider's inside leg and the forehand is slightly to the inside of the track being taken by the quarters. Viewed from the front, the horse's hooves should be on three tracks. This means the inside fore leg makes one track, the outside fore leg and inside hind leg make the second track with the outside hind leg making the third.

## TEACHING THE MOVEMENT

With a novice horse, it is best to start work on new movements in walk, even if the ultimate desire is to ride them in trot. This gives you time to organize your aids and clearly tell the horse what is being asked of him – it can all seem a bit confusing at first. You can move on to trot as soon as you have got the basics sorted.

Before you begin the movement, ensure you have your horse walking in an energetic and rhythmic way.

It is best to start shoulder-in down the long side. As you come along the short side of the school and turn down the long side, keep your horse bent round your inside leg as if you are going to ride a 10m (30ft) circle. As your horse takes his forehand round, don't do the circle, instead use your inside leg to push him down the long side. He should already be bent the correct way for the shoulder-in. Both the horse's shoulders come to the inside of the track as you push the horse towards your outside rein, but his hind legs stay on the track.

It's hard to know initially how many tracks your horse is on, but don't worry if he is on three or four tracks – four is often easier to get. Just make sure you do the same thing on both reins and that the bend involves the whole body – not just the neck. Having a friend or instructor on the ground is essential to tell you how you are doing. Aim for a few steps at a time.

If your horse becomes tense or stiffens, then ride a 10m (30ft) circle, re-establish control and then carry on. Ride as many 10m circles as you need to up the long side – this just stops the horse becoming stuck. Don't just carry on riding shoulder-in all the way down the long side hoping you will have it right by the end. Instead, always make sure you straighten your horse before you get to the end, even if the movement wasn't really correct. You can always start again.

Maintaining activity and tempo is very important; aim to keep the regularity of the length and rhythm of the steps throughout. Don't allow your horse to back off and lose his momentum.

### INCREASING THE DIFFICULTY

When you have mastered shoulder-in on the long side, give yourself a real test by riding the movement down the centre line. Without the school boundary to help, your horse will probably feel unbalanced and wobbly at first. But if you can get to a point where shoulder-in on the centre line feels as good as one down the long side, you know you've cracked it.

## TROUBLESHOOTING

By far the most common fault seen in shoulder-in is too much neck bend to the inside. Riders tend to try to pull their horse into the movement with the inside rein, but all they achieve is the horse overbending without his shoulders moving onto the inside track – which isn't correct. He will probably fall out through his outside shoulder too. If you can see the corner of the horse's eye and mouth on the inside then you have enough bend. To correct too much bend, take a stronger contact on the outside rein to give support, and ask for less bend with the inside rein.

*Too much neck bend is a common fault*

*Many riders collapse to one side or the other during shoulder-in – almost in an effort to make the movement work. Watch out for this. If you do collapse to one side, looking over the opposite shoulder will help to straighten you up again and get things back on track*

## AIDS FOR SUCCESS

• *Put more weight on the inside seat bone – just push down a little more into your inside stirrup. Your inside leg should be on the girth and is used to push the horse forwards and sideways and keep the correct bend. Ideally you should use the leg as your horse's inside hind leg leaves the ground, but this might be difficult to judge – use a friend on the ground to help. If you continually push with your leg, your horse may lean on it.*

• *Place your outside leg behind the girth to stop the horse swinging out with his quarters or outside hind leg.*

• *Use the outside rein to catch the energy produced by your inside leg. Ensure the contact is elastic, but constant, with a little give to make sure the horse can produce the flexion he needs in his neck.*

• *The inside rein is more or less passive – but it may help if you have this rein in a slightly more open position.*

• *Look up the track in the direction the horse is going – don't look down between his ears. Make sure your weight doesn't slide to the outside, as this would collapse your inside hip.*

Lack of pace and rhythm can become an issue through the exercise, especially if the horse doesn't understand what is being asked of him. If this happens, straighten him and get him working forwards again – try a few transitions to get him thinking and listening to you.

As with any schooling session, if your horse is finding the work difficult, or is getting tense about what you are asking him to do, then always go back to basics. In this case, try a bit of leg yielding. It will get your horse thinking and listening and you will still be moving him sideways – good preparation for trying the shoulder-in again.

If things are really not coming together then forget it for the day, go home, have a cup of tea and try again tomorrow. Never lose patience with yourself or your horse – as with so many aspects of riding, shoulder-in takes time to perfect.

# THE LESSONS

While it's all very well knowing the theory behind flatwork and even knowing how to do many of the moves, it is not always easy to put together a satisfying schooling session that offers you and your horse the opportunity to practise what you know and improve on areas that are less than perfect. Many of us ride into an arena, do a bit of warm up, trot around, do some cantering and then think: What shall I do next? The worry is that your horse will be bored, or that you've concentrated too much on one aspect of his schooling to the detriment of another, or that you haven't worked equally on both reins, or even that you've been asking him to do something and he simply hasn't understood what you want.

With this in mind, the next few pages feature complete lessons that you can try out with your horse. They are not in any particular order of difficulty as every horse and rider combination develops differently and what one pair might find easy another will find a challenge. Some do expect more advanced work than others, so bear in mind your horse's level and don't push him to do something he is not ready for. You should find something to inspire you and, by the end of each session, you should also feel that you have both learnt something new.

## TIPS FOR SUCCESS

• *Remember to start each session with a warm-up and end it with a cool-down period.*

• *If your horse isn't getting something right, consider whether you are explaining what you want clearly enough.*

• *Start each session with an idea of what you would like to achieve, but always be prepared to end it before you get there.*

• *End on a good note, so if something hasn't quite come together during a session finish with something you're both good at.*

• *Don't continue if you start to get cross or frustrated. Again, finish with something you both know, turn your horse out and go home to think about how you can do it differently to get a better result.*

• *Quality is more important than quantity – don't practise something badly just for the sake of practising.*

• *Remember you are supposed to enjoy your riding. If you're not, reconsider what you are doing.*

## PROBLEM SOLVER

**Q** I own a Thoroughbred x Cleveland Bay that is rising five. He is well behaved out on hacks but seems to switch off and misbehave when we have a lesson in the school. He is fine for the first 10 minutes, then loses concentration, pulls against me and refuses to co-operate. Why is this?

**A** The problem with an hour-long session is that you are committed to working for a whole hour on a particular day, at a set time, regardless of how you and your horse feel.

When dealing with youngsters, it is important to remember that an hour is a long time to do something. Think of your young horse as you would a toddler: he needs lots of different stimulation to keep his mind occupied, and he can't concentrate for too long on any one thing.

Introduce plenty of variety in each session and add lots of breaks, too. For example, work on getting a good turn, try it a couple of times, go away and do something else, then try the turns again.

Young horses need time to digest what they have just learned so a change is as good as a rest as far as they're concerned – lots of little exercises intertwined with one another are much better than one long, intense schooling session.

Working in a school can easily become a fun-free activity for a young horse. If he is asked to do something that is too demanding for him, he will soon start to nap and mess around. So make schooling fun for your horse – and keep it fun. It means you'll enjoy it more too. Have 20 minutes of tuition, then go for a five-minute walk up the lane and back before resuming your lesson, for example. Alternatively, school out in the field for half your lesson, then go in the manège for the other half. You could also include some polework to keep him interested.

If you have backed a horse in the spring, you should spend the rest of that year just 'playing' with him.

# LESSON 1
# RESPONSE AND SUPPLENESS

This is a complete basic lesson that goes over much of what has been covered so far in this section, while introducing your horse to some more subtle skills. The lesson focuses on how to ride balanced corners, introduce simple canter changes and counter canter, and how to control medium trot. It was devised by British National Dressage Champion and Olympic rider, Richard Davison.

## WARMING UP

Take time in your warm-up to encourage your horse to stretch forwards and down to release any tension in his neck and back. Make sure you are warmed up too, concentrating on your position so you're relaxed and supple. Let your legs hang down, stretch up through your back and grow tall. Riding on a large circle on both reins, focus on your position, which will also help your horse to relax if he's feeling tense or fresh.

Next ride transitions between walk and trot. Use your upper body to make the downward transitions, rather than using your hands – the latter may cause tension. Make transitions around the circle from trot to walk and back. Keep practising growing tall with your upper body, as this will help your transitions, and use your voice as well as your body to bring your horse back to walk.

Repeat the transitions five or six times on the circle, gradually reducing the number of walk steps before going forwards to trot again. This exercise also helps with the upward transitions to trot. Your horse should become much quicker off the leg into trot, which should help him to maintain rhythm and tempo through the transitions.

This circling exercise is ideal for horses that need to be mentally relaxed. Because you are controlling and influencing your horse through your body, he can keep his head and neck stretched out in front of you. If you rely on your reins too much he may bring his head and neck up against you and become tense.

## LEG YIELD AND INTO CANTER

Still on a circle in trot, reduce the circle to 10m (30ft) and leg yield out onto a 20m (65ft) circle making a transition to canter as you finish the leg yield. After one circle go back to trot and reduce the circle again. Looking ahead will enable you to ride a good circle using your upper body to turn and not too much rein.

*The warm-up is vital for encouraging your horse to stretch and release his muscles, especially if he is tense. It also allows him time to start listening to you*

*Think about your own position as well as your horse's way of going. This gives your horse space to get into the rhythm of the lesson*

If your horse is coping well with canter on a 20m circle you can try going forwards into canter on a 10m circle. Remember to keep a straight line from your elbow to the bit. If you have any angles along this line you will make communication with your horse more difficult. Also be careful not to have too much neck bend on the circle. Canter only one circuit then come back to trot. As you come back to trot keep your hands down and level, and use your body to make the transition – don't support too much with your hand.

If you feel the need, give your horse a brief breather now and think about the next exercise while walking on a loose rein. Don't have too long a break otherwise you will both cool down too much, but beware of slogging on without a rest.

*As you reach the outer edge of the circle go into canter – this ensures your horse is listening to you and doesn't go into auto-pilot*

## RIDING CORNERS AND SQUARES

Go large around the arena in trot. Just before each corner make a transition to walk, walk through the corner and go back to trot. This helps keep your horse's attention. As you approach each corner he should really be listening to you and becoming more obedient.

A couple of times around the arena should be sufficient and you can then move on to riding a 15m (50ft) square at one end. Walk the square a few times before riding it in trot, walking for one or two steps in each corner. This exercise is great for encouraging you to steer with your body and legs rather than your hands. You also need to think ahead – as soon as you are in walk you need to be thinking trot to help get a good transition. It takes a lot of thinking from the horse too. Repeat this exercise on both reins.

The regular transitions in the last few exercises have been preparation for using half-halts, so before having another rest, go large and do half-halts in each corner. Try to keep the rhythm out of the corner, it is tempting to accelerate a bit too much. This has been a lot to concentrate on but your horse should now be carrying more weight on his hindquarters and have a much lighter contact on your hand.

*To ride squares you must be using your legs to steer, so this is a great exercise if you tend to rely on the reins*

## SIMPLE CHANGES

If you are pleased with your progress, after a short break walking on a long rein, you can begin the next exercise, which is to introduce simple lead changes.

Ride a 10m (30ft) circle in walk. As you finish the circle, make a transition to canter and walk as you approach the start point of the circle again, walk a 10m circle and then canter again. Ride this pattern several times. As you ride your 10m circle in walk collect the walk by half-halting. To ask for canter, move your outside leg back slightly. This indicates to your horse that you are going to canter right; it's the inside leg that says canter.

*Rather than going into canter and completing a couple of laps, do simple changes to keep your horse with you and really get his hindquarters working. This is a good preparation for flying changes, too*

Change the rein by asking for walk just before the centre line, changing the bend and asking for canter left. Now put the two together: circle round, ask for walk at the centre line and ask for canter right, circle round, ask for walk then canter left. Ride this figure of eight several times, your transitions will begin to improve. Check you aren't using too much hand in the downward transitions.

## COUNTER CANTER

Ride some counter canter loops down the long side of the arena. If your horse is supple enough you should be able to make these 5m (16ft) loops, touching the quarter line of the arena. It may help to ride the loop in three sections: ride a curve to the quarter line, ride straight and then curve back

### Corners

The deepest corner a young horse should be asked to do is about 5m (16ft). So just after the quarter marker you should be thinking of turning. The deepest corner a Grand Prix horse should do is 3m (10ft). Remember, you choose how deep it is, not the horse.

to the track. On each straight line of the loop give and re-take the rein to test your horse's balance and self-carriage.

Change the rein in trot and repeat this exercise on the left rein. If you have a full-size arena, you can now try riding a 10m (30ft) loop. Make gentle turns at the beginning and end of each loop, so your horse can stay balanced in the canter. The longest line is the middle section of the loop.

*Riding loops in canter is a good introduction to counter canter*

## MEDIUM TROT

To finish the lesson, come back to trot and ask for medium trot down each long side. Think of your horse's frame as an aeroplane taking off. Ask for only a few strides of medium trot to begin with and build on that each time you ride down the long side. To help re-balance and bring your horse back onto his hocks, walk in each corner – this also prevents him rushing and getting stronger along each long side.

*If your horse is new to medium trot only ask for three or four steps along each long side to begin with*

### COOL DOWN

*Walk round on a long rein to cool off and stretch. Allowing time for stretching during your schooling is important. It's good physically for the horse's muscles and periods of walk during your work will help him relax mentally too, before you ask for a more concentrated period of work.*

141

# LESSON 2 – WORKING ON YOUR RELATIONSHIP

Many of us get to a certain level with our horse and things start to fall apart, or they don't go as well as we would like. Perhaps the horse seems to have got to the end of his abilities, or maybe you feel that you aren't getting through to him. It's time to consider taking a different approach.

To school a horse with minimum effort and maximum effect, we must understand the theory of riding. A grasp of the simple biomechanics is essential, such as how the hind legs push under the horse's body to send him forward, and where the horse's neck should naturally flex. So are matters like pressure points and how gravity affects not only our body, but also the horse's body. We must also be logical in our approach. The idea of push-pull, for example, is illogical – you are telling a horse one thing with your legs and the opposite with your hands. Such contradictions can make the schooling process uncomfortable and confusing for horses.

*A clear case of telling the horse one thing with your legs and seat and another with your hands*

## THE FEEL-GOOD FACTOR

The secret of success in schooling is to present the horse with the easiest option, particularly when introducing him to something new. A clever rider will also place her horse in a balance that enables him to respond to her cue out of choice. He learns to respond instinctively to that cue each time he feels it. And all this must feel good! For example, in the early days of schooling we open the right rein to indicate right and the horse moves into it because it feels more allowing. This establishes the idea of positive reinforcement. We can then reduce the cue until it becomes a 'whisper' on the rein coupled with a mere 'touch' of the leg.

*A 'whisper' on the rein allows the horse to do the easy, and correct, thing*

When cues are given in a crude, unpleasant way, they are less easily learned. For example, pulling back with the rein instead of allowing with your hand drags on the bars of the mouth. The horse may obey, but he does so out of resignation rather than motivation. The same is true of constant kicking or pushing with the seat. He's learned that things will get worse if he resists. Some horses are too sensitive or proud to give in and develop behavioural problems.

To test your own methods ask yourself: When I school
**A)** can I gradually reduce the aids as the horse gets to know more?
**Or...**
**B)** do I find I need more gadgets, such as spurs, to get the right reaction?

If the answer to A is yes it's pretty certain you are on track with your schooling methods. If the answer to B is yes, you may not be being clear enough in what you are asking for. If you're somewhere in between, perhaps you need to sharpen up your theory rather than your spurs!

## FOUR GOLDEN RULES

*Before you even begin to school your horse, be clear in your own head what you want to achieve. If things aren't clear to you, they are unlikely to be clear to your horse.*

**Rule 1** *Always sit vertical, square and quiet over the strongest part of the horse. The old masters wrote 'Calm! Forward and straight!' The horse won't hear you unless you are balanced and quiet in the saddle. When you ask him to go forward, you should move off as one. This requires focus and thinking about 'togetherness'.*

*Sit vertical, square and quiet*

**Rule 2** *There can be no straightness without suppleness. This applies as much to the rider as it does to the horse. Joints should be yielding and muscles must learn how to flex, tone and stretch. Only then can the whole body – equine and human – operate to full capacity.*

**Rule 3** *Energy must be channelled. Learn to provide a 'corridor' along which the horse can work from his*

*hindquarters through to his forehand. We must channel our own energy at the same time, or risk blocking or compromising the movement of the horse.*

*Channel your horse's energy between the frame of your body*

**Rule 4** *Feel for the balance in everything you do. The centre of balance changes with each change of direction or transition. In turning, the horse will always try to step under the rider's weight. Your adjustments must be minimal. If you lean or tilt, you will threaten your horse's balance.*

## CIRCLE WORK

Ride a 15m (50ft) circle – and remember that in every step and every segment of the circle, you will only remain together if you remember to turn with your horse. The most common fault is leaving the outside shoulder behind. On the other hand, some people turn too much. Remember to stay central and don't twist your body sideways as though preparing for leg yield.

Instead think forward, look the same way as your horse, and feel your inside hip leading you into the circle. Like the horse, our inside hip is carried slightly in advance of the outside hip.

## TRANSITIONS

Ask for a brisk working trot to test your horse's reactions to your new sense of balance. Think both legs 'on' in a quick active tap to ensure an impulsive upward transition, then 'off', or let go, the moment he obeys. Holding legs will stop a horse, as will legs applied too far back. Once your horse will respond to only 'the breath' of the boot, you are on the right track.

Think about downward transitions: how would you yourself go from a brisk jog or run to a sudden stop? How would you ensure you stayed in balance instead of lurching forward with the momentum? You would draw up, wouldn't you? So pushing down into the horse's back has to be counterproductive. Not only will this discourage him from rounding under you, the opposite may happen – he may drop his back and leave his hind legs trailing out behind.

So what's the difference between sitting tall to go forward and sitting tall to halt? All the difference in the world but it's subtle.

*To halt, sit tall and close your legs*

To move off: sit tall, open the shoulders, and lightly tap the horse at the girth with both legs. Lead from the tummy and think 'project'.

To halt or slow down: sit tall, brace the shoulders and close the legs just behind the girth in a dampening-down way. With your tummy think 'close down' or 'hold'.

Remember… you must remain central and above the horse's strongest point at all times. Carefully preserve the hip, heel alignment and keep all movement to a minimum so the horse can really listen. You should now be feeling a difference in your working relationship with your horse (for more inspiration, see Lesson 3, opposite).

# LESSON 3 – THE RELATIONSHIP BETWEEN BEND AND STRAIGHT

Two of the hardest things to do well in equitation are to ride a straight line and an accurate circle. In the early schooling of the young horse, it is all too easy to put aside any idea of developing further bend in order to concentrate on straightness. However, one cannot be achieved without the other, see Rule 2 (p.143): 'There can be no straightness without suppleness.' Too often these movements start off well but halfway through things go to pieces – either the horse is swinging out too much, or he starts to fall in.

## WORKING ON STRETCH

Horses are generally right- or left-sided. This is not their fault, it simply means they are naturally more soft to one side than the other. If we neglect the stiff side, we do so at our peril. This is a vital link in a chain: no horse can be straight until he is evenly muscled on both sides of his body. If one side is stiff or weak, the hindquarters will deviate. Correct muscling and good engagement can only develop once the horse is supple on both reins. And only then can crookedness be eradicated. Charging about on straight lines – without addressing the real problem – is unlikely to achieve very much at all.

*Our most important goal is to teach both sides of the horse's body to bend, yield and stretch in order to achieve equal muscle development all round*

There is an added complication: even the straightest horse, ridden beside the arena wall without due care and support from the rider, can look crooked. Why? It's because most horses are narrower through the shoulders than across the hindquarters, which means the hindquarters will tend to protrude. However, introducing a slight degree of bend on both reins helps to line up the forehand with the quarters and so achieve tracking up and straightness.

The way to get this slight bend is to school with 'inside leg to outside hand' in mind. Use each corner to help your horse flex gently into the inside rein and have your inside leg acting quietly at the girth.

What if the horse resists? In order to enable good flexion on both reins – to improve all-round performance – you need to school the horse on a circle. Start with big circles for a young horse, making them smaller as he grows more supple.

How does circle work improve straight lines? Think of the gymnastic exercises employed by athletes long before they think of running a race – they do any number of warm-up exercises. Bending and stretching is what hones and builds healthy muscles – and the theory and practice is the same with horses.

*As the horse looks and bends around the rider's inside leg...*

*...his outside stretches into the rider's, allowing supportive contact*

## Discover the effects of bend

While many riders are aware that the inside of the horse has to bend and shorten on a curve, they often forget that the outside of the horse has to stretch and lengthen. Several pairs and groups of muscles are involved.

Try this experiment with the effects of bend on your own body. Stand tall, with your legs slightly apart and arms outstretched. Now, bend or lean sideways a few centimetres from your waist to the left or right. You will feel how your waist shortens to one side, while the opposite side of your ribcage has to stretch and lengthen. It is exactly the same for your horse.

The horse's 'waist' (or bendy part) is just behind his forearm, ie at the girth. Once you have learned to activate him here, he will not only curve around the circle more easily, but the outside of his ribcage should stretch and lengthen too. Remember it is he who has to bend, not you. You must stay upright and straight.

## FIND THE SPOT

When you ask for bend using your inside leg too far back this may allow your horse to fall in through the shoulder or disengage the quarters. You merely want to help him curve and shorten the inside of his body to follow the circumference of the circle; don't push him off it. Just as we are more sensitive and ticklish under our armpits – so is your horse. Around the girth area, there are clusters of nerve endings from the intercostal nerve that help support the horse's abdominals, the ribcage and the back.

A light touch here (think of tickling your horse) with the inside leg should achieve two very valuable results:

• The horse will automatically lift through the forehand (some people refer to this as lifting through the withers) if we tap into the right spot.

• The horse will learn to yield to your inside leg, provided you give him something to bend around.

These reactions are a response to pressure. Be careful, as too much pressure may put your horse off. Work with him to learn what is right for him.

## THE CORRIDOR

The 'corridor' (Rule 3, p.143) can be straight or circular, the outside wall being as important in its supporting role as the inside wall. When you ride a circle try to visualize your horse's legs. Be aware that the inside hind has to step deeper underneath his body for balance, so don't lean in and block the all-important engagement. Feel how sitting up and quiet helps.

Test your ability to keep the corridor theory working in all you do. Ride two or three circles of 20m (65ft) on both reins. Then change the rein through the diagonal. Later, link up your circles through a figure of eight. Always ride the horse well up to the track and feel how your inside leg helps place him there. As you do the straight line through the diagonal, carry the idea of bend and stretch that you had on the circle. Stretch and bend will also help you to negotiate corners more effectively, as well as turns and changes of rein.

*Imagine the corridor continuing into the turn – left turn, touch with the left leg allowing the horse's left hind leg to step under*

---

### CORRIDOR CHECKPOINTS

• *Reins – on either side of the neck – frame the horse.*

• *Weight in the stirrups – keep your feet level for all straight work and pointing forward – frame or stabilize and balance your corridor.*

• *Knees and thighs – look forward – establish the boundaries.*

• *Hips – kept square and forward-facing by toned abdominals – support or give direction.*

• *Shoulders – squared back and down – carry the arms and also support or give direction.*

• *Hands – level and about a bit's width apart – connect the energy from the hindquarters and ask for flexion.*

# INTRODUCING SERPENTINES

Once your circles have improved, introduce serpentines into your schooling programme. Good serpentines are a real test of your horse's ability to bend, stretch and straighten. You will recognize success when you feel the horse's energy being channelled in whichever direction you wish and your riding will take on a new dimension. Remember, no aid is given in isolation, there is a back-up to everything we do.

**1** *Start on the track, nice and straight, but think inside bend.*

*Aid: Inside hand asks the horse to look, or flex, into the movement.*

*Back up: Outside hand tells the horse how far to look or flex.*

**2** *Prepare the horse with a little more pressure into the inside stirrup for the first turn.*

*Aid: Inside leg (on girth) asks for direction and bend through the forehand.*

*Back up: Outside leg (behind girth) keeps the quarters pushing under.*

**3** *Turn away from the track with the outside leg and rein gently closing in.*

*Aid: Inside hip supports and leads the horse into the bend.*

*Back up: Outside hip opens outward to allow, and make room for, the outside stretch.*

**4** *Test again for straightness as you head across the school. You should be dead straight by the centre line, but you will quickly need to move into the new bend as you approach the opposite track, so don't forget to change the aids.*

## GIVE AND TAKE

Good schooling is not always about asking more, it's the learning to 'let go' that can make all the difference. A little give and take is more conducive for flexion than a constant nag, with hand or leg. Experiment with your weight aids. You may be surprised how easily the horse responds.

• Think of opening doors and inviting the horse to go through.

• Refrain from pushing; resistance will be met with resistance.

• Remember to show your horse the way and make it easy for him to respond.

• Don't fall into the trap of asking him to do something, then shutting the door before he has a chance to do it.

## PROBLEM SOLVER

**Q** My instructor has told me that my six-year-old New Forest x TB is beginning to work on the bit. I have not done much schooling and am unsure how to develop what I've already got. On a circle my horse lifts his back and drops his head, is this the beginning of working from behind? Are there any exercises to develop my horse's topline?

**A** It sounds as if you are doing well so far. Your horse's hindquarters should be propelling him forwards and your job is to contain this energy without causing resistance. This will give you more control and, as your horse gets stronger and more accustomed to carrying himself in this way, he'll start to develop the correct muscles. Transitions from one pace to another, or within a pace (lengthening and shortening the stride), are an effective way to improve the engagement of the hindquarters. The beginnings of lateral work, such as turn on the forehand and leg yielding, will also help in the following ways: to improve the obedience to your leg aids, with engagement of the quarters; and to improve suppleness.

Working up and down hills and on different terrain out hacking will also help your horse's balance and ability to carry himself. Jumping, trotting poles and gridwork will also be of great advantage.

At first, keep your schooling sessions fairly short so that your horse does not get tired. This would only cause him to resist and stiffen against you and would undo all your good work. For the last few minutes of each session allow him to work in a long, low outline (imagine a horse making a really good shape over a big fence), not flat and fast. This will allow him to stretch after working.

If you are unsure, ask your instructor who will be only too pleased to explain the most effective way of ensuring that your horse continues to work correctly. (See Lesson 4 pp.152–155 for lengthening.)

*Once your horse understands what you want, your schooling will progress in leaps and bounds*

# LESSON 4 – WORKING ON LENGTHENING

This lesson is ideal if your horse is still a bit of a baby and hasn't done much, but you're keen to get started on some dressage. One of the movements expected of novice dressage horses, lengthened strides are also a preparation for medium and extended paces, which come later in training. The idea is that the horse is accepting the rider's aids by taking bigger, not faster steps, while keeping the rhythm and balance of his trot.

Learning any dressage movement takes practice and know-how. Even when you're teaching your horse the smallest things, it's important to get them right. Bear this in mind as it will make everything you do with him in the future easier and more likely to be successful.

## THE WARM-UP

Start by working your horse deep, this will help to remove any tension in his body and to get him soft and relaxed. It is also a good suppling exercise. Gradually give the reins to encourage him to stretch his neck forwards and down. You don't want to allow him to get on his forehand, so remember to keep your leg on to keep his hindquarters active. If your horse is working correctly he should be able to maintain his rhythm and balance. If there is tension in his neck and back he'll find it rather more difficult to stretch down.

## CONCENTRATING ON BALANCE

Once he is warmed up, give him a canter to help to liven him up and get him in a more forward-thinking mood. This will make it easier when you ask for lengthening. Young horses can become unbalanced when making transitions into canter, often flinging themselves into the pace far from smoothly. If this is the case, work on getting a better transition by making sure the trot has a good rhythm first. It will also be easier for your horse to pick up the canter if he is correctly bent to the inside. Asking for canter on a circle will make it easier still for you both to keep everything together.

*Allow your horse to stretch down to loosen any tension in his neck and back before beginning schooling work*

Be careful not to confuse speed for impulsion. When you're asking your horse to be more energetic, think of containing the energy rather than letting it all run away. If the canter becomes hurried, sit on your bottom and push your hips forward. Think of having your shoulders behind your hips. Keeping your weight in the saddle will help your horse get his weight off his forehand – the cause of his rushing – then his hind legs can provide more power.

*Be prepared to take time over this stage and do a few transitions until you get a nice one like this*

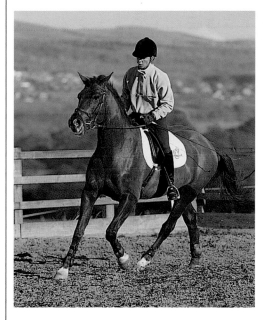

*Canter transitions don't always go smoothly*

## FIRST LENGTHENED STRIDES

When your horse's canter is balanced and he is working nicely from his quarters, you can try for some lengthening.

Trot him on a 20m (15ft) circle. This helps to keep the energy and impulsion. Use your legs together to ask him to lengthen his stride and cover more ground. Ask with your legs in the rhythm of the trot. Then, once he's lengthening, be ready to adjust your aids.

Allow him to stretch his neck but don't let the reins get too long. Think of keeping the bit in the corners of his mouth. Hold your reins slightly out to the sides, with your hands wider apart, to help you to keep the contact. Be conscious of your upper body. Try to sit up so you're not putting all your weight over his shoulders.

*Preparation pays dividends when you get your first lengthened strides with impulsion and in balance*

## WATCH YOUR RIDING

• Be careful not to get into the habit of holding an unbalanced horse in place with the contact. Use little half-halts and give your inside rein occasionally, just to keep him loose and soft, rather than allowing him to get set in his neck.

• Holding your hands out to the sides makes it easier to maintain the contact and also helps the horse with his balance. It is particularly useful when you're asking more from the horse with your legs, otherwise he can feel restricted – rather like you've got the handbrake on.

• Before you ask for lengthened strides, make sure you have a good quality trot. It should be nice and powerful and free from any tension. Prepare your horse for the transition with a half-halt, this gets him listening to you and encourages him to really activate his hind legs.
• Use your weight and both your legs smoothly and at the same time, to push the horse forward and encourage him to take longer steps. The rein contact should not be affected, but be ready to give with your hands as the horse stretches and lengthens his frame.

## ALONG THE EDGE

Another way to practise lengthened strides is to do it down the long side of the arena. However, you need to be careful as it's easier for the horse to get long and flat in his outline when he's not lengthening on a circle.

Prepare by riding a circle and get a good active trot first. When you're happy with the trot, ride down the long side and ask for some lengthening.

When a horse is still learning to do lengthened strides and doesn't quite understand, you may have to let him run faster into it a little, just until he gets braver. As soon as you feel him take a couple of longer steps, bring him back and reward him so he gets the idea.

When you're pushing him forward, remember not to let all the energy run out the front door. It helps if you don't let your reins get too long.

Riding a few transitions helps to keep the trot active and relaxed. Break up your lengthening work by practising some canter transitions. These will also help his balance, which in turn will help his lengthening – everything in a horse's training is connected. If he's capable of using his hind legs to power his body into canter, he is capable of using them to take longer steps.

*When he's working well you will feel a great sense of power coming through from the hindquarters*

## FINISHING OFF

Remember to allow some time for a cool-down. Go back to some well-established work if you like, especially if your horse has found lengthening particularly difficult. Reward him well when he gets it right and give him plenty of breaks. Don't expect to achieve lots of lengthened strides at first, be content with just a couple – it's far more important that what you do get is of a good quality.

*Cooling down is equally as important as warming up*

# GETTING GO MASTERCLASS

This class may seem to be a bit out of place among the more conventional lessons described so far, but there is no doubt that students of Pat Parelli's methods achieve a great deal with their horses, and when you get stuck trying to teach something to your horse, it is well worth looking at different ways to get where you want to go. Think outside the box – as that popular management-speak saying goes.

## ENGINES AND SYSTEMS

What do you do about the horse that doesn't want to go? Is he dull, lazy, stubborn...? Probably none of these things. Think of an engine: it needs three ingredients to work – air, fuel and fire – and you know that if any one of these systems isn't working, the whole engine won't operate properly. Horses also have three systems: the respect system, the impulsion system, and the flexion system. If there's a problem in the second system, impulsion – so he won't go – look for the problem in the first system, respect.

If you haven't already done them, prepare for the session by working through Pat Parelli's Natural Horsemanship games (see pp.84–87). They can be good fun and it's always interesting to work your horse from the ground and watch how he moves and responds to you. This tells you a lot about what your relationship is like and your horse's attitude should greatly improve because of the new level of communication, trust and leadership you achieve with them. Once you have a working knowledge of the seven games you are ready to start with impulsion.

## THE CLASS

Most people are told to kick a horse to go, which is ridiculous when you think about it from a horse's point of view. Imagine if you were kicked in the ribs on the way to the dance floor... what would your attitude be towards that dance partner? Would you even want to go unless you knew the punishment for not going was even worse?

Through you using four distinct phases of assertiveness you can quickly make the horse a willing partner – happy to take your lead on the dance floor.

**1 Smile** with all four cheeks! Take a long focus, stretch your hand out in front of you with the reins, and tighten your

### About whips and emotion

Please bear the following in mind: whips are generally used incorrectly as punishment. Phase 4 (see opposite) used without emotion is assertion – prey-animal behaviour. Phase 4 used with emotion is aggression – human-predator behaviour. Never use whips, sticks and strings with negative emotion (such as anger or frustration), use them with rhythm. For example, when a jockey uses a whip in a race he is using it with rhythm to encourage the horse to go faster and not to punish him for going too slowly. If he is deemed to have used it as punishment, the jockey will be fined or banned for a number of races.

cheeks. If the horse does not move forward from this suggestion, continue through the phases and be ready to release as soon as there's forward movement.

**2 Squeeze** with your legs, starting at the top, then all the way down to your heels (turn your toes outward to make smooth contact). This is not a strong squeeze. If you are straining or getting cramps, it's too strong! Remember, a horse can feel even a fly land on him.

**3 Smooch** Make a kissing noise while holding the squeeze.

**4 Spank** Start by spanking yourself lightly. Slap your shoulders from side to side with the end of a rope (see photos right). Remember, rhythm is important here. Allow the rope to grow longer and keep up the flapping rhythm until it starts touching your horse on the sides of his hindquarters, letting it get progressively stronger if he has not responded. The moment your horse responds, release your legs, stop spanking, and keep smiling.

If your horse stops or slows, repeat the phases again. Always begin with phase 1. After a while he will get the message that when you smile he needs to take action. This builds what Parelli calls the seat connection. You can then transfer this reaction to all your flatwork sessions.

## TROUBLESHOOTING

• Probably the most common mistake riders make is kicking out of habit – this will quickly lose whatever respect you just earned so really watch out for this. Another mistake is to keep squeezing and/or spanking after the horse has made the effort to go forward. This confuses him because then he won't know what the right behaviour is – you have made his correct response wrong in his eyes.

• Be sure to put slack in the reins. It's a common habit to put contact in the reins when the horse goes forward. This is enough to confuse a horse trying to do the right thing.

• If you are not being effective, you won't get results. Begin each time at phase 1 and be prepared to go to phase 4 (see box 'About whips and emotion', opposite).

*Keep smiling when your horse goes forward and make sure you put some slack in the reins*

• Remember your own frailties in being persistent enough to get the result. If the horse doesn't understand your request you are not making yourself clear. In the same way that talking louder to a non-comprehending foreigner doesn't work, you will find the same problem with your horse.

• Finally, be sure there's enough 'life' in your body when you ride. Think about how fast you want your horse to go and simulate that with your body… then let the squeezing, smooching and spanking support it. Your horse will learn very quickly how to get in tune with you.

Just reading about this will not fix the problem. Go out and play with your horse. You'll both find a new level of respect for and communication with each other.

# LESSON 5 – CREATING FREEDOM AND FLEXIBILITY

For your horse to move with freedom and flexibility he needs to be relaxed and supple. Any areas of tension in the rider or horse will alter his way of going and he will find it difficult to carry out movements like circles and turns. A horse needs to be supple in two ways – longitudinally and laterally. Longitudinal suppleness means his hindquarters are engaged and he moves with a supple, rounded back. This can only occur if he moves forwards willingly, is relaxed at his poll and accepts the rein contact. This allows him to lengthen the muscles along his back and neck by becoming rounder in his outline. Lateral suppleness is the horse's ability to bend around the rider's inside leg and show freedom of movement in his limbs and shoulders.

Start your flatwork session by loosening up on both reins in walk, trot and canter. Take this time to assess yourself and your horse before starting work on the following exercises.

### 1 Counter flexion

Counter flexion is a fantastic exercise for horses that are stiff through their necks and it should result in you having a softer feel on the inside rein. Ride down the long sides of the school with your horse looking to the outside (counter flexion). Then correct this and ride him straight on the short sides. This will encourage him to relax on the inside rein rather than be stiff and holding. Practise this in walk, before trying the exercise in trot for five to ten minutes. Make sure that your horse is straight in his body. In this photo the horse has responded to the counter flexion by moving his hindquarters into the school.

### 2 Leg yield in canter

This exercise builds on the first one and helps to prevent your horse leaning on the rein and to become softer in the contact. Begin by turning up the long side and leg yielding across the school in trot. Remember not to let your horse's quarters lead the leg yield.

It is a good idea to combine the leg yield with the counter flexion exercise. So as you reach the track, ride down the next long side with your horse looking to the outside. Repeat this exercise in trot several times – you should feel your horse becoming softer and easier to direct – before trying it in canter. Canter work is particularly useful for putting more energy into your horse, especially after doing some intense lateral work.

Come back to walk and have a rest on a long rein. Change the rein and go into canter on the other rein. Repeat the bending exercise on this rein, bending your horse to the outside down the long side and, again from the corner, leg yielding across the school.

## 3 Canter a circle with counter flexion

Ride a 20m (65ft) circle in canter with slight counter flexion. Practise reducing the size of the circle and then leg yielding back out onto a 20m circle. This will encourage you to ride and direct your horse with your legs rather than relying on your hands.

Spiral inwards making the circle smaller. Do this by asking your horse to move his shoulder across. Think slightly shoulder-in on the circle to help position your horse's shoulders in the correct place. Keep your contact on the inside rein light and bend him slightly to the outside. You should now be moving your horse with your outside leg, not pulling him round with your inside rein. Then increase the size of the circle by leg yielding on a circle. Again, use your legs, not your reins, to move your horse out and maintain a bend to the outside.

## 4 Test the contact

If your horse tends to be heavy on the inside rein, exercise 3 will lighten him. Try riding him straight to test this. If he becomes heavy in the inside rein, bend him to the outside. Then, once he takes the contact on the outside rein, ride straight again.

Finally repeat the 20m (65ft) circle and spiral. Remember to sit tall, thinking of rising up out of the top of your hat not your shoulders, open your knee and keep your legs under your hips. Go large around the arena and come back to walk before cooling off on a long rein.

### DON'T ALLOW LEANING

• *It is a common problem for the horse to lean on the inside rein, and one which riders often respond to by increasing the contact. This is not a good solution as you should be relying more on your legs than your hands to guide your horse.*

• *When a horse is truly on the bit it comes from the contact on the outside rein, rather than that on the inside one.*

# LOWERING TENSION MASTERCLASS

Everyone has seen or experienced fizzy or tense horses. They overreact to the most minor of situations and are often spooky or nappy. They carry their head high and their neck is tight. They get distracted easily, so their ears are often pricked forwards and their eyes are 'on stalks'. They can be tight in the back, so may be unable to move properly. This results in short, hurried, choppy strides, which are not very easy to sit on. A tense horse will react, sometimes quite violently, to the slightest of leg aids or changes in weight in the rider's position. The rider needs to be quiet and secure.

## THE CLASS

### 1 Get on the lunge

The aim of any work with a fizzy or tense horse is to provide a structure in his training in order to remove any nervousness and to build up his confidence. Don't expect things to be perfect straight away, but with gradual build-up of exercises you will see an improvement pretty quickly.

Initially, lunge in an enclosed area using a lunging cavesson with side reins. Lungeing from a cavesson removes any fear your horse may have of the bridle and will make it easier to analyse if this is a problem for him. Don't have the side reins tight as this will cause your horse to become even more tense.

Do most of the work in walk with only small amounts of trot to start with – you don't want him to think that everything has to be done at speed. When your horse can cope with sessions in walk and is working in a relaxed way (look out for a swinging back and a stretched neck) start to do walk to trot transitions – lots of them.

### 2 Rider on board

The next step is to lunge your horse from his bridle with side reins. Elasticated side reins are best, as these reward the horse when he works properly by yielding when he takes up the contact. You want your horse to stretch willingly into the contact, freeing up his back and neck. Do the same walk work and then walk to trot transitions until you are happy that he is

*Lunge work will help to break the horse's habit of 'go, go, go', and get him working with a longer, more relaxed frame. Look for a relaxed neck first, which will then have a knock-on effect on his back and eventually on his whole body*

*Work on getting your horse to listen to you. Be sure to give him plenty of opportunity to do well by making the work easy for him*

accepting the bridle and is not rushing, spooking or becoming tense.

Then put a rider on board – still keeping your horse on the lunge. The aim of this is to put the horse and rider in a controlled situation. The person lungeing should initially take control; the rider can take up the reins but with no contact. Practise lots of transitions. If your horse is rushing, give a rein aid from the lunge line to check him. Because the check is not being given by the rider, the horse is not being pulled backwards and so won't resist or become tense. This teaches him that contact is nothing to worry about.

When your horse is working in a consistent way without rushing, it's time to let the rider take the reins – still on the lunge. Ask the rider to use short rein contacts to check the horse, then release. Again repeat these until he responds happily.

The aim is to communicate with your horse to slow him down and get him concentrating without making him tense.

*The rider starts to use short rein contacts to check the horse, then immediately releases again*

## 3 Leg work

Many fizzy horses will overreact when the leg is applied so it is well worth building up your horse's tolerance to it. He needs to learn that when he feels the leg against his side, it doesn't mean that he can run off. Do this by applying the leg at the same time as giving short contacts on the rein – so effectively 'holding' him between your hands and leg.

If he rushes off, bring him back to a slower pace, or halt if needed and try again. It is worth dedicating whole schooling sessions to this as your horse will need the repetition to understand what it is you want of him – and don't expect results straight away. Concentrate on calmness and stillness in yourself to instil this in him.

### Causes of tension and fizziness

• **Breeding** Thoroughbreds are usually sharper and more sensitive than other horses.
• **Difficult work** A horse may become tense if you ask him to do more difficult work than he's used to. This indicates a lack of understanding or experience and you may need to take things slowly or move back a stage.
• **Routine and diet** Feeding nothing but ad-lib hay for a week or two may help you work out if feed is the cause. Provide plenty of turnout.
• **Tack fit** Anything that is causing pain or pressure will increase the risk of tenseness.

**4 Figure work and repetition**

Spend plenty of time in each schooling session riding circles and figures. Horses find it much more difficult to rush on a circle than in a straight line. Aim for good tempo, rhythm and balance, whatever gait you are in, as this will build your horse's confidence. Decide what tempo to work at and make sure your horse sticks to this – he needs to know that the rider is in control. It's the repetition of exercises that will help your horse to relax – so stick at it and don't stop just because you're bored with them.

*Plenty of figures and circles will have a calming effect*

**5 Going large**

Moving on to riding large around the school is the next stage – your horse will find it easier to rush and spook during this exercise so only attempt it when you feel confident that you can stay in control. And get it right in walk before attempting trot or canter. If he rushes, breaks into a faster gait or tries to take control, always make a downwards transition. Make this a rule so that every time you school, your horse realizes that rushing isn't an option.

When in trot, rise slower than you need to for the speed you are going – your horse should slow his steps in response.

## REWARDS AND TESTS

As you become more in control of the situation, try releasing the rein by bringing your inside hand forward to pat your horse's neck. This exercise can be done in halt first and then in walk and trot. Use it to check that your horse is responding to you and isn't going to run off at the first sign of a soft or released contact. It also acts as a meaningful reward for your horse when he has done some nice work – use it for this and he will really appreciate it.

*Don't forget to try releasing the reins if you feel your horse is beginning to listen to you*

## PROBLEM SOLVER

**Q** My 15.1hh, eight-year-old mare has a naturally high head carriage, so I ride her in a running martingale with a jointed eggbutt snaffle. She will come on the bit for short periods but slips above or behind the bit very easily.

She evades my rein contact by opening her mouth, tilting her head and neck to the side and chewing on the bit. She also tends to lean on the bit and can be strong in trot and canter. I would like to do some dressage with her but unless I can sort out these problems we are never going to get anywhere. When I show her in ridden classes I use a ported-mouth pelham with two reins. She never tries to evade me in this bit and goes in a lovely outline – but I'm not allowed to use it for dressage!

**A** For a horse to work in an outline you must engage the hindquarters, allowing him to work softly through the back and bring his head forwards and away from his body. No amount of strong bits or gadgets will give you a long-term solution, even if they do give a short-term fix.

You need to school your horse. Work her on the lunge using correctly fitted side reins – not short to pull her head in but fitted so you can work her from behind – so she starts to seek the contact and stretch forward into it. This may take a few weeks so intersperse it with hacking and other work.

When, and only when, she is working correctly on the lunge, you can repeat the same work under saddle. Try to find a good instructor who can help.

If your horse is fizzy you may be tempted to hang onto the reins, but avoid this at all costs. Get your mare swinging through from behind and don't get obsessed by her head position. When she is forward and relaxed this will come.

*Working like this is not comfortable for you or your horse. Help her find a more comfortable way of going through*

# SUCCESSFUL DRESSAGE

When your horse's work reaches a certain level, you may start to think about entering dressage competitions. Each movement in a dressage test reflects a training ideal, and is evaluated by the judge. Rather than viewing the competition as an end in itself, you should look at it as a way of assessing you and your horse's progress.

Dressage is a word usually associated with a horse's training but it can also be used to describe the overall improvement of the horse. This improvement comes through the daily use of gymnastic exercises to increase his physical strength and develop greater impulsion. School work, such as transitions and lateral movements, are the exercises we use to ensure our horse gains the physical strength and ability to work with balance, suppleness and in self-carriage. Mentally, he should become obedient because you build a relationship based on co-operation and consistent communication.

## WHAT A JUDGE LOOKS FOR

• **Relaxation:** When a horse is relaxed and engaged he will produce longitudinal flexion, which is often called being 'on the bit'. This means he is rounding his back, lifting his hind legs under his body and working

*Canter pirouettes are the extreme of collection. To perform them the horse must be at the peak of athletic fitness as well as perfectly trained. Olympic dressage rider Richard Davison shows how it's done*

through to the bridle. He is submissive to the forward-driving aids given by the rider.

• **Balance:** A judge will be looking to see if the last step of a gait (canter, for example) is as clear and balanced as the first step of the new gait (trot, for example). If they deteriorate, balance is missing.

• **Rhythm and tempo:** These should be consistent throughout. Any change of rhythm is an evasion. By increasing or decreasing the tempo, your horse is avoiding engagement of his hindquarters as well as lateral flexion, as he needs that lateral flexion to engage.

•**Impulsion:** This is achieved by gradually encouraging increased flexion and movement in the joints of the haunches. This way, you can teach your horse to move with greater animation, yet with decreased speed. Remember, speed is the enemy of impulsion.

• **Suppleness:** This is the effect of your horse moving fluently, with a round back and flexed joints.

• **Engagement:** This occurs when the haunches accept the majority of the weight, with a lifting of the forehand. Daily exercises to increase engagement will ultimately produce collection and extension of your horse's natural paces.

## SIX STEPS TO IMPROVING YOUR DRESSAGE
## PERFORMANCE

**1** Think of your horse as an athlete. He should be fit, supple and physically capable of doing what you want. You can achieve this through daily progressive training, but these qualities cannot be forced as and when you need them.

**2** Always think from your horse's quarters. Riders often focus on the front end alone. However, being truly on the bit involves a supple connection from the hind leg, over the back and into a secure contact.

**3** Work with your horse as a partner and friend. If there is a problem in your performance, it is probably being caused by a communication difficulty rather than your horse trying to be awkward.

**4** Take time to study the classical riders and aim to develop a greater understanding of your horse and his training needs.

**5** Never think of a dressage test as an end result, or learn movements simply because you are riding them in a test next week. The movements are in the test for a reason, which is to demonstrate a specific level of training.

**6** If you feel your horse has performed well, be satisfied. Winning or being placed is just the icing on the cake.

*'Ask for much, be content with little and reward often.'* French classical rider Captain Beudant.

# JUMPING SKILLS

For many equestrians, the thrill of jumping is hard to beat. It's fast, it's exciting and it's fun. Jumping is when your horse really becomes your partner – you can do plenty of preparation work to ensure he learns to jump to the best of his abilities, but when it comes to clearing the fence, it's down to him and his decisions about what to do with his legs and his body. Because of this, jumping is a skill that cannot be learnt, taught or performed half-heartedly. You might be able do the occasional shoddy turn on the forehand or a slightly wiggly straight line and get away with it, but if you don't do a jump right, you really know it. This section covers all aspects of jumping, from grids to cross country, as well as providing plenty of advice to help you cope when things are going awry.

# MAKING A START

Just as they can do most flatwork movements naturally, horses can actually jump without being taught. However, once you put a rider on board and start to ask them to go over several obstacles at a time and sometimes quite high ones at that, then they need careful training to be able to do it well and without losing their nerve.

## JUMPING SECRETS

Good flatwork is one of the keys to good jumping and should never be neglected. All the responsiveness, suppleness and athleticism that is so vital in achieving a good jumping round comes from excellent flatwork schooling. Having your horse balanced, supple and obedient is not just for dressage – it's vital for jumping too. As you ride round a course of fences you need him to go forwards and lengthen his stride or slow down and shorten his stride. There will also be several changes in direction, so it's important you can turn him. To manage this he has to be obedient and listening to you at all times.

Impulsion is also required and this energy comes from his hindquarters. It's easy to mistake speed for impulsion, but if you push your horse out of balance and rhythm he will find it difficult to jump fences cleanly. If he doesn't go forwards willingly into a soft rein contact it will make jumping much more difficult for you and him.

In jumping there are three things that the rider must concentrate on:
1 The quality of the canter – a jump is an exaggerated canter stride.
2 Rhythm – imagine walking along a path and coming to a kerb. Without thinking, you keep walking in a regular rhythm and step down it, taking it in your stride. A horse should do this when he jumps.
3 The line to the fence.
And the horse has one job to do: Jump the fence!

**Important:** Always have a helper on the ground when you're jumping – you don't want to have to get off to adjust the fences. Also, it's sensible to have someone there in case of an accident.

## THE WARM-UP

As always, give your horse an initial period of loosening up work, where you ride him in walk, trot and maybe canter. Check his responses by doing shallow loops and serpentines, and walk and trot a couple of circles on both reins to ensure he has plenty of bend and stretch throughout his body. You are aiming to get your horse's muscles warmed up but also to make sure he is obedient to your aids. He should move forwards and slow down when you ask.

## Test your know-how

**Where is the correct take-off point for a jump?**
The optimum take-off point is half a horse's stride in front of the fence. An average stride is 3.65m (12ft) so he should take off 1.8m (6ft) before the fence.

## STRAIGHTNESS EXERCISE

Next use this exercise to work on straightness, and influencing the horse's pace: ride a line 5m (15ft) inside the track on the long side. Once you have made the turn onto the 5m track, ask the horse to bend to the outside for a couple of strides, before straightening him up and riding him forward for about five strides.

After that collect him up for a couple of strides. The bend only needs to be a small one, but what it does is emphasize your use of the outside aids. Doing this exercise will ensure that your horse is truly straight when you ride him forward, rather than having his shoulder inclined towards the outside of the school as is so often the case.

Do this exercise in walk and trot, and possibly canter on both reins.

## RELEASING STIFF MUSCLES

As you warm up, feel your horse moving under you and make sure that he is really supple. Try a shallow loop along the long side of the school to check that he moves freely. Often a horse will move stiffly through having a tense neck, which can be released with a simple flexing exercise. As you walk round the arena, ask your horse to flex his head and neck to the left for two to three strides and then to the right. Use your legs to keep him moving forwards and straight.

*Bending your horse to the outside will increase straightness*

# JUMPING POSITION AND BALANCE

For your horse to jump well, you need to be in balance and ensure you go with him all the way over the obstacle. Here are the basics:
- Lift your seat out of the saddle
- Put your weight into your heel
- Soften your knee

*The jumping position*

It is well known that your riding position should be such that you would remain standing up were the horse removed from under you. A common fault in jump riders is to lean too far forward over the fence – when this position is replicated on the ground it is clear that the rider is far from balanced (below). Imagine what it's like for the horse when the rider throws their weight forwards like this.

*If your horse disappeared when you were jumping, would you land in balance on the ground?*

Your stirrup leather should hang vertically with your weight in your heels and your knee at an angle of about 90 degrees. By bringing the lower leg forward and relaxing your knees, you will

*This rider is gripping with her knees when jumping, which is causing her to rock forward onto the front of her seat bones.*

*Bring your lower leg forward for a more secure jumping position*

sit tall and secure. A secure lower leg, enables you to use your legs effectively. If your horse tries to stop or run out, you will be in a good position to control him. Keep your head up and look where you're going. Your head is the heaviest part of your body, so its position will influence you and your horse's balance.

Keep your back straight to increase your security. In addition, practise standing and sitting in the canter for a set number of strides, for instance, coming out of the saddle for four strides, and then sitting lightly for four strides, to develop your sense of rhythm. Be accurate with your counting, and light with your seat. This exercise will make you more athletic, and give the horse's canter more spring.

# BEGINNING WITH GRIDWORK

The discipline and repetition needed to encourage your horse to take gridwork seriously and do it accurately will make a vast improvement in the way he jumps, whatever the circumstances. Gridwork influences and improves the way you ride a course of fences – even if the grid is as basic as one or two canter poles and a couple of small crosses. And, any regular difficulties you encounter when you jump, whatever your level, can usually be solved by the careful planning and use of grids.

## SETTING UP

Begin your schooling session with some very basic work. Put up as many small bounce crosses as you can. A grid of seven fences is ideal as it makes the changeover to more advanced exercises easier. But be practical and set up as many as your material will allow.

Don't be too rigid about the distance between fences as smaller horses may find it difficult to reach at first. You can reduce it to 3.35m (11ft) or even shorter if necessary, but remember if you intend to jump competitively a course builder will base his combination and related distances on 3.65m (12ft). It is essential that distances are identical, as this encourages consistency. Most riders eventually learn to pace their distances. Once you have measured your distances, pace them a few times until you get a feel for each distance – this will help when you're walking a course.

### Test your know-how

**What distances are generally used by course builders?**
Bounce distance: 3.65m (12ft)
One-stride related distance: 7.3–7.6m (24–25ft)
Two-stride related distance: 10–10.9m (33–36ft)
Three-stride related distance: 13.7–14.6m (45–48ft)
Four-stride related distance: 18.2m (60ft)
Five-stride related distance: 21.9m (72ft)

The average length of a horse's stride is 3.65m (12ft). A related distance is the natural length of a horse's stride between fences.

## GETTING IT RIGHT

• Make sure you use the grid to allow your horse to learn. Don't be too bossy about making him canter too soon, or telling him exactly where you want him to take off.

• Concentrate on encouraging your horse to go forwards in a straight line and allow him to sort out his legs. The more you can ride him from your leg into a supportive, consistent contact, the more willing he'll be.

• If necessary, reduce the number of crosses in the grid to make it easier for your horse. With a little persuasion from your leg, not a stick, you should find that he'll eventually get going.

• Introduce a novice horse to grids by starting with poles on the ground between wings, graduating to low cross poles once he gets the idea.

*Ride down the grid keeping in the middle and as straight as possible. Looking straight ahead will help you to stay straight and don't anticipate the turn at the end as this will alter your balance and send your horse off to one side*

Position your grid beside the arena or field fence if possible, then you'll only need to worry about your horse ducking out on one side if he baulks. Also, it will make it easier for you to ensure that the grid really is in a straight line.

If you can't build the grid against a fence, buy a builder's 30m (100ft) tape and use it to set up your jumps. Peg the end to the ground and unroll it where you want the grid to be. Not only will this help make sure your jumps are in a straight line, your measurements can be accurate to the centimetre. With no fence line, you could do with a bit of help on your approach and exit so place some strategic poles at the beginning and end of the grid. Place the first pole at the beginning on the outside to prevent the horse bulging out or overshooting the approach. Another pole at the exit on the inside will help prevent the horse from leaning in and cutting across after the grid.

You don't need a great long run at the grid. Allowing extra room on the approach gives you far too much time to fiddle with the stride and rhythm and lose the impulsion necessary to do a good job. A short approach can work in your favour as there is less time to get it wrong! If you ride a decent corner on the approach to the grid, keeping the horse working into a supportive outside rein, his inside hind leg will come through strongly as you come off the turn – hopefully with lots of impulsion. It seems only logical then that if the grid is just four to five strides off the turn, it will be easier to maintain this impulsion all the way to the first obstacle, rather than having to keep up the momentum for eight or 10 strides.

171

# GRIDS FOR A NOVICE HORSE

Before you ask a novice horse to start jumping, he must be able to walk, trot and canter obediently on both reins. Don't even attempt fences until you have this established. Work on improving his balance, suppleness and obedience by schooling over grids of poles. They are also a great introduction to jump work, and using them regularly as part of your schooling will help you and your horse find jumping easy and fun.

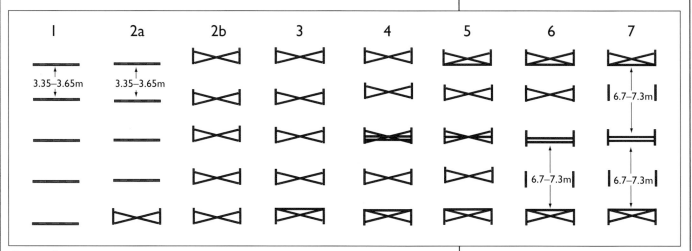

## GRID 1

Place five poles on the ground at 3.35–3.65m (11–12ft) apart and approach in trot. Even if he is suspicious, do not let your horse turn away. You need to establish, right at the beginning of his jumping career, that there is no option but to go forwards. Continue asking until he goes over the poles, however long it takes. A little patience at this stage will pay dividends later on. Remember to repeat this on both reins. It doesn't matter if he breaks into canter, all you are asking for at this stage is a willingness to get on with it.

## GRID 2

When you're happy with his attitude, gradually make the poles into cross fences, starting with the last one (2a) and building backwards until all five poles are altered (2b). Go at a sensible pace and don't rush to get all the poles altered. The cross poles should encourage the horse to jump in the centre and should be around 30cm (1ft) high to start with. Everything you attempt at this stage should be small enough for him to step over from a standstill if necessary. Refusals and run outs must be prevented from becoming a habit, so insist on him going through the grid, even if he knocks everything down. If this happens don't worry, just keep repeating the exercise.

Work on both reins until your horse finds the poles easy to negotiate without too many rattles. If he stays in trot, don't worry. It is better for him to find the easiest way by repeating the exercise rather than bullying him into canter. Allow the canter to develop naturally, just make sure you ride him forwards with enough impulsion to give him confidence.

*When you begin going over cross poles, allow your horse to find his own style*

*Some horses quickly progress to a complete grid of cross poles. A bolder horse will progress faster than a less confident one, but the end result should be the same*

## GRID 3

Add a horizontal pole to the last fence, slightly higher than the middle of the cross. If you have established his confidence over the smaller poles, this should prove to be no problem for him. If he hesitates or becomes anxious, just go back a step. Repeat the earlier exercises until you feel he is ready to move on without any worries – flexible progression is one of the main benefits of starting a novice horse with gridwork.

## GRIDS 4–7

Grids 4 and 5, making the middle fences parallels and adding a pole to the first fence, are your next progression. Once your horse is happily jumping these, try removing the fourth element (grid 6). If all is well, remove the second cross pole (grid 7). As you can see from the diagrams, you will end up building a small, simple combination.

*When you work methodically on grids you soon progress. You horse will experiment with his technique, getting neater and more confident as he goes*

If at any stage your horse starts to get overconfident and hurry, or if he becomes anxious and backs off, go back to jumping the crosses. You need to keep him confident but not cocky. Remember, you are allowing him to learn, not trying too hard to teach him. By the same token, encourage him to manage his own legs through the grid. If you over-organize him, he will become too reliant on his rider to get him out of trouble. Concentrate entirely on approaching the grid with impulsion and allow him to choose where his best take-off point will be. Of course he will make mistakes, but let him learn from them. Don't be tempted to plot his approach with placing poles – he's not going to find them in the ring. Far better to have the grid fences small enough so that any mistakes are not too punishing.

---

### DISTANCE WORK

• *The distances recommended are conventional and are what you would expect to find in doubles or combinations at a novice show. However, the distance of 3.35–3.65m (11–12ft) can be shortened initially if your novice horse finds it difficult. Once he has more confidence, gradually increase it to 3.65m (12ft). Increase it by centimetres if necessary. One day he will have to cope with doubles and combinations at a distance of 7.45m (24½ft), so it is as well to try to establish this early.*

• *It is unwise to lengthen the distance to accommodate a longer stride or bolder horse. A horse with a big stride will need to adjust it to a conventional distance once he starts show jumping. If your horse has a long stride, don't be tempted to remove any cross poles from the grid until he can cope with grids 2b–5. The crosses will naturally help regulate the slightest hint of acceleration or over-lengthening. Take advantage of this, rather than over-checking or fighting with him. When he is more established, you should find him much easier to keep in a rhythm.*

---

## ESTABLISHING GOOD WORK

Set at a very low height, a grid of small bounces is a perfect exercise to teach a novice horse how to manage his legs – and work out for himself that the more obedient he is to your leg, and the more he goes forwards, the easier he'll find it. If he is really reluctant, set the poles really low, but still high enough at the ends to make a cross shape, even if it's only a few centimetres high. Always insist that your horse jumps the fence more or less in the middle.

Once he gets into the swing and rhythm of things, guard against him starting to rush. Don't be afraid to say 'steady' and think 'wait'. You won't put the stoppers on him if you have your leg on, and the more leg you have without going faster, the springier your jump will be.

When your horse is going nicely over the crosses, think about your exit strategy. It would be ideal to come out of the grid at the same speed and rhythm that you went in, and it is sensible to establish that he comes out straight at this stage. If your grid is against a fence, he will know which way he's going to turn when he lands. He's not being naughty if he leans in and tries to cut off the corner in the direction he's going to turn. He's only using his brain, and you need to be sensible about telling him how you want him to proceed. As you approach the end of the grid, ensure that you have a little more feel on the outside rein, and keep your inside shoulder up. You don't want both of you on the slant. Your horse should be encouraged to stay straight and only turn in because you have asked, not because he anticipates the direction.

Being level and feeling a little more outside rein also has the added benefit of encouraging your horse to land on the correct lead. Making it easier to take the correct lead is a very good habit to get into.

*Ride your horse as straight as possible and begin to concentrate on the approach to and departure from the grid*

## TIPS FOR RIDING GRIDS

• As you approach the grid, ease your seat slightly off the saddle and allow all your weight to drop down into the stirrups through your hinges, or joints (ie your hips, knees and ankles). You should still find it easy to encourage your horse to go forwards from your leg.

• Have a bit of a 'float' to your position. Keep your chin up – this will stop you being too far forwards over the horse's shoulder.

• Keep hold! Your hands will allow more than enough 'give' as the balance of your body absorbs the movement of your horse.

• Try to keep a consistent contact with the reins, not too strong but very supportive.

• Aim to have the same supportive feel on the reins all the way through the grid. It's the consistency of the feel that you need to achieve, not a change in style.

• A longer grid will give you more 'goes' and practice at finding a comfortable working position. If you don't have enough material for six or seven crosses, two or three is better than none.

• Once you're confident, raise the ends of the crosses to give a slightly more exaggerated 'feel' from the horse. You don't need to alter your position or what you're doing, just adjust the timing so you allow for the horse being that little bit more extravagant over the crosses, and longer in the air.

• Be comfortable and effective with the amount of leg into your consistent contact, the balance into your stirrups, and your horse's pace and impulsion.

• If you start off trying to achieve the ideal position over a small cross, it will be so much better if you don't need to adapt or change that position when the jumps get bigger.

## PROBLEM SOLVER

**Q** I have a nine-year-old 14.2hh mare that I've owned for just over a year. I ride her in a lesson twice a week and spend a lot of time hacking. She loves to jump and when I'm out hacking she will jump anything, but I can never get her over more than 0.68m (2ft 3in) in the school. She clears this with lots to spare but if I try anything higher she flings her head up and runs straight through the fence.

I've tried jumping from trot, using placing poles, getting a lead from a friend's horse and letting other people jump her, but the results have been the same.

I've had her tack, teeth and back checked and nothing is wrong. Is she just being naughty? I've been told I should smack her every time she doesn't jump to teach her to behave.

**A** Horses refuse to jump for a variety of reasons, mainly through pain, fear, or lack of ability or understanding. Horses that tend to jump very big over small fences find it hard to jump larger ones. This indicates a lack of training and is not necessarily a sign of nappiness or of the horse being awkward.

The first thing to remember is that the height your horse can jump is totally irrelevant. What you must be interested in is the style and technique with which she does it – and this requires training.

You need to go back to basics, so use trotting poles. Put about three in a row, 1.2m (4ft) apart. Get her to work over these until she remains quiet, soft and relaxed. Try putting poles around the arena too so you can occasionally trot over them when you're schooling her.

*If your horse lacks technique, jumping for both of you can be rather uncomfortable*

When you're jumping, use placing poles about 2.75m (9ft) away from the fence. Try jumping small doubles from trot and canter and progress to using grids to teach your horse to be more athletic. As her athleticism improves, her ability to jump higher fences will come. The use of parallel and spread fences is very beneficial in improving a horse's bascule and technique.

Build up the work nice and slowly. At all times you must give your horse complete freedom over the fences and remain in good balance yourself.

# GRIDS FOR TURNS AND ANGLES

Once you're in charge of your horse's direction through a straight grid – not allowing him to hang to one side or the other – and can steer him properly through the exit, you're ready to be more ambitious. The work described here will increase your horse's balance and athleticism while also introducing him to the sorts of turns that he will need to make in a show jumping ring. If he tends to rush, a figure of eight grid will make him think more carefully and he won't find it as easy to get away from you on curves as he does on a straight line.

With only four jumps arranged in the three grids shown in this section, you and your horse can learn virtually all of the skills you'll need to jump a full course proficiently. Nearly every problem a course builder can throw at you as far as the track is concerned can be practised using these grids. The turns and angles required will also teach you both to be proficient in all the skills you need to do well in a jump off.

*Resist your horse's desire to motorbike around corners as it will unbalance him for the next obstacle*

## 1 INTRODUCING TURNS

Set jumps A and B on a three-stride related distance (see table, p.170). Ideally, use an arena or position the jumps against a fence. Alternatively, leave some spare poles lying on the ground to represent a barrier alongside the jumps to prevent your horse bulging wide to the outside of them.

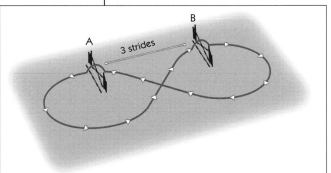

• Begin by jumping from A to B in a straight line several times, making sure that you're riding consistently with strong, active strides.

• Introduce your horse to riding turns. Start with fence A and approach on a diagonal line on the right rein. Head for a spot about 1.8m (6ft) in front of the fence. The close proximity of the arena perimeter or guiding poles will help to square you up and make you jump the fence in the middle.

Once you've landed, turn on a half circle and head across on the diagonal to jump fence B. Take care not to 'motorbike'. Again, aim to a point 1.8m (6ft) in front of fence B to allow enough room to be able to square up on the take-off point.

The difficulty of this angled approach will depend on the size of the half-circle on the landing side of both jumps. Try not to drift too far out or the angle to the next jump will be more difficult.

Repeat this exercise four or five times on the figure of eight to establish some consistency, and aim to make your turns and approaches similar at each end.

*As you jump fence A look ahead around the half-circle. Be careful not to collapse to the inside*

## GETTING A FLYING CHANGE

This exercise is great for teaching horses to take the correct lead and learn flying changes. If you work in canter (and don't get uptight about the correct leading leg), you'll give your horse the opportunity to work out his legs for himself. If you constantly come back to trot to establish the change, he'll never learn that it's simply easier to lead on the right leg.

The more you lean into your horse's turn, the less likely you are to encourage a successful flying change. Keep your inside shoulder up and keep pushing with your inside leg into a very consistent outside rein. It may not happen immediately. If your horse doesn't change legs then by the time you come round the next turn, he'll be on the correct lead again. Stay relaxed rather than force the issue as it will work eventually.

## 2 ANGLES

Reverse your route, trying to follow more or less the line you rode for exercise 1. As you approach jump A, you should already be looking across the diagonal and planning how much of an angle you'll need to be able to ride a balanced half-circle for the approach to jump B. If you cut in too much, your half-circle will be tight. If you go too wide you'll find it difficult to keep your rhythm and impulsion all the way.

This exercise will give you a guide to how much turn you can ask for without being over-ambitious. You will find it more difficult on this route to stop your horse cutting in on the approach to the next fence, so you'll have lots of opportunity to practise looking where you are going (see box, p.180). Turn your head to look for the next fence, but keep your inside shoulder up. Your horse may try to lean in because he's sure he knows where he's going and is keen to get there. He needs to learn that it will be easier for him to jump if he allows you to hold and support him by his outside rein, so that his hind leg remains active underneath him.

Repeat this figure of eight exercise four or five times before you have a breather. If you remain consistent in your riding, it will become easier.

### STYLE GUIDE

• The arena perimeter or guiding poles will help you to square your approaches, but don't be too reliant on them. When you jump a course, you need to be able to look where you're going and steer independently.
• Keep your shoulders level, without easing your outside rein forward, and you should land in an active and working canter, mostly with the correct lead. Don't worry if your horse is on the wrong leg or is disunited. Instead, concentrate on pushing him consistently into his supporting outside rein. He will either change legs or he won't, but your outside rein will keep him balanced if he isn't leading on the leg you hoped for.
• Keep your weight level when you're in the air, and don't anticipate the turn. Land and support your horse with your outside rein all the way round the turn. If you ease the outside rein forward to help you steer, you'll lose the power from your horse's inside hind leg.
• Take around 16 to 18 strides between landing, turning and taking off at the next jump.

*Keep your shoulders level and maintain a contact on the outside rein*

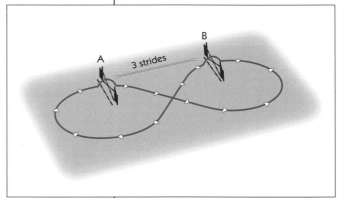

*Your horse needs to listen to you asking him to turn after landing and not become distracted by the fence in front of him*

178

## 3 STEERING AND RHYTHM

Once you feel happy and competent with the basic grid, add two more fences – C and D. Measure a four-stride distance (see p.170) from the middle of C to the middle of B, and from the middle of D to the middle of A.

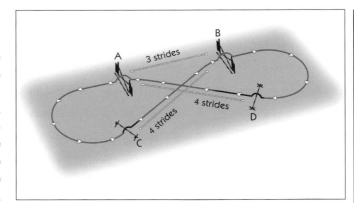

Start at A, then practise your steering, rhythm and impulsion around the corner to enable you to jump C square on. Look across to jump B so that the line between C and B is direct and straight. Remember to aim for a point slightly in front of B to enable you to square up on the approach. Land and then work hard around the corner to D.

The quicker you balance after each jump, the sooner you'll be able to establish the impulsion needed to make it easy for your horse to turn and keep jumping.

Try not to rely on the perimeter fence (or guiding poles on the ground). If you're looking far enough ahead, the route should be straightforward. If you find it too difficult to start with, give yourself a bit more room on the half-circle as this will give you more time to practise looking where you mean to go.

Stay in canter and repeat the exercise four or five times until you feel confident that you can maintain a strong impulsion all the way round.

*It is vital to look far enough ahead while keeping up the rhythm*

## 4 MOVING ON

Repeat exercise 3, but in the opposite direction so you'll have jumps C and D to steer for. Make sure you ride all the turns with a strong outside rein and insist on your horse not leaning in. Hopefully you'll find that as you progress with all the exercises, his canter leads will improve. The extra jumps, C and D, will help your horse to land on the correct leg in canter. If they don't at first, keep going and allow things to improve – don't try to force the improvement to happen. Allow your horse to recognize for himself that it's easier to be on the right leg.

The difficulty of this grid can be varied by altering the angle of jumps C and D. As you become more proficient, alter the angles very slightly to ride a more acute angle or a wider circle – whichever needs more attention and practise.

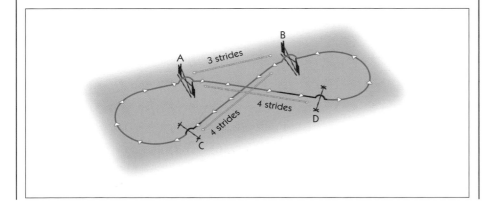

# 5 TWISTS AND TURNS

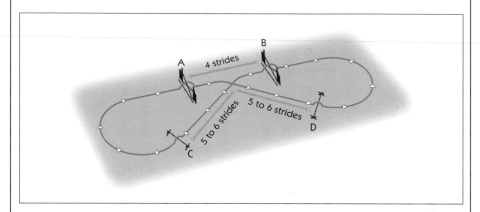

This final exercise is based on exercises 3 and 4 but with different distances, giving you the chance to practise riding slightly straighter approaches.

The routes here are similar to the exercises you have already done, but there's more room between each fence, so you can have a straighter approach to take-off.

Pace the distances between C and B, then D and A on your own two feet at first. Decide where you should aim for on the approach across the diagonal to give you the most beneficial stride. You'll find it easier to have at least one, or even better two straight strides on the take-off side of A and B.

Look ahead on both routes so that you jump the centres of all four fences. Your inside leg working into a supporting outside rein will be the key to success on all your turns, so keep up the consistency of your riding.

## TO FINISH

However hard you try to encourage your horse to listen to you, it will be almost impossible to stop him anticipating his turns. So after doing all this twisting and turning make sure that he will still go in a straight line. To finish, ride a small combination of fences in a straight line – incorporating the line between jumps A and B. This will help to make sure that your horse is genuinely listening to you, so make sure you tell him clearly what you want. See a straight line through the combination and remember how you worked hard on a straight grid to keep him active and accurate.

*Your horse should really be listening to you by now*

## MORE STYLE

• It seems obvious, but practise looking where you mean to go. As soon as you land, turn your head and get your eye round the corner, looking across to the next jump. Don't ride round the turn and then look for the next jump – it might not be where you expect it to be.

• When you ride a whole course, your horse won't know where to go until you tell him. If you practise turning your head in plenty of time, he'll pick up on your slight weight change. This will act as an early warning and indicate to him what you're going to ask.

• Through repetitions your horse will start to anticipate where you want him to go, so make sure you don't allow him to lean into his turns. Remember how you rode the end of your straight grids (pp.172–175) – telling your horse when to stay straight, and asking him to turn, rather than allowing him to choose when he turns.

## PROBLEM SOLVER

**Q** A while ago I was given a 12-year-old, 14.3hh TBx to bring back into work after having a foal. The problem is that every time she sees a jump, no matter what height, she heads for it at top speed. She will happily walk and trot over poles but once there is any space between the pole and the ground, she just speeds into it. I have had everything I can think of checked and have been told she is perfectly healthy and her tack is the best fit it could be. I also tried changing her bit but it didn't make a difference.

Anyone who sees her jump says she's dangerous and I shouldn't bother. But I think she is a very talented mare, capable of jumping 1.5m (5ft) or more if she learned how to slow down.

**A** Rushing into fences is often mistaken for enthusiasm, but it is normally a sign of a lack of confidence. The problem escalates when the rider tries to slow the horse down, restricting him in the process. The horse needs to use his head and neck to balance himself. Restricting this movement is equivalent to us having our hands tied behind our backs.

Changing your horse's bit and other equipment may bring a temporary improvement, but a programme of schooling designed to increase her confidence will bring the only permanent change in the way she goes.

You say that your mare is happy over poles, this is a good place to start. Work over a grid, starting with poles and building up to a series of small jumps. The idea is to use distances that encourage the horse to jump correctly so that you have to make the minimum of corrections.

As your mare's confidence grows you can progress to single fences and then string some together. At all times, try to remember how it feels when she is jumping correctly and replicate this in new situations.

It may be worth getting some experienced help as it is difficult to set up the jumps and ride at the same time. It is very important to set the distances correctly, as if they are incorrect it may upset your horse more. Having some help on the ground is doubly useful, as it's often easier for them to see what, if anything, is going wrong.

*A horse that rushes at fences is showing concern. Take her back a few steps and work on increasing her confidence with exercises she can do well*

*All that gridwork really pays off when you start to jump courses. Your horse will be able to keep straight over all sorts of obstacles, maintaining a good rhythm, jumping cleanly and adjusting his stride as necessary*

# THE LESSONS

*Whether you like cross country, jump cross or show jumping, the skills you and your horse need to develop to be successful are very similar*

When you have a problem with your jumping, it usually comes out when you are at a competition and there is no possibility of working on it. Then afterwards it can be difficult to know what has caused the problem. Because horses are natural jumpers and we have to leave the getting over the fence aspect of jumping to them, it is easy to take a step back from other areas, such as the rhythm and balance, and become more of a passenger than a partner. Left to their own devices, most horses will not hold a line to a fence, or come away from it with impulsion and intention. It is up to us to train them how to do the bit between the fences to the best of their ability – and it is the bit between the fences that makes the difference between having fun and success and just getting round by the skin of your teeth.

The next few pages focus on training particular aspects of jumping. The lessons vary in difficulty so always be aware of what your horse is capable of and build up his skills slowly and methodically. You should find something to inspire you and, by the end of each session, you should also feel that you have both learnt something new.

## TIPS FOR SUCCESS

• *Remember, it is human nature to prefer to do things we are good at, so if you think to yourself, 'I don't fancy doing that,' ask yourself 'Is this the very skill we should be working on?'*

• *It is wise to have a helper on the ground to move jumps, replace fallen poles and give you information about your progress. It is also safer to have someone around when you jump, in case of an accident.*

• *Start each session with a warm-up and end it with a cool-down period.*

• *When setting up any of the exercises described over the next few pages, remember that accuracy is important to ensure that you get the most out of the lesson.*

• *Getting over the jump without knocking it down is not as important as giving your horse the training he needs to do his best. Horses that have problems with jumping often simply haven't been taught the basic skills they need.*

• *In jumping, your fitness is as important as your horse's. You will let him down if you are not fit enough.*

• *Don't continue if you start to get cross or frustrated. Finish with something you both know, turn your horse out and go home to think about how you can do it differently to get a better result.*

# LESSON 1 – CIRCLE AND DOWN THE CENTRE LINE

This lesson is based around an exercise that provides a simple and effective way to practise giving your horse clear directions into and after the fence. Many jumping problems are simply a case of the rider being disorganized and not giving the horse a definite indication of where she wants him to go, which means the horse often starts to take charge, and the results become hit and miss. Because this exercise gives you a pre-planned pattern, you can soon see if you and your horse are going on the correct line. When the rider influences the horse constructively, the horse starts to feel more secure and will relax and become more attentive.

This exercise might seem to be quite basic and straightforward, but it is actually quite challenging, especially when the jump is in place. It really makes you focus on your steering – you will soon know if you don't have as much control over direction as you should.

### QUALITY AND FOCUS

*The aim of this exercise is to test the accuracy of your lines and develop your awareness of what is happening underneath you. It requires you to concentrate on what you're doing, and influence the horse in a useful way. Always remember that when the horse has jumped well, it's better to stop sooner rather than later. Aim for quality, focused work, and then reward him for a job well done.*

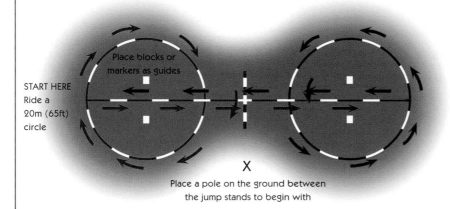

Place blocks or markers as guides

START HERE
Ride a
20m (65ft)
circle

X

Place a pole on the ground between the jump stands to begin with

*Trot through X making sure your horse is responding enthusiastically to your aids*

## THE WARM-UP

Position two jump stands at X, a pole on the ground between them. Start by making a 20m (65ft) circle to the right at one end of the working area. Then turn up the centre line and ride through the jump stands. On reaching the other end, turn left and make another 20m circle, before returning down the centre line. Check that you are clear about your line before you start jumping.

Test that the horse is responding to your forwards and controlling aids by making changes of pace in walk and trot. Pay attention to the quality of his reaction. Does he respond to your leg aids with enthusiasm? Does he slow down with you becoming more vertical with the top of your body and a light squeeze on the reins? Is he flexible when you make soft loops and turns around the arena?

Once your horse is trotting over the pole in an uncomplicated way, give him a short break. Ask your helper to put up a small cross pole. If you don't have a helper, you can do this exercise with just a pole on the ground.

## THE EXERCISE

Test that your horse is alert for your leg aids. Give him a friendly nudge with your heels. He should respond with enthusiasm. Then balance him up and start the exercise.

Repeat the warm-up pattern, but this time go over the cross pole. Ideally, if you trot into the cross pole, you want to land and move away from it in canter. If the horse has landed on the correct lead, continue on the pattern and make a neat circle in canter, before coming back to trot and making another circle, during which you re-balance the trot, before making your next approach. Getting into the habit of re-balancing the horse between fences will serve you well when you come to jump a whole course.

Aim to jump the cross pole two or three times, looking for quality each time. Be as meticulous about your line after the fence as you are about the line before it. Many riders are so relieved to have got to the other side of the fence that they forget themselves, get out of balance and let the horse wander about. Remember that when you are jumping a course, the getaway from one fence is part of the approach to the next one. This is why it is particularly important to ride a good line after the fence, even when you are only practising over a single obstacle.

## INCREASING THE DIFFICULTY

Once you've done the exercise satisfactorily in trot, give your horse a breather and a walk on a long rein, while your helper changes the fence into a small upright. You are now going to repeat the exercise in canter. Take a moment to rehearse in your mind the line you are going to ride.

Strike off to canter and make your preparatory circle. Be sure that your horse's canter is bright enough to jump. Test him with your leg or voice, and, if necessary, make another circle before jumping.

On landing from the fence, softly move the horse forward with your legs to enhance the straight line, and then use the circle to prepare him for the next jump. For instance, if he was bit sluggish into the fence, then he needs a friendly kick to wake him up. If he was running on, you need to sit up and re-balance him.

You can repeat this exercise with a bigger upright or a parallel. Between each stage, give your horse a walk on a long rein. This gives him a chance to recover, and you time to assess what just happened, and how you can improve your performance. If you feel your horse is losing interest in the fence, change the look of it, perhaps by putting a slanting rail underneath it. In addition, if you started the exercise on the right rein at the bottom end of the school, change to beginning at that end on the left rein when you re-start the exercise.

*When you start jumping, blocks on the ground will help your accuracy*

*It is better to do one jump really well than lots badly*

# LESSON 2 – CIRCLE AND ACROSS THE DIAGONAL

Accuracy and confidence are among the basics that your horse needs for successful show jumping. He also needs to work in balance at the correct pace. This lesson works on training these qualities, while also developing your own feel for a stride.

The best way to create confidence is by starting exercises in their simplest form, building them up a step at a time, so that any training session becomes a series of victories. Accuracy is achieved through riding clear lines of your choosing. Feel for the right pace is learned by analysing what happened in the approach, over and after the fence. And you can develop your feel for a stride by improving your balance and sense of rhythm, and by doing exercises with correctly measured distances.

Your horse should have some jumping experience in order to do this exercise. He needs to be fully confident about jumping a variety of fences on a straight line before he is asked to do so at an angle.

## THE WARM-UP

Start by doing some straightforward warm-up work in walk and trot. Then pick up the reins and work your horse in an outline. Work him in circles and turns to increase his suppleness, and also pay particular attention to his straightness after a turn. For instance, if you ride a 15m (50ft) circle with a soft bend to the left, be sure to apply your right hand and right leg when you ride out of the circle to ensure that he is truly straight. It is also worth introducing some half-halts as part of your warm-up routine, starting in walk and then – when he's listening – moving on to trot and canter. Practising these communications with your horse before you start jumping will make it much easier to balance him when you are doing the exercise.

*Work on your communication with your horse before you start the exercise*

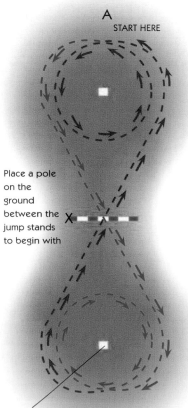

A
START HERE

Place a pole on the ground between the jump stands to begin with

X

Place blocks 15m (50ft) away from the fence on either side

### FOCUS ON CLARITY

A lot of the value in this exercise comes from making a distinction between the circle line and the diagonal line, so that it is obvious to the horse when you mean him to jump and when you mean him to circle. If he looks at the fence when you are on the circle, it means that your line is indistinct to him, and you need to change it so that you leave him in no doubt as to where you want to go.

Make a point of using your outside aids when you turn onto the diagonal. A clean turn with the horse truly straightened up makes it easier to see a stride, whereas losing the shoulder in the turn can lead to a run-out.

## INTRODUCING THE EXERCISE

Place the jump stands at X, and put markers on the centre line about 15m (50ft) away from it on either side. The markers will signify the centre of the circles. Start with just a pole on the ground in between the stands. Not only does this help you get your line right without having to worry about the fence, but the way your horse steps over the pole gives you feedback about the quality of your trot. If he steps over it confidently, with just an increase in the elevation of his trot, it lets you know that your trot has a good rhythm and that he is in front of your leg. If he has to reach for the pole, or chips in a short stride before it, he is behind the aids. If he speeds up towards the pole, then he is rushing away from you and is out of balance. All these faults need to be rectified before you start jumping, otherwise they will just be carried forward into the jumping, where they will be much more problematic.

To ride this exercise, start the circle about 5m (16ft) inside the track at A. Ride one complete circle and, as you come to your start-off point, take the line out several metres in order to turn back on a diagonal towards the fence (see diagram). Make a point of applying your outside aids to truly straighten the horse on the diagonal, and then trot over the pole in the middle of the jump stands. Ride the whole diagonal, before repeating the circle and the rest of the pattern at the other end of the school.

### MAKING A JUMP

When you are satisfied with the line you are riding, your helper can change the pole on the floor into a cross pole. Make a preparatory circle in trot, and then approach the fence on the diagonal. Jump the fence and, on landing, softly move away from it in canter. Follow this by making one circle in canter, followed by one in trot, during which you re-balance your horse to prepare him for the next approach.

This work is quite intense, so repeat the exercise a maximum of four times before having a break. Take this time to assess how the horse is taking to the exercise, what your lines are like and what could be improved.

## INCREASING THE DIFFICULTY

If the trot jumping has been satisfactory, you can progress to doing the exercise in canter over a small upright. When you land from the fence, move the horse forwards, but then take the opportunity on the circle to test his collection in the canter. Once satisfied with the quality of the collection, put some sparkle into the canter, before taking your line out again to turn onto the diagonal and jump the fence.

You can progress to a bigger upright and a parallel. Make the parallel fairly narrow to start off with, as your horse will already be dealing with the added width that comes from jumping on a diagonal.

Each time you re-start the exercise, go on the opposite rein from last time. This means that if you started on the left rein at the bottom end of your schooling area the first time, now start on the right rein at the bottom end. This increases the variety of approaches, even though you are jumping the same fence.

*Achieving straightness on the diagonal is an important part of the exercise*

*Move forward after the fence, thinking about your line*

187

# LESSON 3 – GOING FORWARDS TO THE JUMP

**A common problem with jumping is the horse not fully engaging with the rider and so not being able to jump a full course of fences. Some horses will back off from one jump and be able to recover, but most find that being able to keep up the momentum over a series of obstacles is too much for their athletic abilities and their balance and rhythm.**

## WARM-UP AND CANTER WORK

Begin with some walk and trot in straight lines and circles, making plenty of transitions before moving on to canter. Make sure your horse is responsive and listening to you before you start the canter. A good canter is one where you could be drinking a cup of tea and your horse would keep cantering! Remember to look up and ahead. When you start jumping, it's essential that you're looking up to your fence so you can ride the correct line.

If your horse's canter is a bit fixed, loosen it up by asking him to move forwards more for a few strides and then shortening him. Repeat this down each long side and then ride a circle in canter. Change the rein and repeat the exercise. Vary where you do your circles – don't always go the same route as your horse will start to anticipate, and he needs to listen to you.

Beware of niggling with your legs every step, and make sure your horse is reactive to your aids. He should go when you say go and stop when you say stop. If he doesn't respond to a light leg aid, give him a short, sharp kick and then keep your legs still.

*Being able to adjust the length of your canter stride will help you when you are jumping a course of fences*

*Trot over the poles on the ground until they lose their novelty value for the horse – that is he stops thinking they're going to jump up and bite him*

## POLES ON THE GROUND

This exercise is great for horses that worry about jumps as poles on the ground are much less scary. They can have a good look and learn that they aren't dangerous. Trotting over poles is a good way to get lift in the stride and encourage a horse to stretch through his back and hocks. Begin by walking over four poles on the ground. Keep walking up and down over the poles until he will cross them quietly. Once your horse is more confident, go over the poles in trot. Trot over them a few times from both directions. Now you are ready to jump.

## A SIMPLE CROSS POLE JUMP

Make a low cross pole jump in the centre of the school. Put a placing pole in front of it to help you reach the best take-off point. Approach the cross pole in trot. Your horse must go forwards on landing, so don't allow him to grind to a halt. Remember you're in charge. Most horses will not find a single cross pole a problem, but those that tend not to like jumping a complete course will try to stop moving after the jump and this is what you need to address.

Repeat this jump a few times, each time making sure that your horse keeps moving after it. If possible simply keep trotting and come around and over the jump again. Don't overdo it though. If you have a helper on the ground ask them to move the ground pole and repeat the exercise on the other rein.

Once he is responding well, give him a short break walking on a long rein and then try the jump again, this time in canter. Make sure you have a good responsive canter from which you can ask for a short or long stride. Don't allow your horse to get long and flat. If the canter gets too long he will lose impulsion and balance. Remember to maintain the canter after you land.

Depending on how well it is going, you can ask your helper to move the placing pole and make the jump bigger so that you can repeat the work on the other rein.

## GOING OVER UPRIGHTS

With a real novice horse, a few jumps over a cross pole will be enough for one day. However, if your horse is more experienced then you can move on now to tackling uprights. Use your canter to ride over the upright. Don't change the way you ride just because the fence has changed. It is vital to keep your horse coming forwards to the jump. This will teach him to quicken over the fence. If necessary give him a sharp kick at the placing pole, but don't throw your upper body forward too far. Ride round and jump the upright a few more times so you both get the idea.

Focus on sitting up, and press with your legs, then even if you are on the wrong stride your horse should still jump the fence.

*The departure from the fence is every bit as important as the approach*

*Cross poles encourage a neat jump over the centre of the fence*

*Two poles in front of the fence should put some spring into your canter*

## PUTTING SPRING IN THE CANTER

If your horse tends to be rather flat in his canter, this exercise will help to increase his spring. Simply add another pole in front of the upright, so that there are two poles on the ground. He may be a bit wary of the extra pole being there, so use your voice to encourage him to go forwards. If your approach goes wrong, don't panic. Instead, maintain your position, keep the contact and use your legs – and your horse will still jump.

## NEATENING THE FRONT LEGS

To help your horse become a little neater over the fence, ask your helper to put two poles on the upright to form a 'V' shape. This will encourage your horse to go into the centre of the fence and to bring his front legs up more cleanly. Again, some horses will probably look at this, so as you come around to jump it have your leg on, keep hold of your horse and stay upright on your approach.

*A neat jump is encouraged by two poles making a 'V' shape into the jump*

Remember that he has to go over, so if necessary kick him up to the bridle. Don't fall into the trap of throwing him at the jump and then dropping your contact – keep your position and ride positively. If he gets the idea your helper should see him really snapping up his front legs over the jump and looking neater and more careful. If you find the second ground pole is a distraction, ask your helper to remove it at this point.

## To finish

If all has gone well up to this point, you might like to finish the lesson by asking your helper to add a back rail to the jump to make it an oxer. Think about the quality of your canter as you approach the fence. A good canter is the key to jumping success, both before and after the fence. Use your leg more to create the energy if necessary.

Finally, ask your helper to remove the placing pole. Focus on the canter rhythm and let the fence come to you. See if you can maintain the canter stride into the fence without the placing pole to guide you. Repeat this last exercise a couple of times before spending a few minutes on cooling down.

*Whatever the jump in front of you, ride it in the same way, concentrating on rhythm, balance and impulsion*

### In summary

• *Focus on the quality of your canter, lengthening down each long side of the school. Your horse must be obedient to your aids.*

• *Ride over poles on the ground before you start jumping. This will help you and your horse to ride forwards in a good rhythm.*

• *Use a placing pole in front of a cross pole. This will help your horse to find the optimum take-off point. Approach in trot first and, when you are happy, try it in canter.*

• *When the fence is altered to an upright don't change the way you ride. Maintain your position, with your legs on, to give your horse the confidence to jump even if the stride isn't quite right.*

• *If you need help getting a good canter, add another placing pole. This extra pole will add more energy to your canter. Don't be afraid to use your voice to encourage him to go forwards, as well as your leg.*

• *To finish, jump an oxer with a placing pole. Then remove the pole and see if you can maintain your canter rhythm.*

## PROBLEM SOLVER

**Q** My 15.1hh mare is five, and I've had her since she was three-and-a-half. I brought her on slowly and, until recently, she was jumping 0.76m (2ft 6in) classes clear. I moved to 0.84m (2ft 9in) classes, but she started stopping at the first part of a double or in the middle of a combination. We're doing gridwork at home, but she stops mid-way through the grid. She's had her teeth and back checked. Help!

**A** Over smaller fences, your mare won't need to make so much effort to jump in and through a combination, so you won't become unbalanced on landing. Over a bigger fence, I suspect that you're not recovering quickly enough after the jump to enable you to ride a non-jumping stride between fences consistently.

In addition, your mare is probably lacking enough impulsion to do what you want. If she's sensitive, she won't want to go into a double if she's worried about getting out comfortably over the second fence.

I suggest you try an exercise that will help you get back in balance more quickly after landing, so you can ride a better non-jumping stride in the middle of a double.

Build a small single fence and then place several canter poles on the floor after the fence at 3.65, 7.3, 10.9 and 14.6m (12, 24, 36 and 48ft). As you land, make a huge effort to look up and give your horse a good nudge as quickly as possible, so that you continue over the poles. The sooner you can get your leg on after the fence, the more impulsion you'll produce, and this will make it easier for your horse when she has to cope with another fence. As you become more capable, gradually remove the canter poles one by one, starting with the pole nearest to the fence. When only the furthest one is left, you should be reaching it in three strong non-jumping strides.

# LESSON 4 –
# IMPULSION NOT SPEED

Which of these describes your horse? He's enthusiastic and confidently approaches each jump with his ears forward, jumping clear. He charges round, taking strides out and finishing on a cricket score. Use this lesson to work on removing tension and rushing from your horse's jumping.

A common rider mistake is to ride too strongly with the leg and seat, or not ride in a balanced position. So spend some time working on your flatwork before going back to basics with your jumping. When you're schooling, use lots of transitions to make sure your horse is obedient to your leg and stops when you ask him. Check that he steadies when you use a half-halt and that you can easily lengthen and shorten his stride. Also, make sure that he's supple and that you can turn easily.

## SUPPLING AND RELAXING

After a few minutes of warm-up – doing plenty of walk and trot transitions, circles and straight lines – start the lesson. Taking more of a contact, canter around the arena – riding in a light seat for a few strides, then sitting for a few strides. Check that your horse stays in balance and that the rhythm doesn't change as you alternate between a light seat and sitting. Keep the weight in your heel and your lower leg forward slightly. Once the rhythm's consistent, introduce circles – still repeating the light seat/sitting exercise. Think about maintaining a forward canter.

This exercise will encourage your horse to use his back and help you maintain the correct canter rhythm as you change position (most riders have a tendency to slow as they sit up). Asking your horse to bend on the circle will help to supple him laterally.

Next, come back to trot and ride smaller 10–15m (30–50ft) circles around the arena. Shorten the trot for five or six strides then go forwards to working trot again – this will improve elasticity and get your horse working under you. Encourage your horse to take the contact forward and down so he stretches and relaxes the muscles along his back. Come back to walk and let him stretch on a long rein for a few minutes.

## IMPROVING THE RHYTHM

This really simple exercise to regulate your horse's stride consists of placing a pole on a 20m (65ft) circle and cantering over it. After a few circles you'll begin to feel the quality of your canter improve. Your horse should start to maintain an even stride length and rhythm, and he'll learn to look and adjust himself so he doesn't touch the pole.

Keep looking ahead on the circle so you ride a good line, and concentrate on maintaining a soft inside rein contact. Ride this exercise in a light, forward seat so you don't drive or push with your seat, which

*Cantering on a circle is good for lateral stretching as well as to instil a good canter rhythm*

will upset the canter rhythm. Some horses will see the pole and automatically lengthen their stride in order to reach it quickly – again, a light seat means you're not tempted to drive him on.

Repeat this exercise equally on both reins, until your horse no longer finds it exciting and his canter rhythm stays the same the whole way around the circle.

If he keeps hitting the pole it may be that your horse is relying too much on the inside rein contact, so relax your inside hand – even if you find that this means he bends to the outside. You may also be using too much inside rein to help him turn: try hooking your inside hand into your breastplate (if you use one). This will encourage you to use your outside hand to control the speed and will also help you stay in a balanced position.

## JUMPING ON A CIRCLE

Ask your helper to put up a small upright with a placing pole about 2.2m (7ft) in front of it. In trot, on the left rein, ride a 20m circle. As you ride the circle, jump the upright. Remember, the shape of your circle is more important than the fence. So, instead of looking down at the placing pole, keep your line of sight on the line of your circle. It's also important that you have a good quality, forward-going trot. Repeat the circle and jump on the other rein.

This exercise makes you think about the approach and departure from a fence and takes the emphasis away from the jump, which will help you and your horse to stay calm and relaxed.

## DISCIPLINE AFTER THE FENCE

This next exercise will help stop your horse rushing off on landing. Ask your helper to put up a second and third upright spaced out in the school – on a large circle there's space. Trot over an upright, ride a circle, bring him back to trot, go over the next upright, then circle again. Aim to bring him back to trot on the second stride after landing. By staying in trot, you're making it difficult for your horse to judge the take-off point, so this makes him really use himself. Lots of riders don't like jumping from trot, but it does have its place when you're helping a horse to use his back and jump off his hocks.

If your fences are on a large circle you should now jump all three fences on one circle, still coming back to trot on landing. (Alternatively, ask your assistant to re-build them into a circle.) Keep thinking ahead to your approach to your second and third fence. Remember to maintain your position, and that you are riding a circle. If you ride the right shape it will make jumping the fences easy for him.

Once you have repeated this exercise on both reins, give your horse a walk on a loose rein and allow him time to cool down. If things have gone well this time, try the exercises on pp.194–195 next time.

*Monitor your horse's rhythm, line and straightness over the canter pole. If he starts to rush, lighten your seat a little and keep a soft contact on the reins*

*Don't let yourself down after landing. Think ahead to the next jump and maintain a good trot rhythm*

## Try this next time

Begin by warming up and doing the simple cantering over a pole exercise (see Improving the rhythm, p.192). If you are both feeling relaxed and focused, you can now try the exercises here.

### Four jumps on a circle

Position four small jumps on a circle, with one stride between each. Have a placing pole on the ground around 3m (10ft) before the first jump, and a landing pole around 3.65m (12ft) after the fourth fence. This exercise will test whether you're looking where you're going. You'll need to focus on the line you are riding all the time, and look much further ahead than you would normally – at least two fences ahead.

Keep the jumps fairly small to begin with – this way, if you're struggling to keep your line, you'll still be able to jump the fences. Make regular changes of rein and have your helper alter the fences for you. Once your horse is happily and calmly jumping the fences you can put them up. Adjust alternate fences, so your horse has a chance to recover if he has a problem. Also, if he is inclined to rush, constantly changing the fences will help to keep his concentration. Once he's happy and relaxed you can put the second and fourth fences up. Finally, you can add another – one jumping stride from the last fence.

Keep thinking of your rhythm and guide your horse, looking ahead in plenty of time. Also, keep your posture up as this will help your horse to bring his shoulders up too. Remember to hold him with your outside rein and keep the inside rein contact soft and relaxed.

### Going higher

You can adjust the height of the fences once your horse is going confidently. If he's finding it difficult to stay on a curved line now that there are five jumps, it may help to add a guide pole on the third jump to help him turn without you having to use too much rein. Keep things slow and easy. When you change the rein, remember to move the guide pole to the opposite side.

### Down to three

Still working on a circle, remove two jumps so you have three fences with three strides between each. Make the middle fence a parallel. Don't worry if the distances look short. This exercise is intended to teach your horse to adjust his stride – shortening it if he needs to. It will help him learn to make decisions and sort himself, so you don't have to help him too much. You may find that your horse starts to back off his fences as he is more relaxed, so be ready to use your legs to keep the quality canter. Some riders struggle to look far enough ahead. Get your line to your placing pole on the first fence and then look to the next fence. If he's struggling with this distance, ride an outside line and you'll get the three strides. Use your posture to steady him, not your rein.

### Working with parallels

If you prefer you can use single fences to make progress. Ask your helper to set up a drop-fronted parallel in the centre of the school. Approach this parallel off a circle in a relaxed canter – but making sure your horse is in front of your leg. If all goes well you can now take a straighter line to the jump. Be careful you don't let it get too quick. If it does get fast, approach the fence off a circle again to restore your good canter rhythm. Once you get the relaxed rhythm, keep it and approach on a straight line again. Don't let the canter open up just because you have a longer approach. Canter a circle after the fence to bring your horse back to you and re-establish your good canter again.

*This drop-fronted parallel with double rails at the back is a good training fence for horses that are stiff or tense in their back. The lower pole at the front won't punish the horse if he gets it wrong. It also makes the obstacle a spread fence rather than an upright, which horses find easier to jump*

Next you can try a true parallel and work through it using a circle and a straighter line as before. Always be prepared to go back a stage if your horse starts rushing or your approaches or departures begin to go awry. It is best to do good quality work, even if it feels like you are making slower progress. Don't let your horse run off after the fence – you need to behave as though you're riding a course of fences. If you allow the canter to become faster, your approach to your next fence won't be good.

Finish off by doing a more simple fence, such as jumping a small upright from trot and then walking over it on both reins. Keep a good walk rhythm to the fence, then just trot round the arena on a long rein to let your horse cool off and stretch.

# LESSON 5 – CONFIDENCE BOOSTING

**It is easy to mistake worry for enjoyment in a jumping horse. Horses that rush fences may be trying to get the whole thing over with, while those that appear to be very spooky may simply be lacking in the necessary skills, which will lead to a loss of confidence. Such horses may not really know what is expected of them. Lessons 1–4 will help build your horse's confidence, and should be attempted before doing this lesson. (Stick to the smaller, simpler jumps in Lesson 4 if your horse lacks experience, too.)**

## EFFECTIVE WARM-UP

With a spooky horse it is doubly important to use the warm up to make sure he's relaxed and listening to you before you go on to tackle any fences. Walk, trot and canter on both reins, but don't be in too much of a hurry to move from one gait to the next. It's best to get your horse listening and working properly in one gait before you move on. This means having a nice rhythm and working the horse through from behind into a soft but constant contact.

When you move into canter, take your weight off your horse's back by standing in your stirrups slightly. This will help him to use his back properly. Also, make sure you don't rest your hands on his neck – this is cheating. You should be able to canter in a forward position with your hands in their normal place. If you can't then you aren't in balance (see box, p.169).

Do five circuits of the school on each rein in canter, checking your balance all the time. Ask your horse to lengthen and collect his canter to improve his balance and elasticity. The collection will help to bring his hind legs underneath him – where they need to be for jumping. It'll also give you confidence that you have control over his speed.

## CANTER POLES

As with the previous lesson (see p.192), canter poles work wonders with horses that have issues with jumping. Unless your horse is an experienced and proficient jumper, it is always helpful to do some canter poles at the start of a session.

Place two poles three strides apart (see table, p.170) and canter

(see box, p.169).

---

### THINK POSITIVE

• *If your horse tends to refuse, ride him right to the moment of take off. Horses often refuse because their rider has stopped riding a stride or two away.*

• *If your horse refuses, don't automatically assume he'll do it on the second attempt. This will stop you riding him effectively and positively. Think of every approach to a fence as a new start.*

• *A horse may knock a fence because you're panicking and not riding him all the way. This is a particular problem when you jump a double. Sit up and use your legs. Think about raising your chin as this will straighten your back and put you in a less vulnerable position.*

*If your horse naps, calmly ride him through it. Give him a pat for reassurance, but then use your legs to push him on – he has to accept that you're in control*

196

over them, keeping your horse as calm as you can. Try to get an even three strides in between the poles. When you can do this easily, alter the number of strides. You'll need to have a big, onward-going canter to get three strides in, and you'll need to use your seat and legs to collect your horse to get four strides. If he gets excited and tries to rush, circle him away from the poles and try again.

## THE FIRST FENCE

Ask your helper to set up a simple fence with a filler. If your horse is spooky, he might want to take a look at this fence first. Keep the fence low, so you don't have to worry about him not being able to jump – just keep riding him forwards. If you feel your horse might stop, keep your leg on and ride him positively forwards. Be careful not to throw away your contact.

If you're worried about him going too fast into the fence, be careful not to slow him down too much and lose impulsion as then he'll find it more difficult to jump. Instead, canter a circle and get your rhythm – this will make your approach easier and more balanced.

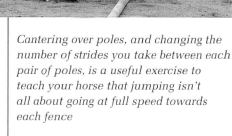

*Cantering over poles, and changing the number of strides you take between each pair of poles, is a useful exercise to teach your horse that jumping isn't all about going at full speed towards each fence*

*Lack of confidence in the rider often leads to a stop*

*Take control and be positive – your horse will be able to tell the difference*

*Keep your eye on the centre of the fence and try to keep your horse straight*

## STAYING IN LINE

A horse may refuse, or run out, if you allow him to drift towards one side on your approach to each fence. He may also be straying to one side because he's putting in an extra stride and getting too close to the jump. If this is the case, don't worry about seeing a stride – instead, keep your eye on the centre of the jump. Keep your leg on and keep your horse straight. Think about riding the jump as you would cross-country fences. Really move on. Make sure you are organized – have your reins short enough to keep an even contact. Tackling show jumping fences in the same way you would cross-country jumps will help if you tend to back your horse off a bit. It may be that you're not confident enough to let your horse go forwards as you're worried about him stopping. But, by being too careful, this is exactly what will happen. Think about the sort of canter you would need to jump a cross-country fence and try to replicate this.

# CONSIDERING CROSS COUNTRY

When riding cross country there's a fine line between feeling exhilarated and terrified. Cross-country obstacles are unforgiving, so it's important that you have a trusting, positive relationship with your horse. You need to know that your horse has the ability and know-how to jump each fence, and he needs to know that he's got a confident, knowledgeable pilot on board. This relationship will crumble if either horse or rider, or both, are lacking in any of these areas.

While the next few pages outline the various skills you need to go cross country and how to cope with the type of obstacles you will find, there is nothing to beat having good instruction. Having someone on the ground telling you what to do will boost you and your horse's confidence, and an experienced instructor will turn each lesson into a positive experience.

## WHAT YOUR HORSE NEEDS TO KNOW

It's very important with young horses that their training is progressive, building up slowly. If the basics have been done correctly, when he is ready, the horse will have the confidence to jump bigger and more technical fences with no problems.

• Gridwork (pp.170–180) and the jumping lessons (pp.183–197) will introduce your horse to the foundation skills he will require to jump cross country.

• Your horse needs to be fit to be able to complete a cross-country course. An unfit horse is more likely to make mistakes as he tires, which can be dangerous.

• Good flatwork training is also necessary to build his athleticism, responsiveness, balance and rhythm – all vital for safe and successful cross-country riding.

• To ride cross country effectively, your horse needs to be able to perform three different canters, ranging from quite a collected canter to medium canter. The aim is then to adjust the canter for different types of fences (see also Check your canters, p.200).

*When you ride cross country the obstacles are unforgiving, so it is vital that you and your horse know what you are doing and have plenty of confidence in each other*

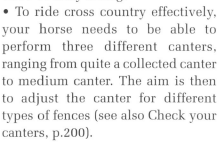

*The quality and adjustability of your horse's canter is very important when you are going across country*

## YOUR RESPONSIBILITIES

The rider is responsible for three things when riding cross country:

**1** A good line to each fence.

**2** Creating the power to jump the fences — but not mistaking speed for power.

**3** Having a forward-thinking hand to allow the horse to use his head and neck.

*Work in partnership with your horse. Set him up well before the fence and then allow him to do the jump unhindered*

## A SECURE POSITION

A secure position is essential for safe cross-country riding. In between fences you'll see experienced cross-country riders bringing their seat out of the saddle and staying in balance without relying on the reins. However, as they approach each fence they will change their position to help prepare for the jump. Their upper body is upright and their seat comes back into the saddle. As the rider adopts this more upright position, you will see how it balances the horse and he may shorten his stride, but the rhythm should stay the same. Horse and rider should maintain this position all the way to the fence.

*As you approach the fence, bring your seat back into the saddle, maintaining an upright upper body*

You need to be sure that your lower leg is underneath you and that you are over your horse's centre of balance. If your lower leg is under your body weight, you have a good support base on which to balance. If your lower leg position is not secure and moves forwards or back, you will feel insecure. You need a good bend in the knee to absorb the movement as you jump and as you are riding between fences. Your weight should be down into your heels to help make your lower leg position strong.

It's important to learn to balance your horse by using your weight and legs rather than pulling on the reins. If you rely on the reins it will slow him down and you will lose impulsion, making it more difficult for him to jump. He may even resist your rein contact by putting his head up, so taking his focus away from the jump in front of him.

In addition, your attitude is important. You need to be attacking and determined, but also to adopt a 'defensive' body position, trying not to push your shoulders forwards on take-off. This will move your weight ahead of your horse's balance and will also cause your lower leg to move. Keep your shoulders up so you are ready for any slight mistake that might happen, and leave the jumping to your horse.

*Between fences, have your seat out of the saddle and balance without relying on the reins*

# CHECK YOUR CANTERS

To ride cross country successfully there has to be a good foundation of trust between the rider and their horse. On most courses you will encounter a variety of different fences including accuracy fences, ditches, steps and water. Your horse will look to you to tell him it's OK to jump these. If you ask him to jump technical fences before he is ready it won't be long before you run into trouble. Take time to build both your and your horse's confidence over small, simple fences. When both of you are completely happy, start to ask him to jump bigger and more technical fences. Training in a progressive way, you and your horse should have lots of fun when you are out competing.

## WARM-UP

Before you start jumping, warm your horse up in walk, trot and canter. During this time, concentrate on getting him listening to your aids. He should move forwards willingly and slow down when you ask.

## GOING THROUGH THE PACES

Having an adjustable canter is very important (see p.198) so a good way to start a cross-country session is testing that your horse's canter is flexible and balanced.

For the first fence choose something nice and straightforward, such as a brush fence, to give you and your horse confidence. Ride into this fence in a working canter so you jump it out of a natural rhythm.

*Approach a brush fence with a coiled-spring of a working canter. Think balance and engagement*

For the next fence try something a litle more challenging, such as a spread. For this you need a medium canter. As you approach the fence, put your leg on and open up the canter so your horse sails over like a bird. This will make it easy for him to make the spread.

*The approach to this spread is downhill, giving the canter impetus but requiring careful balance. This partnership makes a lovely jump over the fence*

Depending on how you went over the spread, either go on to the next fence – choose an upright – or repeat the spread and then go on to the next fence. An upright requires a controlled engaged canter. Adjust the canter after jumping the spread. This should be done subtly between fences.

Move on to another spread, such as a set of sloping rails. You need to approach this type of fence on a lengthening stride, but not too fast. It's important to keep looking ahead: keep your eyes up.

*Organize yourself before you start approaching the fence, rather than when you turn into it, otherwise you encourage your horse to rush*

# NARROW FENCES

On many cross-country courses you will find some form of arrowhead or narrow fence. It's important to practise jumping these types of fences so you are prepared when you are competing.

Before tackling your first narrow fence, test your accuracy by jumping a specific point on any fence. Practise this until you can do it easily, then jumping a narrow fence will be much easier. Collect the canter before the fence. If you approach too fast you will be less in control and more likely to have a run-out.

## ARROWS

Everything hinges on the turn and approach to arrowhead fences. If you get it wrong it may result in a run-out. Practise riding accurate turns to the fence, training your horse to stay straight, in a collected canter and jump in the middle of the fence. Keep looking at the fence on the approach so you get a good turn and ride straight.

If your horse tries to jump to one side or the other, it suggests that your turns are not accurate (see pp.177–180 and 186–187 for working on turns and accuracy). You could also carry a whip to tap him on the relevant shoulder to try to keep him straight. If you are practising in an arena, you can use other equipment to channel your horse to the correct spot, but he will eventually need to go straight without this help.

Keep an eye on your canter. Make sure it is not becoming flat in your attempts to get an accurate jump. Ride positively towards the fence.

*Two barrels at each side of this arrowhead channel the horse into jumping the pallet and barrel in the middle*

*Build a corner fence, making it quite narrow to begin with. Gradually make the corner wider so you can practise jumping accurately*

## CORNERS

A corner is another popular type of cross-country fence, used to test your accuracy and control. Corners can be re-created at home. Initially, make the jump quite narrow from front to back and practise jumping it accurately. If you do well, try jumping it closer to the outside edge to test your accuracy. Carry your whip in the relevant hand in case your horse tries to run out.

Gradually, make the corner wider by moving the wings apart. Again, the turn and approach are vital. Imagine there is another rail running down the middle of the corner. The line you want to take is 90 degrees to that rail.

# DITCHES MASTERCLASS

If you are planning to compete at cross country, you are bound to come across a variety of fences, some of which include a ditch in some shape or form. The sooner a young horse is introduced to ditches the better, as long as he has enough basic education to go forward when asked and stay straight.

Ditches are well known for causing difficulties, usually because the rider is tempted to look down into the ditch and this makes her nervous. The fear transmits to the horse and can cause him to become wary of this type of fence. The secret to jumping ditches is to keep looking up and ahead so your cross-country rounds become trouble-free.

The types of ditch you have available to you for practice will determine which of the following exercises you can try. However, the general advice is relevant to tackling most obstacles that include a ditch.

*Most cross-country courses have a ditch and it's easy to simulate one at home to practise over, simply using empty feed bags and poles on the ground. Approach in trot initially, as your horse may spook, and then canter, once he knows what he is being asked to do*

## THE CLASS

**1** Start with a simple rail fence with a ditch underneath. The one shown here is a relatively easy introduction. The rails form an ascending spread, making it easier to judge and jump. As long as the first rail is close to the ground and the majority of the ditch is covered up, the horse has no idea there is a ditch there at all, which will help him to jump it more confidently. Don't ride this type of fence any differently from other cross-country fences. Don't think: 'Will he?', think 'He will!'

Approach this fence with plenty of impulsion, so that if your horse backs off a little he will still have enough energy to jump it. Remember to allow him to use his head and neck as he jumps. Keep your arms soft, allowing them to move forward, and be giving with the contact.

Building up your horse's confidence over this type of fence will reap rewards when you come to negotiate more complex ditch fences.

### Test your know-how

**What is a coffin fence?**

A coffin fence generally consists of three elements: usually rails, followed by a ditch and then another set of rails. This type of fence tests the horse's boldness, agility and confidence. The degree of difficulty is dictated by:
• The siting of the fence
• The steepness of the slope on either side of the ditch
• The distances between the rails and the ditch
• The dimensions of the ditch
• The height of the rails
• The going

**2** Next try a plain ditch with no camouflage (right). A small natural ditch is often more appealing to jump than a man-made, lined one like this, which can look a little spooky. This one is approached on a downhill slope, so both horse and rider get a good look at it beforehand.

If your horse threatens to grind to a halt at this sort of obstacle, remember to keep using your legs. Don't push him as far as the ditch and then stop riding as he will wonder what's wrong. Keep your eyes forward and focused on the landing side; don't be tempted to look down into the ditch. If you need more confidence, imagine you are negotiating a spread fence, increasing the impulsion as you get closer to the fence (ask for a bolder trot or even a few strides of canter just before take-off). Repeat this ditch until you are popping over without any trouble. Eventually, you can approach in a controlled canter.

*Be ready to kick your horse on if he is tempted to stop in front of an open ditch*

**3** Now progress to a combination. The one here (bottom, right) is a coffin combination, approached downhill. A lot of cross-country courses include a rail-ditch-rail combination, and it is used to test your ability to approach in balance, with sufficient impulsion and at the correct speed. (If you are new to coffins, see Introducing coffins, p.204.) This one is a classic coffin with a set of rails in, one stride to the ditch, then another stride to the rails out. Because of the sloping ground into this particular coffin, the canter needs to be steady on the approach, as it may be slippery, but it must be forward going – otherwise the rider will not have enough impulsion to negotiate the rails.

Ride positively all the way through. Sit quietly but use your legs to make your horse go forwards. Don't be tempted to use your seat too hard as this will make him hollow.

*Remember to allow with your arms. Because this jump is new to her and a bit of a challenge, this horse really uses her neck to get over the fence – it is vital that she isn't restricted*

## INTRODUCING COFFINS

*When introducing a horse to a coffin combination for the first time it is best to do it in three stages:*

*• Pop over the ditch on its own*

*• Then jump the ditch and the rail out*

*• Finally, put all three elements together*

*Only move on to the next stage when your horse is confidently popping over the elements in the previous stage. Your approach is very important. The horse must be in balance and straight, and you should not approach too fast as the first element may be hiding the ditch, which your horse won't know is there. Approach in a good bouncy canter with impulsion so he will find it easy to jump.*

*The rider's position is also important – don't get ahead of the movement on the approach. Stay soft in the knee so your lower leg is secure, let your horse do the work and wait for him to take off before folding forwards. If anything does go wrong you are in a secure position and you can ride forwards positively. Always look up and ahead. As with all ditches – don't be tempted to look down into the ditch: where you look is where you go!*

**4** A trakehner (above) makes a good progression from a coffin jump. Trakehners are no more difficult than plain ditches – in fact they can be easier if you can make yourself focus on the rail, not the ditch. However, this type of fence is designed as a 'rider frightener' to confuse you about where you should be looking. Approach in a balanced canter with plenty of impulsion, keep looking ahead and your horse will produce a confident jump.

This trakehner is situated off a right-hand turn on level ground. It consists of a telegraph pole over a lined ditch. Sit up and ride forward round the corner and ride positively toward the middle of the fence. Remember to keep looking up!

### Trakeheners

This type of fence is most often a telegraph pole or log placed on an angle over a ditch. There are various factors that will make it more difficult:

• The approach to the fence
• The size of the ditch and whether it is lined or natural
• The thickness of the log or rail

## GETTING IT RIGHT

Blyth Tait suggests you need to treat open ditches like spread fences. It's really important not to approach them too fast or you will startle your horse and this will lead to difficulties. Take time to build up his confidence over ditches — as well as your own. He should answer your leg and jump over the ditch in a smooth and flowing action. Initially, you should approach in trot and take up a steady canter about five or six strides away.

A rail with a ditch in front should be treated as a parallel. Close your legs on the approach to encourage your horse to lengthen the stride and he will find it easy to jump the fence. Remember to keep looking up and ahead not down into the ditch.

*Be prepared for a big jump and be ready to let your horse use his whole body to get over if he needs to. After a few repetitions he will not want to work as hard as this*

*Fences before or after a ditch can be easier, as you and your horse tend to focus on the fence rather than the ditch*

# DROPS AND STEPS

Drops and steps are popular with cross-country course designers and they really test the partnership you have with your horse, as well as your ability to stay balanced and keeping a contact while allowing your horse the freedom he needs to jump downwards. Drop jumps that are positioned at the top of a slope which goes downwards again after the jump are particularly challenging as you are asking your horse to jump into space. However, with a careful build-up to these advanced fences and plenty of practice, your horse should be quite happy to do them for you. Most water jumps are forms of drop fences (see pp.208–209), but need a slightly different introduction because of the added element – water.

## INTRODUCING DROPS

When you introduce your horse to drops, start small and build up in size as he progresses and becomes more confident. Initially approach drop fences at the trot and simply ask your horse to step down. This is why you should start small. When your horse has worked out what is required you can start to approach in canter. Make sure that you have a steady canter and that as you reach the drop you come slightly behind the movement. This stops you from overbalancing your horse as he drops down. Practise various types of drop fences, such as steps, so you learn to approach them with the correct amount of impulsion to jump easily.

*For success over this small drop you need to go with your horse, keeping yourself organized while letting him do his job*

## TIPS FOR RIDING STEPS

### DOWNHILL STEPS

• *Start by introducing your horse to one step down.*

• *Approach in either a collected canter or trot. Ensure that your approach is straight and keep on looking straight ahead.*

• *As your horse drops off the step, allow him to stretch his head and neck.*

• *Don't allow your body to be pulled forward*

– *keep your lower leg forward with your weight in your heels.*

• *Once you are confident you can move onto riding down several steps.*

### UPHILL STEPS

• *Approach uphill steps with plenty of energy so your horse can jump up them easily.*

• *As he jumps up each step he may land a bit shorter, so you need to keep using your leg to push him forwards.*

• *Angle your weight slightly forwards up each step to help him jump and keep looking forwards where you want to go.*

• *It is even more important to keep you eyes focusing ahead if there is another fence to jump after the steps. Looking ahead will help you ride accurately to the next obstacle.*

## STEPS UP AND DOWN

To step down, begin by approaching in trot. Make sure it's a balanced trot and not too rushed, and allow your shoulders to go forwards as you go down each step. When your horse knows what to do, he will find small steps quite easy to pop down.

The technique for steps up is, of course, different to steps down. Your horse will tend to leap up steps individually but it is easier for him if you can keep him in a flowing canter by keeping your leg on so that he doesn't lose impetus. Be positive. Remember again to allow with your arms. Don't use your hands to balance yourself on his back.

*Practise adjusting your position as you jump up and down steps, while remaining in balance. Think about how you might use your body to run up and down stairs and allow your horse the freedom he needs to do the same*

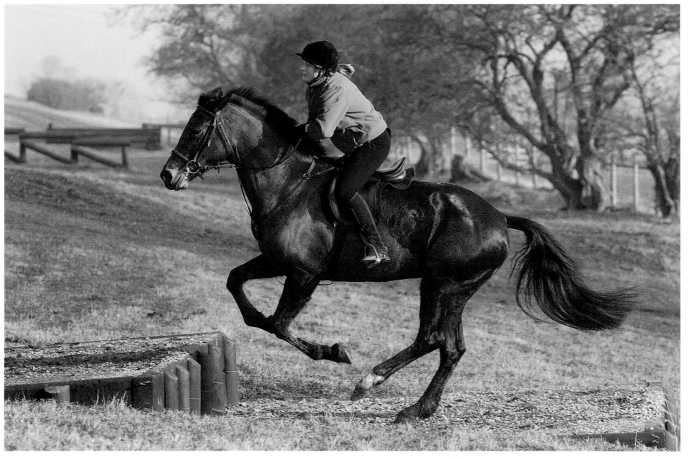

# DROP COMBINATIONS

Cross-country fences are rarely simply straightforward steps or drops. Builders often combine drops with fences, such as a drop to an arrowhead, or a bank then drop then step up combination. These fences are designed to test your versatility and impulsion as you have to be thinking about riding out of the combination while you are entering it, making sure that you can adjust your horse's canter and keep him going throughout. Water jumps (opposite) are among the most challenging of drop combinations.

*This combination consists of jumping up onto a bank then a jump off the bank, two strides and up again. The jumps up can be looked upon as upright fences. You want to spring up the step, so you need plenty of impulsion. As you jump up, keep your seat out of the saddle with your weight in your stirrups. This will give your horse the freedom in his back to jump up the step. As you step down, land with your weight in your stirrups and keep focusing ahead to the next element*

*A drop to an arrowhead is a tough question – you need to be absolutely straight as you come off the bank otherwise you have no chance of making the arrowhead*

# WATER

At the big cross-country events the water jump is always popular with spectators. Perhaps it's because they like the splash of the water on a warm day, or maybe it's because they know that plenty of cross-country riders find water a bit of a challenge. Horses always seem to know what's coming and can sense the rider thinking, 'Please don't let me get wet today.' They don't stop to cause trouble, but just because the rider's thought introduces a hesitation in their riding and a horse is extremely sensitive to this. However, there is no reason for a horse not to perform well into water. As with everything else, it's a matter of introducing him to it slowly and building his confidence before you start jumping into it.

## MAKING A START

Begin by walking in and out of the water before asking your horse to trot then canter. Let him get used to the splashing around his legs. It is important that it doesn't put him off his stride. It may take several schooling sessions before he is confident enough to jump in and out. Until then play around in the water, focusing on keeping him balanced and not allowing his stride to become long and flat. (See also Water, pp.236–237.)

## JUMPING THROUGH WATER

When you feel he is ready to take a water jump, you can try a small step into it. Remember how you rode down the steps. Keep the contact and encourage your horse forward with your legs. Watch out for your horse getting keen at this point. He may decide he knows what's required and stop listening to you. Keep control. Don't let him run – you need to keep him balanced.

Continue in stages. Introduce a step out – prepare for this as soon as you land in the water. Gather your horse together and push him into the step. Now combine a step in with a step out. Try a small log into the water and out up a step.

It is easy to become a bit untidy when negotiating water jumps so you need to practise being organized, keeping a contact, especially to a step, as some horses can misjudge a jump out of water if their stride has become too long.

*Make sure your horse is happy going through in walk, trot and canter before you try jumping in and out of water*

# COMPETITION AND CONFIDENCE

Jumping is a very popular equestrian sport. It's fast and fun, but it can also be frustrating. There are plenty of riders who enjoy jumping practice at home and do quite well but find it all falls to pieces when they enter a competition. It might be their nerves or it might be that the horse is distracted. Among the most common problems are a lack of confidence, either in the rider or in the horse, stopping, running out and rushing. If you are finding that your jumping performance is not as good as you would like, the information provided throughout this chapter should be enough to enable you decide where your problem lies and begin to work towards a solution. These two pages feature some key problems and training suggestions, which might help you to get to the heart of your jumping.

## RUSHING AND REFUSING

**Q** I own a 14.2hh Connemara x Thoroughbred mare who is an experienced jumping pony. She rushes towards her fences and is very fast over jumps. However, as soon as a filler is added she refuses.

**A** Even though your pony is fast, pace will not get you safely and accurately over a fence unless you are actually working her from your leg. Try setting up a line of canter poles 3.35–3.65m (11–12ft) apart and practise cantering over them, without looking down. If your pony rushes, repeat the exercise until she settles. All the time, ride her from your leg into a consistent contact so she learns that you are not going to throw the reins away and abandon her. Until she accepts that it is your leg that tells her to go forwards, you are unlikely to make any progress.

Try hard to keep the same rhythm and pace, even if it's on the fast side, so that the canter feels the same whether you are going over the poles or not. When you have established a working canter and feel that you are a partner rather than a passenger, start jumping some fences. It is very important to keep your leg on into the fence, however fast you are going. You are looking for power rather than pace and you won't get it without enough leg.

When you introduce a filler, try to make it small enough so that you can jump it from a standstill if necessary. Keep your leg on all the way to the fence, and don't look down or drop your contact. If your pony stops, don't get agitated or turn away, just encourage her to pop over from a standstill. If you let her know there is no other option, she will get into the habit of accepting your wishes and getting on with the job.

## GET IN BALANCE

- If you think you may be interfering with your horse's jump, try this exercise to improve your jumping position:
- Put a neck strap on your horse and stand in your stirrups when you trot. Hang on to the neck strap so that you don't catch your horse in the mouth.
- Think about letting all your weight hang from the stirrup bars. Imagine three-quarters of your weight being below the waist.
- As your horse trots be conscious of allowing all the hinges in your body to soften and relax. Your ankles, knees and hips should all be acting as effective shock absorbers, enabling your lower leg to stay in position.
- If all your weight is in the stirrups, balancing to the trot should really increase your joints' flexibility, making it physically difficult for your lower leg to slide out of position.

*Rushing and refusing are common in horses that lack technique and don't listen to their rider*

## STAGE FRIGHT

**Q** My 10-year-old Welsh gelding refuses to enter the ring when we go show jumping. He kicks up a huge fuss – going backwards and sometimes even rearing. He is stubborn and strong-willed by nature and I know he's not in any pain. Once he's in the ring (I have to get off and lead him in) he loves it and usually goes clear. I'm now having to cancel my regular shows because of this behaviour. Help!

**A** What a pity your gelding has this little quirk which is making your show-jumping performance a bit of a lottery. There is no logic in this behaviour, but it is happening too often for it to be a momentary lapse and is becoming a serious nap. If, at the moment, the only way to get him into the ring is to lead him, then do it. It would be sensible to have a word with the judges first and let them know your difficulty. It would also be useful to be followed in by someone to give you a leg up.

Make sure you are sensible in the collecting ring and don't let him get planted at the entrance. Hang back and walk about until it is actually time to go in and hope that he keeps on moving. Don't chat to anyone or walk round the collecting ring with a friend – this would give him a chance to hang towards the other horse. Make sure you are independent and keep his attention on you at all times.

## HE RUNS OUT

**Q** My horse jumps well at home but often runs out at fences when we enter a competition, especially the first fence. He always feels tense and nervous when we enter the ring, however he jumps nicely in the practice arena. What can I do?

**A** Obviously something is going wrong when you and your horse get in the ring. When you say he is tense, ask yourself why – is he anxious? Is it because you are giving him different signals at a show? Is your show kit unfamiliar? Perhaps he jumps well in the practice ring because you are more relaxed? The running out may be due to your riding – horses only run out because they can. If you hold him right to the fence he might stop, but he would not be able to nip out of the side door.

Here are some suggestions:
• Get kitted up in your competition gear when you school at home: make sure your horse is familiar with all of it, including his tack.
• At home, practise jumping lots of pretend 'first' fences. Work out a warning system so that your horse knows he is about to be asked to jump. Having a warning system ensures your horse is ready to go when the start bell is rung. When practising at home, before you approach your first fence, do something: touch your boot or your horse's shoulder with your stick – as a signal. If you do this four or five strides away from every first fence you come to at home, your horse will be ready to go over it. Use the same signal in the ring.
• Hire an unfamiliar arena and practise all these ideas in a different place, but without the pressure of a show environment.

*Napping is an annoying habit that needs consistent work to overcome*

*With regular practise and a well-structured training programme, both you and your horse should relish your jumping experiences*

# OUT AND ABOUT

An enormous number of riders keep a horse (or borrow someone else's) simply to have the enjoyment of going out for a hack. One of the greatest pleasures in life is riding down a country lane, along a bridlepath or across an open space on a warm day with the birds singing, the sun shining and your horse willingly walking, trotting or cantering underneath you. This is when all that hard work in the yard pays off – or does it? Few of us can claim to have the perfect horse, and even if we mostly have a wonderful time out on the trails, there are usually one or two things that we wish our horse would do better, or that he wouldn't do at all. As well as giving you some advice on fitness and competing, this section focuses on some of the less fun aspects of hacking and how to overcome them.

# WORKING ON FITNESS

If you've ever reached the top of the stairs puffing and panting, you'll know that being out of shape is no fun. And it's simply not fair to expect a horse to work hard without building him up gradually so he becomes accustomed to the extra exertion. Not only will your horse find his work more enjoyable if he's in good physical condition, but he'll be able to concentrate more on what you're asking him to do. Being toned and strong puts far less strain on a horse's heart, lungs and legs, and greatly reduces the risk of injury.

Whatever the reason for his lack of fitness, the first couple of months in a horse's training regime are crucial. It is then that muscle is developed, legs are hardened and the heart and lungs are strengthened for longer, faster work (see also pp.10–13). Any hurrying or cutting corners can result in injury, so it's well worth taking your time and doing the job properly.

*As you and your horse grow fitter you'll build a close bond and he'll develop the trust to do as you ask him*

## Why *hack* for fitness?

Allowing your horse to see the world and learn to cope with it has huge benefits in any discipline, from endurance to showing. Coping with natural hazards such as hills, uneven terrain and water teaches a horse to think for himself while at the same time building a good working relationship between you. Hacking gives you time to get to know each other in an unpressurized environment. It will also give your horse a change of scene if he's worked hard over the competition season and perhaps become a bit stale.

## BEFORE YOU BEGIN

Make sure that your horse's feet and teeth are in good condition and that he is generally sound and in good health before embarking on a fitness programme. If you have any qualms about any aspect of his health, consult a vet beforehand. This programme is unsuitable for a horse under six years old, as it is easy to overwork a youngster and cause problems later in life. If you have an oldish horse, be very considerate about his needs and stay alert to any signs that he is not coping.

You must also be sure that all your horse's tack fits well and is comfortable. This goes for all riding, of course. A horse cannot work properly if he is being pinched or rubbed by an item of tack.

## WHERE TO START

The first step is to establish your horse's current condition. Is he starting from scratch or already able to cope with a reasonable workload?

• A horse that's spent the last few months in his field with just the odd trip out at the weekend is likely to be in a 'soft' condition, which means he has little strength, stamina or muscle tone – start at 1 (overleaf).

• A horse that's been busy over recent months but only because he's been working in the indoor school won't be accustomed to hacking and may find road work, longer distances or difficult terrain more of a problem than you imagine – start at 1.

• A horse that has been in regular, varied work will have a reasonable level of fitness – compare his daily schedule with the programme descriptions to find out the best point for you to start.

*If your horse has been doing a reasonable amount of hacking out, he may already be quite fit*

### Measuring progress

• To monitor his fitness, record your horse's pulse, temperature and respiration at rest, and his weight (see pp.12–13). Record these on a weekly basis – it will help you check your progress and decide whether you are progressing at a fair rate, too fast or too slow.

• Do exactly the same ride once a fortnight, at the same pace, noting how your horse copes. Take his pulse before you untack him, allowing for any change in weather that might make the ride harder. Then take the pulse again five minutes later. The quicker it falls to his base (resting) rate, the fitter the horse.

• Watch your horse's general appearance – he should have a healthy bloom to his coat and a bright, alert attitude.

# THE PROGRAMME

Although the suggested exercise rates here should be acceptable for most horses, you know your horse best. Tailor the programme to suit him and beware of expecting too much too soon.

### 1 Walking – 30 minutes, increasing to one hour

Half-an-hour of good walking is ample for the first few outings. Aim for an active and engaged walk on a long rein, making sure your horse is swinging along. Just sit quietly, encouraging him if necessary with a schooling whip or a pair of short spurs rather than nagging him every step of the way. Keep your hands steady but soft.

Work your horse five days a week, lengthening the duration by 10 minutes or so at a time until you are walking for an hour. This could take around three weeks with a completely unfit horse.

Keep a close eye on how your horse is shaping up. He should be relaxed but interested when out and about, and cool on his return to the yard. Check for rubs, sores, lumps and swellings as you groom him after returning from each ride.

### 2 Trotting – one hour of walking, building in short periods of trot

The next step is to introduce short periods of trot into your hour of exercise. Stick to a couple of minutes at a time to begin with, building it up gradually. By week four or five you should be covering 9.5km (6 miles) within an hour, which equates to an active walk interspersed with a few trots. To calculate the distance, take a piece of thread and a map of your hacking area and work out a 9.5km (6 mile) route from home. Then see how long it takes you to complete it. Calculate a few different routes with varying terrain.

*Build in short periods of trot in week two or three, depending on your horse*

Begin to incorporate some hills. Hills are hard work, so walk up to start with. If your horse finds it easier, allow him to trot and let him walk on a long rein at the top to get his breath.

Tailor your programme to your local terrain. Hilly areas can really take it out of a horse so you may have to go a bit easier. Similarly, road work is more tiring than work on springy ground, so build up the trot very gradually if you're doing a lot on tarmac or a hard, stony surface.

### 3 Upping the pace – 10 minutes of trotting within the hour, working up to 1¼ hours in total

As you move into week six, build up your trotting to a good 10 minutes in the hour, allowing your horse to move on at an active but collected pace.

If all is going well, increase the length of your hack each outing until they last 1¼ hours, incorporating longer periods of trot. Within that time your horse should be covering 13km (8 miles) without too much effort.

Pay attention to how he behaves when he returns home. You're aiming for a happy, relaxed attitude, not the look of a horse that's just done a marathon.

## UP A GEAR

If all the signs are good that your horse is happy with his workload, it's time to push on. Over the next few weeks you can take your horse from a basic level of fitness to a stage where he really is fully muscled and raring to go.

Even the most careful programme can be interrupted by unexpected health troubles. Don't panic at a sign of illness or injury. Investigate the problem thoroughly and seek expert advice if necessary. Never be tempted to press on with the training regardless.

*When you introduce canters, keep them to short, calm bursts to begin with*

### 4 Introducing canter – plenty of trot and one or two short canters in a 1¼-hour outing

Introduce canter for just a couple of minutes at a time at first, aiming for a springy, controlled pace. Try to remain balanced in the saddle and keep your contact light and steady. Excess movement on your part will only make the job harder for your horse.

### 5 Longer distances – building up to 1½ hours

Increase the canter gradually. You should now be doing longer periods of trot and canter, interspersed with shorter recovery periods at walk. A good day's work will by now consist of a 1½-hour ride incorporating all three paces, with your horse moving forwards at around 13–16kmph (8–10mph).

## WARMING UP AND COOLING DOWN

He may not be doing much activity in the early stages, but your horse still needs to be loosened up before he exerts himself. When you leave the yard, walk actively for a good 10 minutes and always start your trot at a gentle pace.

As horses get fitter, they can get fresh and impatient to move up a gear. How you deal with this is up to you, but if it's safe to do so, it is a good idea to allow your horse to trot on gently for a few minutes to settle. It will give him more to think about and you are asking him to do something rather than saying no all the time.

Arriving back at the yard cool is a must, so walk the last mile home to let your horse wind down.

*As long as the water isn't stagnant, let your horse drink if he wants to when out on a hack*

## TROUBLESHOOTING

• **Jogging** (see p.241).
• **Napping** (see pp.232–233).
• **Lameness** – Typical problems include bruised soles or corns, both of which your farrier can help sort out. Windgalls can occur with increased work but the effects are usually just cosmetic. Ask your vet about anything more persistent that is worrying you.
• **Overtraining** – We all have off-days and a horse is the same. If he has become a little jaded, he may benefit from a holiday with a couple of days' turnout. (In any case, when your horse is really fit he will benefit from as much turnout time as possible.) If he's still lethargic, reassess his training and diet. Consult your vet if he fails to perk up after a short break.
• **Tack** – Your horse will be muscling up and changing shape, so check the fit of your saddle regularly. Deal with rubs as soon as you see them. Check his mouth for bit sores and alter your bit if necessary. Keep all saddlery and accessories clean and supple.
• **Drinking** – If the water is clean, allow your horse to drink when he wants to when out hacking. There's more danger in denying him water and then letting him gulp down a full bucket when he gets home. If your horse drinks from a cold stream, go steady for a few minutes to allow the water in his gut to warm up.
• **Boredom** – Avoid the onset of any behavioural problems by varying the route and the direction you go in, and riding out both alone and in company.

> **Sample weekly workout**
>
> **Day 1** Mixed ride including trot and canter – 1½ hours.
> **Day 2** Mixed ride including trot and canter – 1½ hours.
> **Day 3** Hill work: just hills, walking up and down – 1 hour.
> **Day 4** Rest and turnout.
> **Day 5** Mixed ride including trot and canter – 1½ hours.
> **Day 6** Long ride – 2–2½ hours.
> **Day 7** Rest and turnout.

*If you can ride on a beach, stay half a metre or so above the waterline. This reduces concussion during fast work. You get wet but that's half the fun*

# SPEED

We invest a lot of time and money improving our riding on the flat and over fences, but spend little or no time on what is potentially the most dangerous aspect – riding at speed. However, it is possible to train your horse to gallop without pulling or running away. Trainer Mark Smith uses the techniques described here, having developed them mainly from his racing days. He encourages his pupils to spend time watching some of the racing greats – in particular Frankie Dettori.

'Frankie has a fantastic technique and constantly watches his races back and practises on a mechanical horse to improve his riding,' says Mark. 'He uses his body position to influence the speed of the horse, keeping him steady at the start of a race with his bottom up out of the saddle. If he wants the horse to go faster, he'll lower his bottom closer to the saddle, then at the end of the race he stands up and lets the reins go longer so the horse steadies naturally.'

Mark explains that incorporating fast work into your riding programme will improve both your fitness and that of your horse. This is important as an unfit horse and rider will both lack control over their bodies – which is vital if you're riding cross country.

## Safety first

If you can't canter in control in an arena then don't attempt it in an open space, and get help from a good instructor. If your horse is strong when you canter you need to break the cycle. Horses are creatures of habit; with the right training, they soon learn that going slowly is an option. But it's important when you first take your horse into an open space that you don't rush things. Do some trotting first, so your horse learns that he isn't always going to bomb off. Once you're happy with this, quietly ask him to canter.

*Fast work can be exhilarating, and if you train your horse to do it well slowing down won't be a battle*

## FOCUS ON POSITION

Your position is crucial when you're travelling at speed, especially with regards to your lower leg. If this is correct then you'll have control over the rest of your body. Practise riding with short stirrups to build up the strength in your calf muscles. When you're out hacking, ride with your stirrups short and trot standing up so you encourage the weight into your heels. Trotting like this softens your ankles, which are your shock absorbers when you land over a fence. You want the weight to come down the back of your leg. If your knee creeps forward your lower leg falls back, making your position insecure.

It's so easy to unbalance a horse by using too much hand. When we're training on the flat our aim is to use really subtle aids, so why do we forget this when we go cross country? Use your body weight to keep your horse steady and don't be tempted to get into a pulling match – you must have the confidence to release the contact. Don't give him the option to fight you – remember it takes two to pull. The more you can take the pressure off his mouth the better. Using a half-halt is an effective way to regain control – ask and then soften on the reins, repeating this until he learns to stay in control.

When you're riding in a forward seat try to keep your shoulders over your knees. If you let your shoulders get too far forward it makes your position unstable and you're more likely to fall off should your horse spook. Keep your hands low – it is better to keep a finger in a neck strap than to bridge the reins.

Don't ride with your reins too short. Short reins don't give greater control, and if your reins are too short you can have a tendency to get in front of your horse, and again you risk falling off if you get into trouble over a fence. You need a good length of rein to give your horse the chance to use his head and neck when he jumps. If you ride with your reins too short he can't do this.

*By standing in your stirrups when trotting you can improve your balance and body-weight distribution*

## USE YOUR BODY

During his clinics, Mark Smith uses the lunge to enable riders to learn to use their body weight, rather than their reins, to control their horse's speed. To encourage a horse to trot on, you need to bring your hips forward more as you rise. If you want to slow down, you should make your rising more upright.

Changing the position of your shoulders (putting them back) will also influence your horse's speed, and closing your knees will help to slow him.

Practise this on the lunge with your reins removed so you're not tempted to use them. For safety reasons use a neck strap so that you can steady yourself if you lose balance.

Make sure you're the one giving the commands. Have a couple of markers in the arena – for instance plastic jumping blocks. The person holding the lunge line can then ask you to change pace at the markers to check that the horse is listening to your aids.

*Learn to use your body to control your speed*

# GETTING A FEEL FOR SPEED

Riders often do too much when they're galloping. It's common to see them hauling their horses about trying to get them to slow before a cross-country fence.

'Learn to be more of a passenger,' says Mark. 'I teach riders to create a "speedo" in their head so they know when they're travelling at the right speed.'

This is quite easy to do. First, check what speed you need to be going at – for example, at British Eventing Intro level, for the cross-country phase the speed is 450m per minute. Measure a distance of 450m and put a couple of markers at the start and finish to help you. It might be useful also to have a helper on the ground with a stopwatch.

Most riders go too slowly over the 450m distance when they first start. If you find this is you, try lowering your body slightly closer to your horse to encourage him to go faster.

You can also use this exercise to practise using your body position to influence your horse's speed. As you're cantering, practise keeping your upper body upright to steady him. When you want him to go faster, lower your body closer to him, then come more upright to slow again. Keep repeating this until you're both happy and your horse comes back to you with little or no pressure on the reins.

It may take time to get the correct feeling of riding at the right speed, so keep practising. Once you're covering the distance in the right time, practise in an arena. Depending on the size of the arena, work out how many times you need to canter round to cover 450m – then time yourself.

Once you're happy with this, put a ground pole along one of the long sides to pop over, then make it into a small fence. Before you know it you'll be jumping the fence out of a great rhythm – and at the correct speed. After all this training, all you need to do now is go and have fun riding safely at speed!

*Stay upright to steady your horse...*

*...and lower your body to go faster*

# TRAFFIC

Riding out in traffic can be a dangerous affair. You wouldn't dream of letting a dog loose on a busy stretch of road, no matter how well trained he was, yet every day hundreds of horses are ridden close to cars, lorries and tractors. It's asking a lot of a flight animal to cope with the noise, size and close proximity of traffic, so it's vital that you train him properly. Here's a quick, sobering reminder of why it's so important: there are over 3,000 road accidents in the UK involving horses annually – mostly on minor roads. Around five riders are killed on the road each year and, with roads becoming busier and faster all the time, it doesn't take much to work out that riding a spooky horse in traffic is dangerous.

A busy road is not the place to teach your horse road sense, especially as many motorists don't know how to pass a horse safely. School him at home, in the yard, manège, and on quiet tracks. Taking the time to do the groundwork somewhere safe will help to eliminate any unpleasant experiences for you and your horse when you do venture onto the road.

## LET HIM LEARN

• *Hacking along bridleways is a good way to get a young or nervous horse used to different sights. If your local bridleways are only accessible via roads, box or trailer your horse to an area where there's plenty of off-road hacking.*

• *Keeping your horse in a field close to a main road, or stabling him at a noisy farmyard is a good way to condition him to the sight and noise of traffic. Indeed, teaching him to tolerate any strange noise – for example the sound of clippers – will help to get him used to the odd noises he'll hear out on the roads.*

• *Within reason, don't try to wrap your horse up in cotton wool, the more he sees and hears of the world – with you giving him the courage to accept it all – the more bombproof he will become.*

*Always wear highly visible kit when riding on the roads. Even on bright sunny days it can be difficult for drivers to make out a rider on a dark horse in the shade. Most high-vis gear is light and easy to wear for you or the horse – there is no good excuse not to use it!*

## YOUNG AND OLD

Youngsters have no reason to fear the roads unless they get a scare or you expose them to too much too soon. So training a youngster to accept traffic is quite straightforward. Trying to rebuild an older horse's confidence on the roads can be much more tricky. It's certainly far more difficult than training a young horse to accept traffic for the first time. The advice here can be applied to both youngsters and older horses. With both types take it slowly and be prepared to backtrack if necessary. With older horses you may need to take more time to really instil in them that there is nothing to fear.

## WORKING ON ROAD SENSE

If there's a quiet farm track leading from your horse's yard, this is a perfect place to start teaching your horse to accept traffic. Failing that, make use of an empty paddock or manège. Limit each training session to half an hour and aim for lots of small goals that you can reward, as this will help to build your horse's confidence.

Once you've chosen a safe place, set up a series of hazards – a parked car or roadworking signs, for example – and ride past them. If your horse is really worried about traffic, he may be wary of the stationary car, so treat it as you would any other spooky object and let him have a good look.

Once he is happy to pass the stationary vehicle, ask a friend to start the engine and ride past it carefully again. Take this training one step at a time – never take unnecessary risks. When he has accepted the running engine, progress to having the car moving slowly, then have the car passing the horse. This may take a few sessions, but once your horse has accepted a car going past at a slow speed you can consider introducing bigger, noisier vehicles.

Working in a controlled environment like this will build your horse's confidence. You'll soon get a feel for how much he can tolerate, so bear this in mind and never push him so far he feels he has to run away from the problem. As long as he doesn't get a scare, he'll soon learn that there's nothing to worry about.

*Teach your horse to be happy about passing a parked car in a safe environment*

## PUTTING YOUR TRAINING TO THE TEST

When you feel your horse is ready to cope with road work, choose the route carefully – lanes with flat, wide verges are best. Not only should the traffic be lighter and slower moving, your horse will gain confidence from having plenty of space between him and the traffic. If he is used to being long lined (pp.57–59), you can long line him along the verge first, with an

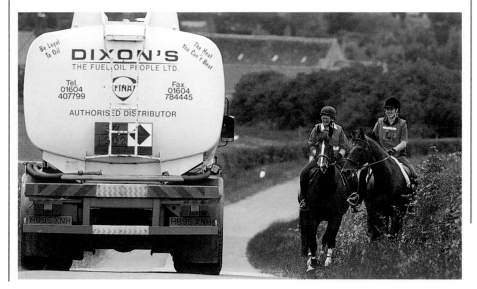

*Wide verges and back lanes are a good combination for early road work. Most lorry drivers are very considerate when passing horses*

223

experienced friend standing at his head. Alternatively, ride him and ask an experienced rider with a quiet schoolmaster to accompany you, and position yourself on their inside. Eventually you will be able to progress to riding out alone along quiet lanes. Keep these outings short to begin with, perhaps asking a friend to drive slowly by, to ensure all your work has paid off.

## PROBLEM SOLVER

**Q** I have a very serious problem with my horse, she is terrified of motorbikes. If she sees one she bolts, spins or tries to run away. It doesn't matter if they are still, going past or have the engine turned off – she goes into a blind panic and doesn't care about anything but getting away. She has never been hit by a bike, it just seems to be a phobia which has escalated out of control. I have friends with bikes and wonder if it would help if we put one in the school or leave one outside her stable, but I don't want to make matters any worse. Can you help?

**A** This problem could take some time to rectify and your mare may never be 100% with motorbikes. You should try hacking her out in company as this gives you someone to go between your horse and the traffic when a motorbike is passing. Your horse should feel more secure in company and, with the protection of the other horse, she may eventually learn to accept the bikes.

*On your road rides, take a friend with a traffic-proof horse and ask them to ride to your outside. This will give your horse confidence and prevent her from tangling with the traffic*

Be careful not to tense up at the thought of approaching motorbikes. Horses are extremely sensitive and she will pick up on your nerves and think that something is going to happen. Try to wrap your legs around her and ride her forward into the reins. Encourage her with your voice if it helps but don't stop riding her forwards. Even if she goes past fast and tense, this is a starting point. Slow her down again and praise her.

Your friends' bikes may help. You could try parking one in a safe area of the yard so that your horse has to pass it each day. I don't advise putting one in the school while you're riding, this could be dangerous for both you and your horse. You will need to be very careful where you put the bike for your own, and everyone else's, safety.

*Before long you will be able to venture out on short road hacks alone*

# SPOOKING

Have you ever noticed how your horse sees things that you do not? You can be riding down the road and, for no apparent reason, he suddenly leaps out from underneath you. Horses are flight animals, and it's their instinct to be on the lookout for danger. Despite domestication, this instinct stays with them, just as when you hear a loud bang it makes you jump. However, while we forgive ourselves for jumping, when a horse leaps out of the way, the rider often punishes him, which only confirms to the horse that he is in a serious position. This does nothing to help the situation; in fact it can heighten his spookiness and make him even more wary.

## STOPPING IT HAPPENING

The key to coping with spooking is to pay close attention to your horse. You will notice that before he spooks, he gives you a warning signal that something is wrong. You need to tune into your horse to be able to spot the sign, as it may be quite small. He might prick his ears more sharply or tighten in his neck. This is your signal to respond and put his focus elsewhere before he has the time to jump sideways.

*You both know it's scary but as the rider you need to pretend that you aren't at all worried. You horse will be looking for reassurance and confidence from you – don't let him down*

You can do a lot to influence your horse's state of mind by dealing with your own. If you tighten up, the horse will too. The first step is to be aware of when you do this, and do something different. You need to remain as calm as you can, and you can achieve this is by keeping your breathing rate regular. It's all too easy to pre-empt the horse's spook by holding your breath, which will make your body tense, sending a message that says, 'Danger ahead!' Instead, keep breathing and look in another direction, preferably the one in which you want to go.

*Remember car drivers don't know that a horse might leap sideways at the sight of a small plastic bag. If your horse is going to be really upset wait for traffic to pass you before you pass the bag – better still, train your horse not to be afraid somewhere safe*

If your horse spooks in the school, try this exercise. Pick a line to ride that goes past the troublesome object but is far enough away that he is not going to have a big reaction. Trot past the object with his head, and your attention, turned away from it. The idea is to get his body closer to the object without forcing him to look at it. When he has gone past comfortably, give him a pat. Next time, pick a line a couple of metres closer, and the next time, get closer still. Each time, pat him to reassure him that he has done well to go past. If he reacts, go back to a line further away.

In a school situation most horses soon relax and accept whatever is frightening them, and you will then have a horse that is mentally ready to start work. Like all training, this requires patience. A few minutes spent acclimatizing your horse to spooky objects before you start schooling will prevent the whole session turning into an argument. Remember that riding lateral movements, both in the school and out hacking, will help keep your horse's attention on you, which gives him less time for spooking. Shoulder-in is the most useful anti-spook exercise there is. Bend your horse away from the frightening object, whether it is real or a figment of his imagination, not towards it.

*Teaching your horse a variety of lateral movements – here leg yield – will be useful when you want to regain his attention and stop him spooking*

## CHECK YOUR RIDING

To avoid being unseated by spooking, you need to sit well at all times, so that you are always ready (or as ready as you can be) for whatever your horse decides to do. If you're stiff in your lower back, or tight in your seat muscles, there'll be loss of flexibility in your leg joints. This means you'll lose the shock-absorber effect in your lower body – an essential for you to be able to stay in balance if your horse spooks.

Aim to keep a soft contact through your reins at all times too. If your reins go loose, your horse may seize the opportunity to spook – only you know how likely this is. So ride him into the bridle, by closing both legs all the way down, and sit up, staying firm through your stomach and lumbar region. Keep your elbows by your sides and maintain a steady contact without pulling back. Have your hands closed around the reins but don't grip too tightly.

## BUILDING A BOND

Now you know how to cope with a spook when it happens, or how to stop it happening when it's imminent, but wouldn't it be great if your horse trusted you so much that he never considered spooking at all? In order to train your horse to overcome his natural flight instincts and to school him to perform effectively in other spheres, you need to begin by building a bond with him. This means spending time with him in the field, grooming him and observing and learning from his natural behaviour. Be fair but firm whenever you handle him, and teach him that you're the boss and what you say goes. This doesn't mean smacking him every time he does something wrong, but instead praising him to show him when he's done something right.

All horses have a strong herd instinct and seek safety in numbers, so it's up to you to establish yourself as your horse's herd leader. In the wild,

### In an emergency

Schooling exercises can help you to get out of a sticky situation you encounter on the road…

• Shoulder-in is useful if your horse spooks. If he's spooking at something on the verge, flex him away from the kerb or hedge, so his shoulders move towards the middle of the road. Keep your right leg on the girth, so you're pushing your horse onto the left rein. This will reduce the risk of him jumping into the traffic.

• Leg yielding will help him become more manoeuvrable, so you can move safely around stationary objects such as skips and cars.

• Turn on the forehand is great for grabbing your horse's attention and encouraging him to move forwards when he's being stubborn and difficult. When your horse performs a turn on the forehand he crosses his hind legs and this makes it difficult for him to stay still or back up.

• Asking for a few steps sideways can also help to encourage a stubborn horse forwards.

horses trust and obey their leader because their life depends on it. Your horse has to know that he can trust you, and that you'll make the right decisions for him. When you ease him on past that flapping bag he needs to know that he's not going to get pounced on and eaten!

If your horse doesn't quite trust you yet, using an older, steady horse as a companion whenever you ride out is a good interim measure. It's a great way to help build his confidence – he'll want to stay with the other horse as he'll feel safer in a group and, if the other horse doesn't spook when he sees a stray bag or dustbin, then your horse will start to realize that he's not in danger.

## DESENSITIZATION

Your horse will only react defensively (spook or bolt) if he feels threatened – and he'll feel threatened when he's pushed beyond his comfort zone. It's your job as his rider and trainer to establish where his comfort zone ends, and what pushes him over the edge. Horses like familiarity, and it's when they're faced with something new or unexpected that they often resist and react with what we see as irrational, spooky behaviour.

You can gain a good idea of what worries your horse by how he behaves when he comes across various objects and obstacles on a hack. You can then work on desensitizing him to these things. To do this you need to gently and safely push him past his comfort zone – he won't become brave if you avoid what scares him. This doesn't mean turning him into a nervous wreck and scaring him, but pushing him until he's just a bit nervous and unsure, allowing him time to accept the object and then praising him warmly.

*Be prepared to push your horse slightly outside of his comfort zone to enable him to gain in confidence*

Never push so hard that your horse can't cope with the desensitization process, and end each training session on a positive note. Repetition is the key. If your horse sees dustbins as scary monsters, for example, put one outside his stable and another on the way to his field so he has to pass them every single day. Eventually he'll be so used to seeing dustbins randomly placed here and there, he'll accept them.

# BOMBPROOFING MASTERCLASS

If you enjoy desensitization work (p.227), you can extend it to encompass a wide variety of objects, even those your horse rarely comes across. As well as teaching him to cope with the various objects, this sort of work will deepen your bond and he will learn to really trust you. It also helps him to use and develop the rational side of his brain, which means he will start to think before reacting. This has a knock-on effect of making him less stressed in new situations. And bombproofing work is great fun too, for both of you.

Whenever you are doing the exercises be careful not to put yourself in any danger and never force your horse to do something. Think of another way to explain to him what it is you want, and always be prepared to make it easier for him if he needs it. This is meant to be fun for both of you.

## THE CLASS

### 1 Cones
• Make a wide path lined with traffic cones and walk your horse through them.

At first he may hesitate and look at the cones, but let him sniff them if he wants and then push him on. Once he's walked through them, try again in the opposite direction. When you're happy going through the cones, make the path a little narrower and repeat the exercise. You could extend this exercise by making a pathway with the cones leading into your horse's stable, so he learns they're nothing to worry about. Barrels are another favourite. Lead or ride your horse between them and gradually make the gap narrower. Eventually he will enjoy knocking them over as he goes through.

### 2 Flapping objects
• Flapping bags and pieces of litter are a common problem when out hacking. Replicate them in a safe place using balloons, preferably ones filled with helium, tied to the cones.

Do the cones exercise first and once your horse is used to this, tie one balloon onto the end cone and walk past it. Expect a lot of hesitation but use the cones to channel your horse towards the balloon. Take your time and don't rush. If you are riding, relax and think about your forwards aids, encouraging your horse every step of the way. Once your horse has walked past the balloon give him a big pat and then repeat the exercise in both directions. When you're comfortable with one balloon, add another onto the other end cone and repeat the exercise. The wind will make a difference to how spooky this exercise is. Start on a calm day and then repeat it on a breezier day once you're both confident.

### 3 Noisy surfaces

• Tarpaulin is great for desensitizing your horse to noisy surfaces and flapping plastic. Place a folded piece of tarpaulin or plastic sheeting on the ground and weigh it down at the corners with cones or poles – again use them to channel your horse towards the tarpaulin.

Ride or lead your horse towards the tarpaulin. At first he may try to jump right over it – so don't be in front of him if you are leading him, and be ready to hold onto his mane if you are riding. Keep going over it until he calmly walks over it. Once he's comfortable with this, open it out so he has to go over a larger surface and repeat the exercise. When you're happy with how you're progressing put all these obstacles together.

*Plastic sheeting is a versatile spooky object to use when spookbusting your horse*

### 4 Umbrellas

• It's a good idea to get your horse used to umbrellas as soon as possible because they're pretty common and they always appear on those rainy, breezy days, when your horse will be feeling that little bit more lively anyway.

Ask a friend to stand in the field or arena and hold up a brightly coloured umbrella. Walk your horse up to it and let him sniff it and familiarize himself with it.

Next, walk around your friend while she opens and closes the umbrella. When you're happy with this, get your friend to

hold two umbrellas open. Again, let your horse sniff them and walk him around them until he's calm.

### Tips for success

• *Begin your bombproofing work on foot with your horse following you past each scary object (make sure you're wearing a hard hat, proper footwear and gloves). Next, use a schoolmaster to give your horse a lead past and then ride past on your own.*

• *If you are going to lead, work on his leading to start with (pp.30–33).*

• *Before you attempt any kind of bombproofing training in the school or field, make sure your horse is attentive to your aids.*

• *Relax – if you tense up your horse will think there's something to be scared of. Ride positively and you'll give him confidence.*

• *Do all the work in walk at first.*

• *If your horse spooks, use your legs to push his body towards the object and turn his head and neck away.*

• *Once you get past the scary item reward your horse by patting him and talking to him gently.*

• *Don't rush things. If your horse is having difficulty overcoming a fear then return to something he's not anxious about. You need to build his confidence rather than push him over his limits.*

*Police horses are renowned for their unflappability in all sorts of stressful circumstances, yet they are just normal horses that have been extremely well trained*

# RUNNING AWAY

Most of us have ridden a horse that doesn't really respond when you ask him to stop – usually from canter or trot. In the end, plenty of experienced riders simply resort to a good hard pull with one rein or turn him in a circle, but then the horse hasn't learned anything from the experience – and next time... off he goes again. Whereas running off like this is usually caused by discomfort or a lack of schooling, bolting is a different matter and is often the result of blind panic in the horse.

## WHY DO HORSES RUN OFF?

The first things you must check are that your horse's tack, teeth and back are comfortable. This includes the bit. A horse can become frightened of the bit (or pain he associates with it).

*Bolting is rarer than running away – if your horse regularly runs off then he is unlikely to be running through fear but running through habit*

Also consider your horse's daily routine. Horses that are overfed and underworked will become far more lively than is natural, which is uncomfortable for them and their riders. Try to give your horse as much turnout as possible and limit his hard feed to what he really needs – most horses can get the calories they require from grass in summer and plenty of hay or haylage in winter. Hard feeds are only really necessary for horses in regular hard work, or those that have difficulty keeping weight on.

When you hack, do you always canter, or trot, in the same place? Do you canter with friends and do you ever allow it to become a bit of a race? If the answer to these questions is yes, then you are encouraging your horse to run off.

## STOPPING IT HAPPENING

If you are sure there is no physical cause for the problem, then you can begin to work on your horse's basic schooling to get him out of the habit of taking charge when you are out hacking. At heart horses are very willing students and good learners, and the chances are that he won't really be enjoying running away – in nature horses only usually run for any distance because they're scared. As he becomes more obedient and supple, especially in his neck, it will increase your control and his acceptance of your aids. If stopping is still a problem, you could try to change his bit to a pelham or a kimblewick – something that acts comparatively mildly but has a curb chain to help you when he decides to run off, but the real solution is to train him to stop wanting to do this.

*When you ride out with friends, keep the mood calm and respectful. Choose your companions carefully and don't go out with someone who has a reputation for riding fast*

When he seems to be more responsive in the school, you can start to hack out again. Go in company if possible as many horses are worried by hacking alone, and go in front. For the time being, don't canter while out and use different routes so your horse doesn't anticipate where he's going. Think of the hacking as a schooling session and use lots of transitions to keep him listening to your aids. When you do canter, vary the places where you do this and ask for a calm walk or trot everywhere else.

*Your horse must learn that it's up to you to choose both when to canter and when to stop cantering*

## CHECK YOUR RIDING

When you have a horse that won't stop it is easy to fall into the trap of hauling on the reins, but then the chances are that you set up a pulling match. Your reins are not the brakes, your body is, and it's only by learning to co-ordinate your rein, seat and leg aids that you'll have control over your horse. If you get it right you'll be able to soften your reins and relax your arms, while still holding your horse together with your legs and back. Holding your back muscles firm and stopping your hips from moving will ask your horse to stop. At the same time, close your legs all the way down and keep your hands in position – don't pull back. This bracing causes a downward transition, and if you brace like this and release it as soon as you feel your horse hesitate, this is a half-halt (see also pp.114–115) – a stop/start movement (like testing the brakes). Once you've released the half-halt, allow your hips to move with your horse.

This is exactly the same feeling as making a transition from walk to trot. You should still be sitting tall while moving your hips accordingly.

## Emergency stops

If your horse is strong, the one-rein stop is a groundwork exercise that may help. It teaches your horse to soften, and stops him using his strength against you. It works not by pulling the horse's head and neck round, but by yielding his quarters away. On the ground, teach this either at the halt, or at walk on a smallish circle.

**1** Work your horse in a halter or headcollar and stand by his side with a loose leadrope.

**2** In halt motion your hand at the side of your horse – where your leg would be if you were asking him to do this as you ride. You may need to use a schooling whip to gently back up your hand signal. When your horse yields his hindquarters, the hind leg nearest you will cross over in front of the other hind leg. If he is stiff and resistant, or tense, he'll shuffle and his legs won't cross well.

**3** Your horse should execute this movement in a calm manner. If he's flexible and soft to you, you should see the movement through his jaw and the whole length of his spine.

**4** You may need to practise this exercise a few times to get it right. It's important to be patient and persist until it is.

**5** The next step is to ask for this yield in walk, and use the yield as a transition down to halt. Ask for this yield from touch initially.

*As your horse begins to understand what you want him to do, your aids can become subtler until you should only need to point at his quarters and he'll yield them*

# NAPPING

Napping is usually a sign of worry or confusion in a horse. Here are two typical descriptions:

'Out on hacks, in lessons and at events my horse will sometimes stop dead in his tracks and go backwards, sideways or spin round. Nothing I do will make him go forwards until he is ready to move. He mostly naps on hacks when he's left behind by other horses.'

'My pony is extremely nappy when I hack him out alone. He leaves the yard without a problem and goes about 50m (55yd) along the road, then he stops. After considerable persuasion he will continue for about another 50m before stopping again. Sometimes he also tries to spin round. He carries on like this for the whole ride.'

From these it is clear that there is a problem in the relationship between the rider and their horse. It may be a lack of trust or it may be a lack of schooling. Either way, work is needed to bring the two sides together.

*Unnerving as it is for the rider, napping is often a sign that the horse is worried too*

### Try long lining

Napping can be scary for the rider, so you could try leading or long lining your horse to build his confidence without denting yours (see pp.30–33 if you need help with your leading, and pp.57–59 for information on long lining). If you decide to long line, ask an experienced friend to walk at his head. She can encourage him forwards if he starts to nap. Pick a route that avoids any busy roads and start with short walks out, keeping everything positive. Eventually you should be able to progress to riding.

*Long lining can be a great confidence enhancer*

## STOPPING IT HAPPENING

A napping horse needs to be taught the skills that will go a long way towards dispelling his fears and confusion. Start with basic schooling. He must go forwards from the leg. If you say trot, he must trot. Make sure you can perform simple transitions (halt–walk, walk–trot) freely and smoothly, then try direct transitions (halt–trot, walk–canter). He must be responsive to the aids and in front of the leg at all times. This way when he decides to stop you know he will go forwards when you put your leg on. If he is not completely forward thinking, then he may be confused about what is required. Be prepared to go right back to basics if necessary.

Start riding out when you feel that he is really responding well to your requests. Work hard on your attitude when riding to really give your horse confidence in you. You can also do this when you handle him, to form a strong and trusting bond. Don't think of him as being naughty, but instead think of him as being confused – this simple mindset-swop will change your approach to the problem.

## CHECK YOUR RIDING

When you start riding out, gently guide your horse forwards with your legs and hands, but don't squeeze with both legs at the same time. Praise every forward movement with a rub on the neck, help him out and be sympathetic, but make the rules clear. If he co-operates and takes a step forward, you stop hassling and say thanks. If he refuses to listen you keep hassling until he does as you ask.

Start small. For example, if he naps on leaving the yard, just look for a few steps beyond the yard gate, give him a rub on the neck to say thanks and then take him home. Gradually increase the distance you ride out. Treat each hack as part of your schooling. Ride transitions and ask him to move forwards at all times. Don't give him the opportunity to make up his own mind about what he is going to do next – keep giving him something else to think about.

With a napping horse that is a bit scary too, it is very easy to sit with a hard rein contact, to stop the spinning perhaps, and kick with both legs in a bid to get him to walk forward. But this type of riding will lead to more resistance. Whenever you feel your horse grinding to a halt, use your left rein to turn his head to the left slightly and back up this aid with your right leg to get his shoulders moving. Then do the same with the right rein and left leg to 'bump start' him. Praise any forwards movement, however small, with a rub on the neck to say thank you for his effort.

## MOVING ON

Once you start to get results you can ask an experienced rider with a quiet schoolmaster to accompany you on rides and take the lead when necessary. Keep rides short to start with and avoid anything potentially scary, such as noisy farmyards. If this goes well, try meeting up with the other rider while you are out hacking. Ride together for a while, then go your separate ways. Hack side-by-side, if it's safe to do so, and don't allow your horse to be clingy towards the other horse. Gradually do more and more of this work, but keep going with the schooling at home too.

### THINK OUTSIDE THE BOX

*One effective method with a horse that is worried about leaving the yard is to lead him calmly away from the yard and then jump on board at a later stage. If he is worried about a particular spot on the hack, do the same. Lead him past and then hop on again. You may need to do this a few times, but it is certainly a confidence booster and you will be starting to break the habit, too.*

*Your horse really won't 'learn how to make you dismount' if you get off him to lead him past scary things occasionally*

• *If the horse is refusing to budge because he is being awkward, getting off and leading him will blow a hole in his strategy. While he is getting results through napping he is learning that he can render you ineffective, so you need to train him out of this.*

• *A lot of people have it drummed into them that if they get off, the horse has won. This is the wrong mindset, as it turns riding into a conflict. Instead, do anything – including getting off and leading – to get the horse moving in the right direction.*

# REARING

Of all the problems that people encounter with their horses, rearing is the most frightening and potentially the most dangerous. Perhaps it's scary because it usually happens at the halt or walk, when we mostly feel we should be safe, or perhaps because it is difficult to do anything about it while it is happening – also, of course, there is that terrible fear that the horse will topple over backwards and onto you, which is why rearing is so dangerous. Rearing is a very serious problem and one that takes experience and courage to overcome. Don't attempt to ride a known rearer unless you are sure that you can cope with whatever he might throw at you.

## WHY DO HORSES REAR?

Obviously, pain or discomfort can be a reason for rearing, as with bucking, so ask your vet to check your horse over. If he gets the all clear and you are sure his tack fits well, then you need to cope with the problem itself.

A horse often learns to rear once he has exhausted all other possibilities. Consider this scenario. Out on a hack you see a flapping carrier bag in a hedge. Your horse is genuinely nervous of passing this so he comes to a halt. His instinct is to run away rather than try to rationalize and deal with the situation, so all of his reflexes are saying 'run'. You, meanwhile, know it is a harmless plastic bag and give your horse a hefty kick to send him on. He then chooses one of several options. In the best case, he closes his eyes and leaps past, so at least it is over for this time. Otherwise he might dive off to the left or right in a bid to escape, or run backwards. All of which inevitably lead to a battle.

You may well manage to bully your horse past the scary, flapping object, but he hasn't learned to deal with it. The next day when you approach the same bit of hedge he thinks, 'Uh-oh, I remember – this is bad news'. As a result, he stops a couple of strides further away from the hedge than the day before, and a repeat of the battle ensues.

If a situation like this is allowed to get out of hand, then once the horse has exhausted the possibilities of going back, sideways or standing stock still, he remembers there's one way he hasn't yet tried – going up in the air. Like all learned behaviour, if he gets the result he wants (he goes home), then rearing has worked for him.

*Beware of letting your horse get into the habit of rearing – try not to push him to the point where he feels there is no other option*

### In an emergency

If you think your horse might rear, don't tense up and pull on the reins as this will increase the risk of him rearing. Instead, ride him in a circle, moving gradually forwards, and use your forwards aids.

If he rears, move all your weight forwards and relax the contact on the reins. Once you're back on four hooves push your horse sharply forwards and turn him tightly – this acts as a strong discouragement. After two or three circles ride straight.

## STOPPING IT HAPPENING

Rearing is essentially an excellent way of ditching the rider and cutting short the ride. If a horse learns the art of going up in the air he will try it whenever he faces a situation that he feels he can't handle.

If a horse rears because he is worried and anxious, the trick is to take him to one degree below the crucial point at which he will freak out and rear. This will help him to face up to his fears and deal with them without the situation turning into a drama. However, it takes an expert to gauge this. If you haven't got the knowledge and experience to school your horse out of this habit, then seek professional help.

When dealing with a nervous rearer, be sympathetic, but not so sympathetic that you can't get the job done. Communicate to the horse that his behaviour is not acceptable. There is no place in the world for a horse that rears and he has to learn that. Keep each hack or training session interesting to ensure that his mind is occupied and give him every chance to get over his problem. The rest is up to him. It is the rider's job to show their horse that life is easier if he doesn't rear, and it is his job to accept this and deal with it.

*Horses may rear through being nervous and being given no other escape route*

### PROBLEM SOLVER

**Q** I've owned my six-year-old TB ex-racehorse for three years and until recently we've been doing very well. However, when I go to change the rein in the arena he rears vertically. It's the same when we hack out: when we get to the end of the drive he rears and bolts back home. I'm an experienced rider but he's starting to worry me.

I had his teeth, back and tack checked, but everything is fine. I know people say once a rearer always a rearer, but I don't want to sell him because who knows where he'd end up. I've heard that cracking an egg on a rearing horse's head will stop the habit, but it must be very difficult. What can I do?

**A** Horses that rear are difficult to change. There are many old-fashioned ideas to cure rearers, which include hitting them over the head with plastic bottles or eggs, but it's difficult to see how these work.

The bottom line is that a horse that goes forwards does not usually go upwards. Your horse must respect your leg and go freely forwards from it. In the school, use transition work to sharpen him up. Make sure your hand is in no way restrictive so he has no excuse to stand up. Working him on the lunge may also help. Try to make his work as varied as possible, hack out in company when you have the opportunity, and make everything as much fun for him as you can.

Finally, check his feed and exercise routines to make sure they are suitable.

*Calm, well-organized and varied schooling may enable you to stop your horse rearing*

# WATER

Considering that they must drink it to stay alive and that it is very common, especially in winter – running down roads and pooling by their gates – it is surprising the number of horses that avoid water. For some, this is just a preference – if they can go around a puddle, they will, but if they have to cross a ford then they're happy to do so – but for others, water seems to be quite frightening and they will do anything they can to get away from it, although rarely, it seems, when it's in a bucket or water trough!

*Who can blame a horse that doesn't want to step into mud? Nevertheless, you don't want to have to get off to lead him through either*

## WHY ARE THEY AFRAID?

There is a theory that horses are wary of water because of an instinctive fear of what may lurk in its depths or lie hidden around its perimeters. In the wild, prey animals, such as zebras and antelopes, are extremely cautious around water holes. They know that if they are not careful, a predator, also there to drink – or to find food – could catch them. Perhaps this caution lives on in our domesticated horses.

## BANISHING THE FEAR

A fear of puddles is a problem you can work through at home fairly easily. Work in an enclosed yard or school and either put a strip of plastic on the ground, or spray a hard surface with the hose to create your very own puddle effect. Work your horse in-hand at first to give him extra confidence, and ask him to walk over the plastic or patch of water.

*Keep your horse's attention focused on the 'water'*

*Allow him to sniff but not turn away. Eventually he will go over*

He is likely to be highly suspicious at first, so give him plenty of time to investigate. He will probably prick his ears, snort or try to turn and run. If he does try to pull away, keep turning him back to the puddle (you may find that leading him in a bridle gives you more control). Allow yourself plenty of time for this exercise and stay calm. Keep correcting him and make it clear that you want him to step over or through the plastic, or water. Every time he considers this scary obstacle – by taking a step towards it or lowering his head to have a sniff – say thanks with a rub on the neck and let him know he's doing well. Remember, this is a big issue for him so he needs plenty of encouragement.

Eventually, he will take the plunge and step over. Be prepared for him to take a huge leap, or rush, and avoid yanking him in the mouth if he's wearing a bridle. Make a fuss of him, tell him how brave he is, then ask him to step back over. He will continue to rush until he realizes nothing awful is going to happen to him.

Repeat this exercise several times, ending each session on a high note. Once he has reached the stage where he is able to walk over the water or plastic, slowly, you can progress to riding him over it, and eventually move on to tackle small puddles on hacks. Choose a shallow puddle you know has a hard base, to avoid frightening him. (For more of this type of work, see Bombproofing masterclass, pp.228–229.)

## PROBLEM SOLVER

**Q** I have owned my New Forest x Welsh pony for five years and have never been able to get him to walk through water while out on a hack. At home, when the area near his field gets flooded, he will walk through it without hesitation. However, when I ride out with friends and come to a shallow puddle he won't go near it. What can I do?

**A** The most straightforward way to deal with this is to find a stretch of water that covers the entire path you are riding along – this ensures that your pony won't be able to go to one side or the other. It is very difficult to get most horses through a tiny puddle when they can see an easier, or safer, way around. Make sure the water is very shallow with a good base and not boggy at the entry or exit.

Arrange to go out to this piece of water with a companion on a horse that you know will go into and through water easily. When you get to the stretch of water the lead horse should go through first. You should then try to follow as closely behind as is safe. If your pony wants to stay with his friend he has to go through the water. If he hesitates, stand him at the edge and keep encouraging him with your legs and voice. Don't let him turn away. If he tries to turn away, keep turning him back to face the water. Eventually, he will decide it is easier to go into and through the water than to resist.

Be patient and don't lose your temper with your pony. You don't want him to associate going into water with a fight. The initial steps may be tentative. Be sure to reward any forwards movement with your voice and allow him to move forwards with your hand. Repeat the process of entering the water behind your pony's friend several times until he feels really confident. Then try it on your own and, again, go in and out several times.

Once your pony has gained confidence you will probably find that he will happily cope with most water obstacles and streams. Find as many different water situations as you can. Always make sure that each water obstacle has a good entry, exit and base so that all the time you are giving him lots of confidence. Don't attempt to force your pony through every tiny puddle you come across – just walk past. Eventually, by not making a big issue out of each puddle, you will probably find that your pony will start to walk or trot straight through them.

*Splashing through water can be fun on a sunny day*

# Separation anxiety

We all know of horses that hate to leave their special friends. As handlers and riders, this can cause us anything from a minor problem to a full-blown major headache that never seems to get any better.

Here is a typical description of the type of problem separation anxiety can cause: 'I moved to the livery yard on the same day as Jill and her TBx mare Question. As the newcomers, the horses were introduced to each other and within a couple of days were grazing in the same paddock. I was especially pleased with my new horse, as he was a gentleman to handle and ride, obedient and responsive. I was therefore completely shocked by the incident that occurred a week later.

Arriving at the yard one evening, I could see Jill hurriedly leading an excitable Question along the driveway from their paddock. In the field, my horse was going berserk, whinnying like a creature possessed and hurtling around the field, barging at the gate. Grabbing a headcollar, I ran to the field gate but as I opened it my horse thrust forward and galloped down the drive. I found him standing outside Question's stable, with his head thrust inside.'

## Why do horses like being together?

Horses don't like being on their own. Mother Nature created them to live in herds where their many needs are met. One of these needs is close friendship. Humans and other animals can, to some extent, provide a substitute friend for a horse but nothing beats the company of their own kind. Within this mix, some horses get on better with each other than with others. It's very much like the difference between friends and acquaintances in people.

A horse's best friend – the one he spends most time with, grooming with, playing with, dozing with and eating from the same pile of hay with – is often of a similar size, age and sex as himself. Such close friendships may be formed for many reasons. Perhaps the horses have lived together a long time or, at the other end of the scale, two horses find themselves together in a situation that challenges them, such as the example above.

## Stopping it happening

If possible, keep your horse in a small group rather than with just one companion. In a group there will be individual strong friendships, but there are less likely to be problems. The horses know that while one may leave the group for a short time, he or she will always return. Regularly visit your horse within the group, and not always to take him away. That way the appearance of a person does not necessarily mean that one of the horses is about to be taken away and the whole herd will stay relaxed.

*As well as being irritating and nerve-wracking, when your horse hates to leave his friends it can severely limit your riding options*

If your livery yard owner will not allow larger groups of horses, you will have to work to show your horse that being separated from his friend is not a huge problem.

## WHEN IT HAS ALREADY HAPPENED...

If your horse frets when his friend is not around, paces up and down the fence line or gallops around madly, you probably think you have a real mountain to climb in re-educating him. However, it is not an insurmountable problem. Each journey starts with one step – and for your horse that first step could be a very small one. However, if you break down the process into tiny steps, which your horse can manage, and you allow him the time he needs, you will make progress.

The best idea is to help your horse to realize that there is no reason to be fearful when his friend leaves the field. This work could take weeks, so be patient and accept that you may not be able to ride your horse for a while – it will be worth it. If possible, enlist the owner of your horse's best friend to help. It will be safer and easier if there are two of you. Always be aware of safety. For example, sometimes the horse being left can become so anxious he may try to barge through the gate with you. If this happens, you are taking things too fast.

**1** *Go into the field and catch your horse. (Don't catch your horse's friend unless you have his owner's permission.) If either horse suffers from serious anxiety, you may see the signs at this stage. Practise catching your horse every day until he accepts it calmly, then move on to step 2. This could take a several weeks.*

**2** *Start to lead your horse to the gate. This may be enough to upset his friend so don't take him out of the field until they both seem happy. Gradually build up to leading him through the gate and then return him to the field immediately. Again, repeat this process until both horses see no cause for concern and learn that they will soon be reunited.*

**3** *Slowly increase the amount of time for which the two horses are separated, constantly watching for signs of anxiety. If you have someone to help you, try giving the two horses a feed when they're apart, but still in sight of each other.*

**4** *Take your horse out of sight of his friend and then return him to the field. Start with just a couple of minutes. Slowly extend the period for which they're apart. Try feeding them when they're out of each other's sight and increase the amount of time they spend alone after their meal.*

*As long as you do not try to progress too quickly, you should eventually be able to take either horse from the field for a hack, lesson, show or whatever without any problems.*

# Weaning

Friendships between horses may be strong, but one of the strongest bonds we break is that between a mare and foal. Weaning can be extremely traumatic for both mare and foal and can have effects that manifest later as behavioural problems. Although it seems to be the practice to wean a foal when he is six months old, many people now believe that it is better to wait until he is a bit older – seven or eight months old at least. Horse owner and equestrian author Lesley Bayley recounts the steps she took to wean her seven-and-a-half month old foal.

• The mare and foal were brought in from the field; the foal was taken into their usual stable and the mare was held outside. We dispensed feeds, with the mare eating from a manger hooked over the door so that she could see her foal and vice versa. A little while after they had finished eating, the mare was put into the stable with the foal.

• After a few days of this, the foal was put into his usual stable and the mare into a stable at right angles to his. This meant that both could see each other. Initially the foal was a little concerned but the appeal of food won him over in a matter of seconds. Once they had finished their food, the mare rejoined her foal.

• Gradually we increased the time between finishing the meal and being put together in the same stable.

• When both were relaxed with this procedure we moved the mare into a stable further away. Both could still see each other but, by this time, neither appeared unduly concerned by the separation.

• We then built up the time that both spent in their individual stables – they would happily eat feeds and hay and then spend time watching the yard activity.

This whole process took about three weeks and culminated in the mare being taken away to another yard for a month. One evening we followed the usual routine and then loaded the mare into the lorry. I took her to another yard while my husband and friend kept an eye on her foal. He was agitated for a few minutes and then settled to eat his hay. The youngster had the rest of his usual herd to look after him and the mare went to a yard where she had lived before and was looked after by me. Neither was unduly concerned about the weaning – a far cry from the stories you hear of foals throwing themselves around stables and calling constantly for their dams.

# JOGGING

Jogging, not to be mistaken for the Western pace between walk and canter, can be the most exhausting and irritating of habits. Many horses start a ride out a bit on their toes but calm down after a few minutes, and even more horses will speed up for the last few hundred metres home. For the most part, we get to know what our horse is going to be like and can work around it or it doesn't really bother us. However, there are some horses that get themselves very wound up. They don't just speed up – they jog. They may also keep snatching at the bit or tossing their head around and generally act unsettled.

## WHY DO HORSES JOG?

Before you start to try to retrain a jogging horse, it is important to have his tack, feet, back and teeth checked. Discomfort can manifest itself in all sorts of ways and unsettled behaviour is one of them. Once you are completely sure that he's not in pain, look for other reasons why he might be jogging. It may be that he's not getting enough exercise, or that he's getting too much hard feed, both of which will mean he has energy to burn. Maybe he is worried by being out on his own and wants to get back to the yard (see Separation anxiety, pp.238–239) or perhaps he is confused about his role. Here are two anti-jogging techniques to try.

## USE IT

Make sure you're in a good position in the saddle, keeping your back and stomach toned. Sit tall and only allow your hips to move as they would if your horse were in walk. If he's well schooled this may be enough to slow him down. If not, try moving your hips at trot speed – the nearest correct gait to jogging is passage (a very collected trot) – close your thighs to collect him and maintain a steady contact with the bit. Use calf pressure to close him up a bit and keep the jog slow, but ride it deliberately. By asking your horse take passage-like steps, you will be working him quite hard – and he should be pleased to walk after a few steps of this. Relax your legs and allow your back and hips to go into

walk motion to let him know what you want. If he won't walk then maintain a controlled, springy trot, which is much less jarring for his joints than continuous jogging. Repeat the passage work every so often, and eventually he should decide to walk. Praise him warmly when he does.

## LOSE IT

An alternative, to use with a horse that jogs towards home, is to turn him around and ride back the way you have come – away from home – for a few metres until he stops jogging. If you repeat this exercise consistently he will get the idea.

If it is not possible to ride in the opposite direction, circle him once or twice and then head for home. If he jogs immediately, circle him again.

The principle behind these exercises is to make it easy for your horse to do what you want him to do, and to make the undesirable behaviour a little more uncomfortable.

Whichever method you try, don't pull on the reins to slow your horse as this will merely antagonize him. Throughout this you need to be patient, clear in what you ask your horse and firm but fair.

*Try not to let your horse jog. Instead, use his energy constructively – a good trot up a hill may calm him down*

# SHOWING

A lot of this section has been about problems that you might have with your horse, so to finish, we look at two fun things to try – showing and driving. Showing is exciting – a chance to show off your horse's looks and paces and all that hard work you have put into training him. Many riders are put off showing because they find it confusing, or think their horse isn't good enough. Well, that's just not true. There's something to suit everyone. Some of the classes on offer include working hunter, mountain and moorland, show cob, riding club horse and family horse. Shows can range from a relaxed and informal village affair that often includes a dog show and a bouncy castle too, to a serious and competitive regional set up, where you mix with some really classy equines.

*There is a class for everyone, so you should be able to compete with horses of a similar type*

## INDIVIDUAL SHOW

Perhaps one of the most intimidating things about showing is the individual show. This is basically putting your horse through his paces in front of the judge. You will be expected to walk, trot, canter and sometimes gallop down the long side of the arena. You will either be asked to ride a set show, or you can ride one that you've made up yourself. To get an idea of the level of expertise required, it is best to visit a few local shows before you enter, but you also need to practise so that your horse knows what is required of him. There's nothing worse than getting into the ring and having your trusted steed refuse to canter, or go into canter and refuse to stop!

When you've finished your indivudual show, never pull your horse up right in front of the judge, or end up with your horse standing too close to her. This is not only off-putting but it restricts the judge's view of your horse. Remember that the judge is only interested in your horse and how he moves and behaves – she isn't interested in how you ride. Always ride quietly so you don't distract her from your horse and if you have to devise your own individual show keep it short and uncomplicated.

### BEING IN THE RIBBONS

Showing is all about standing out from the crowd, so be confident in the ring – a shrinking violet won't get results. When you enter the ring, try not to go in behind a horse that's been doing really well – he may outshine you and catch the judge's eye before she's had a chance to notice you! Entering behind a horse of a different colour will help yours to stand out.

When you're walking, trotting and cantering round the arena with the other competitors, make sure you trot on the right diagonal, don't cut your corners or get in anyone's way. Circle away if you start to bunch up, and keep your eye on the steward. In the line-up, don't let your horse go to sleep or rest a leg. When the rider before you starts her show, this is

*A simple turnout will get you noticed*

the time to let your horse know that it's his turn next – so use your legs a little to get his attention.

In the final walk round, keep smiling and really ride your horse. Even if you are towards the bottom of the line-up it's worth making the effort as judges often have a shake up at the end.

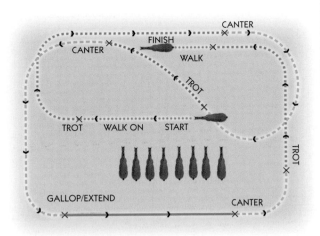

*Keep your show route simple – a serpentine or figure of eight is best. Remember, showing is like presenting a picture in the ring. The way you ride and how your horse moves should look smooth and effortless*

## COMPETITION TIPS

*A good relationship with your horse is essential if you compete, but in the stressful atmosphere of a competition, it's easy to let frayed nerves spoil any bond you've created at home.*

*In order to keep the partnership on track you need to form a plan of action. Dressage rider Carl Hester goes for a quiet hack before a big class to keep his horse relaxed, and event rider Mary King likes to make sure everything is thoroughly organized in order to keep her nerves at bay. So take a tip from the celebrities and form a show plan.*

• *Make a list of everything you need to take. There is nothing worse than arriving at a competition minus something vital.*

• *Take someone calm and efficient to help you. Getting into a shouting match with your sister at the event does not bode well for a good performance.*

• *Practise a warm-up routine at home so that you and your horse know it well by the day of the competition. Going through this routine will reassure your horse and you will be less flustered on the day if you have a selection of prepared exercises.*

• *Arrive in plenty of time to warm up calmly. Keep away from busy areas of the arena to do this. Begin in walk, take deep, slow breaths and check your position, relaxing your shoulders if they have become tense and unclenching your fists if you are gripping the reins.*

• *Try not to clench your jaw. This leads to a tense neck. If you feel stiff through your back, some transition work and slow, collected trot work can help you to move through your back. If you cannot move your lumbar region, neither can your horse.*

• *Learn how to ride courteously with other riders, always passing left to left with oncoming horses. This prevents collisions and stress for you both. Focus on spaces to ride into and don't stare in panic at an oncoming horse. If you are indecisive, your horse will become worried and tense.*

• *When it's your turn to start your show, stay calm and ride your horse just as you did at home and in the warm-up. If it goes wrong, there is always next time.*

• *If you experience problems at a competition, train at home until you feel confident to try again. Competing regardless, every weekend, will not necessarily help to resolve your difficulties.*

*Showing should be about having fun*

# DRIVING

Learning to drive is a great way to broaden your horizons with horses. Whether you aspire to be a competitive driver, or just want to enjoy the countryside, it opens up a whole new world of experiences you can share with a horse. Many people take up driving because they feel like a new challenge, or as a way of expanding their equestrian experience. Whatever your reason for having a go, it's easy to get hooked.

## WHY DRIVE?

Driving is a sport where physical ability doesn't matter. It offers a way to enjoy the company of a horse, even to compete successfully, for anyone who finds riding an impossibility. Because fitness level isn't as important, you can carry on driving effectively and comfortably long after aches, pains or age make sitting on a horse difficult. But driving isn't just a serene pastime. You can also experience all the thrill and exhilaration of tearing round a cross-country course at breakneck speed.

Driving is an excellent option for giving an outgrown pony a new lease of life. Pulling a carriage does not put any weight on the horse's back, so it can be ideal for equines that can no longer carry a rider but still enjoy getting some exercise.

Another advantage is that driving is a sociable sport. It's something that family and friends can easily be included in and enjoy, even if they're not horsey. In fact, most of the time you need to have a helper with you.

### HAVE YOU GOT WHAT IT TAKES?

• *Women tend to make better carriage drivers than men, because they tend to be more dextrous. Good hand-eye co-ordination really helps when you're driving.*

• *Good horse sense is an important factor. The ability to read your horse's body language is vital, especially as you're not able to feel his reactions. You have to rely on seeing what's happening around you and sensing what your horse is likely to do.*

*Whether you want to enjoy the view on a leisurely trip around the countryside, or experience the thrill of racing against the clock – driving is the answer*

## GETTING STARTED

Whether you're curious about what driving would be like, or you've got your heart set on doing it, the best way to get started is to book a lesson. Your local riding school should be able to point you in the right direction of specialist centres.

A lesson gives you the opportunity to ask questions and get a taste of what driving involves. You will be shown how the harness should fit the horse and how to harness up correctly. The instructor will show you how to hold and manipulate the reins before taking you for a short drive.

If you're feeling confident, you will usually get the chance to have a go. Steering a carriage takes some getting used to but most instructors have dual control reins, so you should always be perfectly safe.

### THE RIGHT HORSE

The most important thing about a driving horse is his temperament. A good driving horse is reliable and trustworthy, especially in traffic. Horses that can't tolerate tractors, lorries or other everyday distractions are not really suitable – it isn't going to make them any better and could put you both in a potentially dangerous situation.

Driving horses come in all builds and heights, from chunky cobs to streamlined event horses – suitability is very much down to outlook and temperament. Most native ponies are ideal for driving. Carriages also come in all shapes and sizes and are readily available to fit anything from a donkey or miniature pony to a 17hh draught horse.

Although people often want to start driving with a horse they already own, it's not the ideal situation if you're both beginners. It's better for novice drivers to start with a horse that knows the ropes. Just like riding, a novice driver can learn quickly and have a lot of fun with a horse that already knows what he's doing.

*The harness will feel strange to the horse to begin with. The biggest changes are the breeching harness, which fits around his quarters, and blinkers, which restrict his vision*

### RIDE AND DRIVE

A horse that is already being ridden is usually easier to introduce to driving than a totally unbroken horse. He will have more experience of life – he will have a working relationship with his rider, and he is likely to have seen more traffic and be more used to everyday hazards. The rider will know his character and be able to anticipate his likely reactions in any given situation.

It takes roughly the same amount of work to break a horse for driving as it does for riding. The first step is to introduce him to long lining. This teaches him to be obedient to the commands of someone on the ground behind him. He must also be introduced to pulling a weight and allowed to get used to the noise this makes. Driving skills must be taught slowly, progressively and very carefully, so there is no danger of frightening or confusing him.

## RIDER TURNED DRIVER

Being a rider brings both advantages and disadvantages when it comes to learning to drive. A rider will already have empathy with horses. However, controlling a driving horse is different to controlling a riding horse, which can cause confusion initially. The way the driving reins are held and handled can take a lot of practice to perfect. Most beginners tend to oversteer. Drivers have to learn to be agile with their hands and be able to make tiny hand movements.

When you're riding it's usually easier to control the horse, but it's harder to control yourself. With driving it's the opposite, it's easier for you to control your body, but it's more difficult for you to control the horse. However, just because there's more of a distance between you and your horse, it doesn't mean there's a distance in your relationship. Horse and driver need to have a heightened understanding and communication, and this brings them closer together.

*Training a driving horse takes just as much time and patience as training a riding horse*

# AND FINALLY...

*Enjoy your horse*

The contents of this book should have given you plenty of inspiration and help with your horse. Although you may still have questions, at least you will have an idea of where to start looking for the answers. If you ever get frustrated with your rate of progress when training your horse remember this: the most important thing about horses is probably why we love them in the first place – they are eternally interesting. If we were after something that always did what we wanted – we'd buy a car.

# ACKNOWLEDGEMENTS

This book has been compiled from articles that originally appeared in *Your Horse* magazine. The publishers would like to thank the following contributors whose expertise made it possible:

Jane Baker BHS SM BHSII
Lesley Bayley
Dr Deb Bennett
Ellie Bolton BHSI SM
John Bowen
Jeanette Brakewell
Julie Brown
Jackie Budd
Karen Bush
Richard Davison
Karen Dixon
Ferdi Eilberg/Maria Eilberg
Sarah Fisher
Carl Hester
Andrew Kerr Sutherland
Mary King
Lucy Killingbeck
Charles and Hilary Le Moignan
Claire Lilley
Phillip Lindley BHSI Cert Ed
Sylvia Loch
Nick Locke BHSI Cert Ed
Allison Lowther
Geoff Luckett
Carol Mailer
Helen Milbank
Pat Parelli
Michael Peace
Alison Ritchie BHS Int
Nikki Routledge PGD, BSc (Hons), BHSAI, EBW
Tina Sederholm
Jo Sharples
Heidi Simmons
Mark Smith
Polly Stockton
Peter Storr

Blyth Tait
Jill Thomas
Vicki Thompson
Sophie Underwood
Jane Vargerson BHS SM
Charles Wilson MA, BHSAI

Photography by
Matthew Roberts
Julia Shearwood

Thanks to the many models, including these:
Rebecca Bagnall and Stuart Roberts BHSI (Driving features)
Sam Booth (Issue 261, p.18)
Lorna Cameron (Issue 255, p.88)
Victoria Catling (Issue 274, p.71)
Laura Edmonds (Issue 249, p.96)
Sheryle Elson (Issue 261, p.16)
Cara Haywood (Issue 257, p.104)
Beth Hutchinson (Issue 238, p.84)
Amanda Lane (Issue 264, p.76)
Caroline Lewis (Issue 243, p.92)
Lisa Marriot (Issue 261, p.82)
Kazzy Pfeiffer (Issue 236, p.60)
Helen Pittick (Issue 256, p.76)
Giles Relf (Issue 254, p.76)
Diana Rhodes (Issue 271, p.75)
Angela Sturgess (Issue 270, p.70)
Sarah Walker (Issue 273, p.73)
Sam Weir (Issue 250, p.80)
Caroline Xueereb (Issue 262, p.28)

# INDEX